RUSSELL BAKER, a veteran journalist, has been writing the "Observer" column for *The New York Times* for the past twenty-nine years. Baker is a two-time Pulitzer Prize–winner. His first book of memoirs, *Growing Up,* won the Pulitzer for Best Biography in 1982. He and his wife, Mimi, live in Leesburg, Virginia.

The Good Times

RUSSELL BAKER

A SIGNET BOOK

SIGNET
Published by the Penguin Group
Penguin Books USA Inc., 375 Hudson Street,
New York, New York 10014, U.S.A.
Penguin Books Ltd, 27 Wrights Lane,
London W8 5TZ, England
Penguin Books Australia Ltd, Ringwood,
Victoria, Australia
Penguin Books Canada Ltd, 10 Alcorn Avenue,
Toronto, Ontario, Canada M4V 3B2
Penguin Books (N.Z.) Ltd, 182–190 Wairau Road,
Auckland 10, New Zealand

Penguin Books Ltd, Registered Offices:
Harmondsworth, Middlesex, England

Published by Signet, an imprint of New American Library, a division of
Penguin Books USA Inc. This is an authorized reprint of a hardcover
edition published by William Morrow and Company Inc. Previously published in a Plume edition.

First Signet Printing, June, 1992
10 9 8 7 6 5 4 3 2 1

 REGISTERED TRADEMARK—MARCA REGISTRADA

Printed in the United States of America

To Mimi

At the age of twenty-two I believed myself to be unextinguishable.

—SIEGFRIED SASSOON, "Memoirs of a Fox-hunting Man"

1

Cousin Edwin

My mother, dead now to this world but still roaming free in my mind, wakes me some mornings before daybreak. "If there's one thing I can't stand, it's a quitter." I have heard her say that all my life. Now, lying in bed, coming awake in the dark, I feel the fury of her energy fighting the good-for-nothing idler within me who wants to go back to sleep instead of tackling the brave new day.

Silently I protest: I am not a child anymore. I have made something of myself. I am entitled to sleep late.

"Russell, you've got no more gumption than a bump on a log. Don't you want to amount to something?"

She has hounded me with these same battle cries since I was a boy in short pants back in the Depression.

"Amount to something!"

"Make something of yourself!"

"Don't be a quitter!"

On bad mornings, in the darkness, suspended between dreams and daybreak, with my mother racketing around in my head, I feel crushed by failure. I am a fool to think I amount to anything. A man doesn't amount to something because he has been successful at a third-rate career like journalism. It is evidence, that's all: evidence that if he buckled down and worked hard, he might some day do something really worth doing.

It has always been like this between my mother and me. In 1954 I was assigned to cover the White House. For most reporters, being White House correspondent was as close to heaven as you could get. I was then twenty-nine years old and getting the White House job so young puffed me up with pride. I went over to Baltimore to see my mother's delight while telling her about it. I should have known better.

"Well, Russ," she said, "if you work hard at this White House job you might be able to make something of yourself."

Onward and upward was the course she set. Small progress was no excuse for feeling satisfied with yourself. Our world was poor, tough, and mean. People who stopped to pat themselves on the back didn't last long. Even if you got to the top you'd better not take it easy. "The bigger they come, the harder they fall" was one of the favorite maxims in her storehouse of folk wisdom.

Now, on bad mornings, I sense her anger at my contentment. "Have a little ambition, Buddy. You'll never get anywhere in this world unless you've got ambition."

The civilized man of the world within me despises her incessant demands for success. He has read the philosophers and social critics. He is no longer a country boy, he has been to town. He scoffs at materialism and strivers after success. He thinks it is vulgar and unworthy to spend your life pursuing money, power, fame, and—

"Sometimes you act like you're not worth the powder and shot it would take to blow you up with."

—and it's not true that newspapering is a third-rate career. It has helped him to understand humanity's dreams and sorrows.

"My God, Russell! You don't know any more about humanity's dreams and sorrows than a hog knows about holiday."

The mother-haunted son within me knows she is right. After all, he asks, what is a newspaperman? A peeper, an invader of privacy, a scandal peddler, a mischief-maker, a busybody, a man content to wear out his hams sitting in marble corridors waiting for important people to lie to him, a comic-strip intellectual, a human pomposity dilating on his constitutional duty, a drum thumper on a demagogue's bandwagon, a member of the claque for this week's fashion, part of next week's goon squad that will destroy it.

She has no patience with talk like that, never did. "One trouble with you, Russell, is you always overdo things," she said whenever I yielded to my newspaperman's weakness for overstatement.

To her, newspapers were important and the work honorable. She had pushed me toward it almost from the start. She would have liked it better if I could have grown up to be president or a rich businessman, but much as she loved me, she did not deceive herself. Before I was out of grade school, she could see I lacked the gifts for either making millions or winning the love of crowds. After that she began nudging me toward working with words.

Words ran in her family. There seemed to be a word gene that passed down from her maternal grandfather. He was a schoolteacher before the Civil War in the Northern Neck of Virginia. His daughter Sallie became a schoolteacher, his daughter Lulie wrote poetry, and his son Charlie became New York correspondent for the *Baltimore Herald*. His granddaughter Lucy Elizabeth, who became my mother, was also a schoolteacher. Words ran in the family, all right. That was a rich inheritance in the turn-of-the-century South, still impoverished by the Civil War. Words

were a way out. Look at Uncle Charlie. Words could
take you all the way to New York City.

The most spectacular proof that words could be a
gift of gold was my mother's first cousin Edwin. He
was schoolteacher Sallie's son, and when he first
entered my life he was managing editor of *The New
York Times*. Before that, he had been to Paris, had
traveled all over Europe, had known General "Black
Jack" Pershing in the First World War, and had been
there at the airport outside Paris the night Charles
Lindbergh, "Lucky Lindy," landed *The Spirit of St.
Louis* after flying solo across the Atlantic. Had not
just been there, but had written about it in *The New
York Times,* beginning his story with a three-word
sentence: "Lindbergh did it."

Cousin Edwin proved that words could take you to
places so glorious and so far from the Virginia sticks
that your own kin could only gape in wonder and
envy. When my mother saw that I might have the
word gift she started trying to make it grow. She was
desperately poor, but she found money to buy me
magazine subscriptions to *Boy's Life* and *American
Boy*, and later *The Atlantic Monthly* and *Harper's*. She
signed up for a book deal that supplied one volume of
"World's Greatest Literature" every month at a cost
of thirty-nine cents a book. Poe, Hawthorne, Shakespeare, Thackeray—the full panoply of English literature piled up unread, but treasured, under my bed.

I respected those great writers, but at the age of
ten, eleven, twelve, my heart did not sing when I
opened them to read. What I read with joy were newspapers. I lapped up every word in newspaper accounts
of monstrous crimes, dreadful accidents, and hideous
butcheries committed in faraway wars. Accounts of
murderers dying in the electric chair fascinated me,
and I kept close track of last meals ordered by condemned men.

Though I did not realize it at the time, I was preparing myself to challenge my mother's cousin Edwin in newspaper work. This was such a preposterous idea that I kept it secret even from myself during all the years of my growing up. What was oddest about this was that I had never met Edwin, that my mother had not seen him since before the First World War, that Edwin did not know I existed, and that he probably remembered my mother only as a little girl he had once liked to tease.

"Edwin James was the worst tease I ever knew in my life," she often said. This grievance, like most of the others, dated from their childhoods.

"Conceited," she called him.

"Mean."

"Gave himself airs."

"Always acted like he thought he was smarter than anybody else."

"Edwin James was no smarter than anybody else," she told me so often I believed it.

I had a glimpse into the depths of her anger when we first moved from New Jersey to Baltimore. That was in 1937. I was eleven. She was just a notch above abject poverty, unemployed, but optimistic about finding a job soon. She had rented an apartment on West Lombard Street in working-class southwest Baltimore. Her younger sister Sally, married to a successful, five thousand dollars-a-year insurance man who owned a yellow Buick and had a telephone, visited immediately.

Aunt Sally charged up the steps—it was a second-floor apartment—burst through the door, and, with a wild and desperate expression, cried:

"Good Lord, Lucy, you've got to get out of this place right away."

My mother dearly loved Aunt Sally, whose temperament was in the grand operatic style, but she considered her a ludicrous and shameless social climber.

"This is a terrible, terrible neighborhood, Lucy," Aunt Sally went on, her dark eyes rolling in dismay, her voice quivering so intensely that she seemed about to cry.

"I cannot have my sister living in a place like this."

My mother was amused at first. She was often amused by Aunt Sally's melodramatic cries, gestures, and lectures on how to do things right in high society. Listening to Aunt Sally, I understood that my mother had made an awful mistake in not consulting her about where to live in Baltimore. This mistake had to be corrected right away or there would be ruin. We must get the mover back immediately and have everything trucked to a respectable neighborhood. North Baltimore was the only place for respectable people to live. Under no circumstances could we live another hour in southwest Baltimore, least of all on West Lombard Street. Didn't my mother know anything? Didn't she realize that West Lombard Street bordered on the section of Baltimore known as "Pigtown"?

My mother's laughter at all this only inflamed Aunt Sally to louder argument. North Baltimore, she advised my mother, was where "the James girls" lived. The James girls were Edwin's two sisters, who had moved to Baltimore years ago. I guessed from the way Aunt Sally spoke about them that they were high society.

My mother urged Aunt Sally to settle down and have a cup of coffee, but the idea of drinking coffee in the face of social cataclysm was too much for Aunt Sally. She arched her back, threw her head back, clenched her fists, and cried, "What will the James girls think when they hear my sister is living on West Lombard Street?"

The fury of my mother's reply shocked me. Suddenly all her good-humored tolerance for Aunt Sally's performance was gone, and she seemed to lose control of herself.

"I don't care what the James girls think," she shouted. "The Jameses have nothing to be so high and mighty about. Who are the Jameses to be looking down their noses at other people? Their father was nothing but an old oyster pirate."

Long afterward, this scene helped me understand her dislike for Edwin. Edwin's father had been a financial success; her father had died in failure and bankruptcy. And she had loved her father so deeply.

"Papa was the only man I ever really loved," she told me once when she was furious with me and the whole masculine world, and probably overstating things a bit, but not too much. Dear "Papa's" death had devastated her. He was a lawyer and timber dealer who specialized in supplying walnut veneers for expensive gunstocks. In 1917 he died of a heart attack, leaving nothing but debts. The family house was lost, the children scattered. His wife, Lulie the poet, fatally ill with a tubercular infection that was slowly destroying her spine, fell into suicidal depression and was institutionalized. My mother, who had just started college, had to quit and look for work. Life had been hard ever since. After five years of marriage and three babies, her husband had died in 1930, leaving her so poor that she had to give up her baby Audrey for adoption and move to New Jersey to take shelter with her brother Allen.

Then, in 1932, important events: In April she heard Edwin had just become managing editor of the *Times*. A few weeks later, after two years of futile job hunting, she finally found work patching grocers' smocks at ten dollars a week in the A&P laundry in Belleville.

Belleville was situated just ten miles west of Manhattan, where Edwin stood at the top of the heap. She must have felt mocked by the irony. They had both started from the same Virginia backwater, and both had ended up in this faraway northern place separated by a scant ten miles of geography, except that geography lied about their destinies. The true distance separating them could be better measured in light years: the conceited, arrogant, insufferable Edwin standing on top of the world; my impoverished mother passing her days among baskets of ragged aprons.

Life had always smiled on Edwin. His father had done well enough in the Chesapeake Bay's seafood trade to put his children into college and keep them there. As a child, my mother had felt Edwin patronizing her as well-to-do people so often patronize their threadbare relatives.

As I gradually absorbed her dislike for him, I decided that while famous Cousin Edwin might be a family hero, he was also my mother's enemy. This made him my enemy, for with my father dead and Audrey given away for adoption, my mother, my sister Doris, and I had to stick together in everything.

I had a special duty, because I was the man of the family. My mother started telling me so when I was eight years old, and I soon believed it, and believing it filled me with a sense of responsibility to serve my mother. When she said I had to "make something" of myself, I often thought of her cousin Edwin, who had made so much of himself. In her pep talks about what a great success I could be if I worked hard, lived a clean life, and never said die, she often used Edwin's example of how far a man could go without much talent.

"Edwin James was no smarter than anybody else, and look where he is today," she said, and said, and said again, so that I finally grew up thinking Edwin James was a dull clod who had got a lucky break. Maybe she felt that way about him, but she was saying something deeper that I was too young then to understand. She was telling me I didn't have to be brilliant to get where Edwin had got to, that the way to get to the top was to work, work, work.

". . . and look where he is today."

She was giving me a way to channel my ambition when I was too young to know what success might be. She was giving me Edwin as a model, and in the process she was telling me that success for me would be to go where Edwin was.

Then I was no longer a child, and luck got me into college, and the war came and I left my mother for the first time and in the navy learned the pleasures of the company of men and of the desire for women. The excitement of being grown up freed my mind of childishness. Whole years went by without my thinking or hearing of Cousin Edwin. He became just another hazy childhood memory, without weight or meaning.

In 1947, however, when I wandered into the newspaper business and found I liked it, the childhood memory revived. Edwin, mythic Cousin Edwin, whose success had galled my mother, again took up residence in my mind. I began to entertain childish revenge fantasies. Edwin was still managing editor of the *Times* then. Wouldn't it be delightful if I became such an outstanding reporter that the *Times* hired me without knowing I was related to the great Edwin? Wouldn't it be delicious if my work was so astounding that Edwin himself one day invited me into his huge office at the *Times,* offered me a cigar, and said, "Tell me something about yourself, young man"? What exquisite vengeance to reply, "I am the only son of the woman you once treated with contempt, though you were no smarter than she was: your poor cousin, Lucy Elizabeth Robinson."

This is the story of how I almost made that fantasy come true, and of the people I met along the way, and of the good times when a young man, shameless enough to want to make something of himself, could still go to faraway places on the gift of words, even though he was no smarter than anybody else.

Edwin James at the peak of his career (*New York Times*)

2

Deems

My mother started me in newspaper work in 1937 right after my twelfth birthday. She would have started me younger, but there was a law against working before age twelve. She thought it was a silly law, and said so to Deems.

Deems was boss of a group of boys who worked home delivery routes for the *Baltimore News-Post*. She found out about him a few weeks after we got to Baltimore. She just went out on the street, stopped a paperboy, and asked how he'd got his job.

"There's this man Deems . . ."

Deems was short and plump and had curly brown hair. He owned a car and a light gray suit and always wore a necktie and white shirt. A real businessman, I thought the first time I saw him. My mother was talking to him on the sidewalk in front of the Union Square Methodist Church and I was standing as tall as I could, just out of earshot.

"Now, Buddy, when we get down there keep your shoulders back and stand up real straight," she had cautioned me after making sure my necktie was all right and my shirt clean.

Watching the two of them in conversation, with Deems glancing at me now and then, I kept my shoulders drawn back in the painful military style I'd seen in movies, trying to look a foot taller than I really was.

"Come over here, Russ, and meet Mister Deems," she finally said, and I did, managing to answer his greeting by saying, "The pleasure's all mine," which I'd heard people say in the movies. I probably blushed while saying it, because meeting strangers was painfully embarrassing to me.

"If that's the rule, it's the rule," my mother was telling Deems, "and we'll just have to put up with it, but it still doesn't make any sense to me."

As we walked back to the house she said I couldn't have a paper route until I was twelve. And all because of some foolish rule they had down here in Baltimore. You'd think if a boy wanted to work they would encourage him instead of making him stay idle so long that laziness got embedded in his bones.

That was April. We had barely finished the birthday cake in August before Deems came by the apartment and gave me the tools of the newspaper trade: an account book for keeping track of the customers' bills and a long, brown web belt. Slung around one shoulder and across the chest, the belt made it easy to balance fifteen or twenty pounds of papers against the hip. I had to buy my own wire cutters for opening the newspaper bundles the trucks dropped at Wisengoff's store on the corner of Stricker and West Lombard streets.

In February my mother had moved us down from New Jersey, where we had been living with her brother Allen ever since my father died in 1930. This move of hers to Baltimore was a step toward fulfilling a dream. More than almost anything else in the world, she wanted "a home of our own." I'd heard her talk of that "home of our own" all through those endless Depression years when we lived as poor relatives dependent on Uncle Allen's goodness. "A home of our own. One of these days, Buddy, we'll have a home of our own."

That winter she had finally saved just enough to make her move, and she came to Baltimore. There were several reasons for Baltimore. For one, there were people she knew in Baltimore, people she could go to if things got desperate. And desperation was possible, because the moving would exhaust her savings, and the apartment rent was twenty-four dollars a month. She would have to find a job quickly. My sister Doris was only nine, but I was old enough for an after-school job that could bring home a few dollars a week. So as soon as it was legal I went into newspaper work.

The romance of it was almost unbearable on my first day as I trudged west along Lombard Street, then south along Gilmor, and east down Pratt Street with the bundle of newspapers strapped to my hip. I imagined people pausing to admire me as I performed this important work, spreading the news of the world, the city, and the racetracks onto doorsteps, through mail slots, and under doorjambs. I had often gazed with envy at paperboys; to be one of them at last was happiness sublime.

Very soon, though, I discovered drawbacks. The worst of these was Deems. Though I had only forty customers, Deems sent papers for forty-five. Since I was billed for every paper left on Wisengoff's corner, I had to pay for the five extra copies out of income or try to hustle them on the street. I hated standing at streetcar stops yelling, "Paper! Paper!" at people getting off trolleys. Usually, if my mother wasn't around to catch me, I stuck the extras in a dark closet and took the loss.

Deems was constantly baiting new traps to dump more papers on me. When I solved the problem of the five extras by getting five new subscribers for home delivery, Deems announced a competition with mouth-watering prizes for the newsboys who got the most new subscribers. Too innocent to cope with this sly master of private enterprise, I took the bait.

"Look at these prizes I can get for signing up new customers," I told my mother. "A balloon-tire bicycle. A free pass to the movies for a whole year."

The temptation was too much. I reported my five new subscribers to help me in the competition.

Whereupon Deems promptly raised my order from forty-five to fifty papers, leaving me again with the choice of hustling to unload the five extras or losing money.

I won a free pass to the movies, though. It was good for a whole year. And to the magnificent Loew's Century located downtown on Lexington Street. The passes were good only for nights in the middle of the week when I usually had too much homework to allow for movies. Still, in the summer with school out, it was thrilling to go all the way downtown at night to sit in the Century's damask and velvet splendor and see MGM's glamorous stars in their latest movies.

To collect my prize I had to go to a banquet the paper gave for its "honor carriers" at the Emerson Hotel. There were fifty of us, and I was sure the other forty-nine would all turn out to be slicksters wised up to the ways of the world, who would laugh at my doltish ignorance of how to eat at a great hotel banquet. My fear of looking foolish at the banquet made me lie awake nights dreading it and imagining all the humiliating mistakes I could make.

I had seen banquets in movies. Every plate was surrounded by a baffling array of knives, forks, and spoons. I knew it would be the same at the Emerson Hotel. The Emerson was one of the swankiest hotels in Baltimore. It was not likely to hold down on the silverware. I talked to my mother.

"How will I know what to eat what with?"

The question did not interest her.

"Just watch what everybody else does, and enjoy yourself," she said.

I came back to the problem again and again.

"Do you use the same spoon for your coffee as you do for dessert?"

"Don't worry about it. Everybody isn't going to be staring at you."

"Is it all right to butter your bread with the same knife you use to cut the meat?"

"Just go and have a good time."

Close to panic, I showed up at the Emerson, found my way to the banquet, and was horrified to find that I had to sit beside Deems throughout the meal. We probably talked about something, but I was so busy sweating with terror and rolling my eyeballs sidewise to see what silverware Deems was using to eat with that I didn't hear a word all night. The following week, Deems started sending me another five extras.

Now and then he also provided a treat. One day in 1938 he asked if I would like to join a small group of boys he was taking to visit the *News-Post* newsroom. My mother, in spite of believing that nothing came before homework at night, wasn't cold-hearted enough to deny me a chance to see the city room of a great metropolitan newspaper. I had seen plenty of city rooms in the movies. They were glamorous places full of exciting people like Lee Tracy, Edmund Lowe, and Adolphe Menjou trading wisecracks and making mayors and cops look like saps. To see such a place, to stand, actually stand, in the city room of a great newspaper and look at reporters who were in touch every day with killers and professional baseball players—that was a thrilling prospect.

Because the *News-Post* was an afternoon paper, almost everybody had left for the day when we got

there that night. The building, located downtown near
the harbor, was disappointing. It looked like a factory,
and not a very big factory either. Inside there was a
smell compounded of ink, pulp, chemicals, paste, oil,
gasoline, greasy rags, and hot metal. We took an elevator up and came into a long room filled with dilapi-
dated desks, battered telephones, and big blocky
typewriters. Almost nobody there, just two or three
men in shirt-sleeves. It was the first time I'd ever seen
Deems look awed.

"Boys, this is the nerve center of the newspaper,"
he said, his voice heavy and solemn like the voice of
Westbrook Van Voorhis, the *March of Time* man,
when he said, "Time marches on."

I was confused. I had expected the newsroom to
have glamour, but this place had nothing but squalor.
The walls hadn't been painted for years. The windows
were filthy. Desks were heaped with mounds of crumpled paper, torn sheets of newspaper, overturned
paste pots, dog-eared telephone directories. The floor
was ankle deep in newsprint, carbon paper, and
crushed cigarette packages. Waist-high cans over-
flowed with trash. Ashtrays were buried under cigarette ashes and butts. Ugly old wooden chairs looked
ready for the junk shop.

It looked to me like a place that probably had more
cockroaches than we had back home on Lombard
Street, but Deems was seeing it through rose-colored
glasses. As we stood looking around at the ruins, he
started telling us how lucky we were to be newsboys.
Lucky to have a foot on the upward ladder so early
in life. If we worked hard and kept expanding our
paper routes we could make the men who ran this
paper sit up and notice us. And when men like that
noticed you, great things could happen, because they
were important men, the most important of all being
the man who owned our paper: Mr. Hearst Himself,

William Randolph Hearst, founder of the greatest newspaper organization in America. A great man, Mr. Hearst, but not so great that he didn't appreciate his newsboys, who were the backbone of the business. Many of whom would someday grow up and work at big jobs on this paper. Did we realize that any of us, maybe all of us, could end up one of these days sitting right here in this vitally important room, the newsroom, the nerve center of the newspaper?

Yes, Deems was right. Riding home on the streetcar that night, I realized I was a lucky boy to be getting such an early start up the ladder of journalism. It was childish to feel let down because the city room looked like such a dump instead of like city rooms in the movies. Deems might be a slave driver, but he was doing it for my own good, and I ought to be grateful. In *News Selling,* the four-page special paper Mr. Hearst published just for his newsboys, they'd run a piece that put it almost as beautifully as Deems had.

YOU'RE A MEMBER OF THE FOURTH ESTATE was the headline on it. I was so impressed that I put the paper away in a safe place and often took it out to read when I needed inspiration. It told how "a great English orator" named Edmund Burke "started a new name for a new profession—the Fourth Estate . . . the press . . . NEWSPAPER MEN."

And it went on to say:

"The Fourth Estate was then . . . and IS now . . . a great estate for HE-men . . . workers . . . those who are proud of the business they're in!"

(Mr. Hearst always liked plenty of exclamation marks, dots, and capital letters.)

"Get that kick of pride that comes from knowing you are a newspaper man. That means something!

"A newspaper man never ducks a dare. YOU are a newspaper man. A salesman of newspapers . . . the

final cog in the immense machine of newspaper production—a SERVICE for any man to be proud of.

"So throw back the chest. Hit the route hard each
day. Deliver fast and properly. Sell every day. Add
to your route because you add to the NEWSPAPER
field when you do. And YOU MAKE MONEY
DOING IT. It is a great life—a grand opportunity.
Don't boot it—build it up. Leave it better than when
you came into it."

"It is a great life." I kept coming back to that sentence as I read and reread the thing. No matter how
awful it got, and it sometimes got terrible, I never
quit believing it was a great life. I kept at it until I
was almost sixteen, chest thrown back, delivering fast
and properly, selling every day and adding to my
route. At the end I'd doubled its size and was making
as much as four dollars a week from it.

A few months after he took us down to see the city
room, Deems quit. My mother said he'd found a better job. Later, when I thought about him, I wondered
if maybe it wasn't because he hated himself for having
to make life hell for boys. I hoped that wasn't the
reason because he was the first newspaperman I ever
knew, and I wanted him to be the real thing. Hard as
nails.

3

Marydell Road

We moved out to Marydell Road just before the war, and that ended my career as a foot soldier in William Randolph Hearst's newspaper empire. After Lombard Street, Marydell Road was like walking into a Norman Rockwell landscape. Our place was at the very end of a long, downhill block of two-story brick row houses. Arching maple trees canopied the street halfway down the hill. At the bottom was a broad grassy field bordered on the far side by a bosky, shaded stream where I could walk in solitude and pretend I was a great airplane pilot like Colonel Roscoe Turner or an irresistible rake with the ladies like Clark Gable.

I had never dreamed people like us might live in such a paradise. A steep wooded hill rose from the far bank of the stream. If you climbed to the top and walked through a silent piece of woodland, you came to a small farm. Yet we were still inside the limits of a vast, grim city filled, as I knew from bitter experience, with misery, filth, crime, and deadbeats so unscrupulous they'd move out under cover of night rather than pay the paperboy the seventeen cents they owed for a week's deliveries.

The Marydell Road house itself was a place of many splendors. It had hardwood floors waxed to a high

shine. It had a sun parlor overlooking the grassy field
and the stream. It had a long, roofed front porch
where I could sit in a glider, look up the block, and
watch what was happening on twenty identical front
porches aligned perfectly with ours. On the second
floor it had a bathroom, but not just a bathroom, a
bathroom with a shower. You could stand in the tub
and take a shower right in your own house. The second floor had four bedrooms. Mine was big enough
to hold a single bed, a small desk, and an upright
bookshelf gaudy with my two dozen volumes of
"World's Greatest Literature."

That wasn't all. Located underneath the dining
room was a garage built right into the house. Underneath the sun parlor there was a club cellar, a narrow
room paneled in beautiful pine, mostly below ground
level and a little musty smelling, but a place, nevertheless, to boast about when you met the kind of person
who was impressed by club cellars. The main part of
the cellar was a wonder in itself, with the floor all
covered by linoleum and a big laundry tub connected
right into the plumbing. By turning a couple of faucets
we could do the laundry in the new washing machine,
run it through the electrically powered wringer and,
lo, it was all ready to be dried in the yard.

On Lombard Street we'd had to dry the washing on
a line stretched from the kitchen window to a telephone pole in the back alley. On Marydell Road we
had an elegant new clothes drier, an ingenious wood-
and-rope contraption which we could unfold and stand
upright in a metal socket in the lawn, then take down
and store out of sight when the clothes were dry.

This was living as I had seen it pictured in magazines and movies. We even had dark green canvas
awnings which flared out over the windows to keep
the rooms dim, if not cool, in the steamy Baltimore
summertime. For winter there was an oil-burning fur-

nace which roared merrily into action at the touch of a thermostat. To be able to touch that thermostat and hear the furnace instantly obey was like having a genie at my command.

Such a house, oh such a house it was. We were not just renters there either. It was our house. It was that wonderful "home of our own" that my mother had dreamed about all through the Depression years. Because it cost so much—the price was $4,700—we didn't technically own it yet, but were buying it with a mortgage loan that would take twenty years to pay off.

Herb at Marydell Road

This change in our fortunes resulted from my mother's marriage in 1939 to Herb, a locomotive fireman for the B&O Railroad, and the birth a year later of my baby sister Mary Leslie. Mary was born the day after my mother's forty-third birthday. Herb was forty-six years old. Mary was my mother's fourth and last child, and Herb's first. They were ecstatic about her. She was a blessing bestowed on people who had almost ceased to believe anything wonderful would ever happen to them again. In their amazement, they adored her and immediately set about assuring her an enviable life.

Thanks to Herb's comfortable railroader's pay, my mother finally had an opportunity to bring up a child without hardship. Ten years earlier she had had to give up Audrey for adoption. All through the Depression she had had to train Doris and me to accept hard times and hard work as the natural way of the world. Now, with this beautiful, pink, new baby given to her so late in life, she at last had another chance, a chance to do things right, a chance to create a happy world where a child could grow up happily.

It was easy persuading Herb that their first move must be from the Lombard Street apartment to a whole house in a tranquil neighborhood with trees, grass, and parks. Marydell Road was ideal. It was in the Irvington section of Baltimore, four miles west of my Lombard Street paper route. That meant giving up the paper route. My mother didn't chafe about that. Mary Leslie was not the only person she hoped to spoil a little now that her luck had finally turned. Not that she was going to let me become a complete good-for-nothing. Far from it. I still had a mission in life. I had to make something of myself. Work was vital to keep me fit for the task, so I got a Saturday job doing heavy lifting in a grocery at the Hollins Market.

Still, for a few months it was a golden time, especially for my mother. New baby, new house, new life: It was the happy ending the movies promised, and she basked in the joy of it. There were always guests now, guests for her huge Sunday dinners, guests to play cards at the kitchen table on Saturday night, guests dropping by for coffee and gossip in the afternoon. One Sunday morning she commanded me not to leave the house for my usual Sunday afternoon at the movies, but to stand by freshly scrubbed and dressed in my finest. One of her mother's sisters, Aunt Sallie, was coming to visit that afternoon.

Aunt Sallie? Which one was that? My mother had aunts galore and reminisced constantly about all of them, but they were not real to me. I had never met a single one. They seemed to belong to another time, to be part of another life she had lived in another world. I thought of them as dead, when I thought of them at all, which was rarely, and could never keep them sorted out. There were Aunt Lillian, Aunt Kate, Aunt Rose, Aunt Eva, Aunt Helen, Aunt Estelle, Aunt Edna, Aunt Alice. So this day I had to ask my mother, "Which one is Aunt Sallie?"

"Edwin's mother."

What a thunderbolt.

The mother of the great Cousin Edwin.

Coming to our house on Marydell Road.

What grandeur. What honor. Here was proof that Marydell Road had raised us out of the Baltimore muck. My mother's sister Sally, named after this aged Aunt Sallie who had mothered Edwin, had once been ashamed to let Edwin's sisters know we lived on Lombard Street. Now she was bringing Edwin's mother to sit in our parlor on Marydell Road. Visiting in Baltimore, this grand lady had expressed a desire to see my mother.

For my mother this was a momentous event. Though she disliked Edwin, she dearly loved this Aunt Sallie. Aunt Sallie, her mother's big sister, was a visitor from the happy years of childhood. Almost everything from that time was now long dead or lost or scattered: "Papa" dead since 1917. The wonderful family house, Mansfield, sold to strangers. Her brothers scattered across the continent. "Mama" dead since 1923. That was when she'd last seen Aunt Sallie, at "Mama's" funeral eighteen years ago. That was in another world, another life, another time, before she had been married, and widowed, and sacrificed a baby, and survived the Depression, and brought up two children, and married again, and gained another baby, and finally come into a home of her own.

I had no feel for what my mother's emotions about this visit might be. I knew she carried around a lot of old memories, but I yawned when she started telling me about them. To me, her aunt's visit was just a chance to gaze at a curiosity, the famous Edwin's mother. Funny, I hadn't thought of famous Edwin having a mother. I'd heard my own mother angrily slander Edwin's father as "nothing but an old oyster pirate," but I dismissed that as pure romance. For such a mythic figure as Edwin, however, a mother seemed unnecessary. Well, he not only had one, just like everybody else, but she was about to arrive at our house, my great-aunt Sallie.

My mother had let up on me lately about Edwin James, and I had packed him away in my mind's deep-storage compartment. Now, though, the memory of her old hostility and hurt returned, and I was determined not to show awe when I met this Aunt Sallie, but to let her know in a subtle but polite way, if opportunity arose, that I was not impressed one iota by her son's greatness.

The car bearing her arrived at the foot of Marydell Road in midafternoon. Inside were the two Sallies, Great-aunt Sallie, mother of myths, and just plain Aunt Sally, who was my mother's only sister. Uncle Emil, who was married to just plain Aunt Sally, was driving his latest Buick. A big, florid man who was proud of his Germanic roots, Uncle Emil worked for the most important insurance company in Baltimore and was forceful, dynamic, and opinionated. His Buick spoke of money and power to Marydell Road, which was Chevy, Ford, and Plymouth territory. Fortunately for the younger Aunt Sally's social reputation, Herb kept his 1934 Chevrolet coupe out of sight in the garage.

From an upstairs window I saw the Buick arrive, then retreated to my bedroom while the welcoming fuss went on downstairs, first on the porch, then in the parlor. I was not going to be down there falling all over myself like my mother and Doris to make the great man's mother feel she was doing us a favor with this visit. My plan was to act as though nothing at all special was going on. I would stay in my room reading until my mother called me to come down. Then I would descend casually, greet Edwin's mother civilly, but in a way to let her know I was slightly bored, then excuse myself on grounds I had something important to do.

It was a hard scheme to carry out. For one thing, I didn't really want to read. I wanted to know what was being said down in the parlor, and I couldn't hear anything except Uncle Emil's voice booming away now and then. Uncle Emil usually boomed when he spoke. Uncle Emil had a big voice, which he used to overpower conversations with big, powerful opinions. He sounded more terrifying than he actually was, because of his constant proposals that political problems be solved by lining people up against walls and shooting them.

Had a larcenous gang of political boodlers been caught robbing the municipal till?

"They ought to line them all up against the wall and shoot 'em," said Uncle Emil.

Were conscientious objectors refusing to answer the draft call to report for military duty?

"If I were in charge, I'd line them all up against the wall and shoot 'em," said Uncle Emil.

From behind my closed bedroom door, I couldn't make out whether he was urging the usual sanguinary solutions this afternoon. His rumble was more muted than usual, and there wasn't as much of it. Apparently the women were doing most of the talking.

The book I'd chosen to read was one of the unread classics from my "World's Greatest Literature" set. It was numbingly dull, possibly because I was so busy straining to hear what was happening downstairs that I couldn't concentrate. I had chosen it so that when my mother called me to come down I would be carrying an impressive tome. I wanted this Great-aunt Sallie to notice it, to say with admiration, "Ah, I see you are reading 'World's Greatest Literature.' "

To which I would reply, "Yes, but it's not one of the best. It's just Hawthorne, or Poe, or Shakespeare," depending on whatever it happened to be.

Wasn't my mother ever going to call me, so I could make my languid entrance coming down the stairs? Had she forgotten I was up there?

To remind her, I opened my bedroom door and walked out into the hall and took a few steps back and forth, making noticeable noises with my heels on the wonderful hardwood floor. Then I waited for a reaction downstairs. And waited. Still no call to appear and meet the great guest.

It was finally unbearable. I picked up my volume of "World's Greatest Literature," left the bedroom, and started down. From the top of the stairs I could instantly see our visitor. I was startled. She was so different from what I had envisioned. I had expected a commanding woman of regal stature, square-shouldered, robust, authoritative but youthful, an Amazon, a school principal. Until that first sight of her, I didn't realize that I'd had a vision of what she would look like. The woman I saw, however, gave me the kind of jolt that comes only when some preconceived notion is proved by the reality to be completely wrong.

What I saw was a short, stout old lady swathed in black, with a touch of white here and there, lace maybe, at the neck and cuffs of the gleaming black dress. Her face was a thousand wrinkles, her hair a gray that would never turn silver. It was like looking at one of those old nineteenth-century portraits seen recessed in oval frames in old country houses.

But of course I should have realized that she would be ancient. She was four years older than my grandmother who had died before I was born. Later I learned she was born in 1863, the year of Gettysburg. On my sixteen-year-old's scale of time, that made her seem almost as antique as the pharaohs, though on that day at Marydell Road she was only seventy-eight.

We were introduced. She did not take notice of my book, but appraised me with a professional eye. She had been a schoolteacher, after all. She may have been old, frail, and wrinkled, but her questions were crisp, and her facial expressions suggested an intelligence so superior that I was glad she didn't ask me about the book, since she probably would have understood at once that I hadn't read a word of it.

So I was a senior in high school?

"Yes, ma'am."

I fell back instinctively into the southern form of respect.

And was I doing well in my studies?

Better in Latin than in math, ma'am.

She was pleased to hear I was taking Latin. It was good, rigorous training for the mind, and important to a sound understanding of English.

With that, she was finished with me, and resumed the conversation in progress when I came down the stairs. It was about something that was occurring in Washington, but since I paid no attention to news about government and politics, I had no idea what she was talking about. Neither, I guessed from their withdrawn expressions, did my mother or Aunt Sally the Younger. Uncle Emil, though, seemed to know all about it, and expounded on it forcefully.

Great-aunt Sallie listened to him with beautiful politeness, and, when he subsided, said, "There was a good article on it in *The New York Times* last week which you probably missed. If you go back and read it, you'll have a much better idea of what's involved."

It was magnificent, and even at age sixteen I knew it was. With impeccable courtesy, she had told him he hadn't the faintest idea what he was talking about; she had flattered him with the suggestion that he was a regular reader of *The New York Times,* though she surely knew it was almost impossible to find in Baltimore; and she had let us all know that, though she might look older than Pharaoh, when it came to keeping up with the world, she was miles ahead of anybody in the house.

After that they moved on to easier ground and reminisced about kin living and dead and about times long gone, and it was all "Have you heard anything of—?" and "When was the last time you saw—?" This left no conversational role for me, and I sat gratefully silent, for I knew this ancient lady was too formidable for me to cope with in any way short of utter humility.

That afternoon I had a sobering glimpse of where Edwin James had come from. It made me wonder if my mother had been deceiving me. After seeing my great-aunt Sallie, I began to suspect that, in spite of what she said, maybe Edwin really was smarter than anybody else.

4

Hemingway

In the summer of 1942, I graduated from high school and started classes at Johns Hopkins University. Because of the war, colleges were running full tilt year round, so my transition from high-school senior to college freshman happened immediately. One day I took the commencement tuxedo back to the rental shop and next day I was listening to Professor Francis Murnaghan lecture on differential calculus. This was an alarming experience because, after my first ten minutes in the course, I knew I was going to fail calculus.

Dr. Murnaghan was a spirited, rosy-cheeked gentleman with silvery locks, who spoke with a pronounced Irish brogue. His energetic classroom manner was like a theatrical performance by an Irish character actor with a fondness for pixie roles. He never said "calculus," but always called it "the calcullus" and urged us to think of it as a beautiful machine capable of doing magic things.

"The calcullus, boys, is a fine and smooth machine," he was fond of saying. I liked the poetic idea of mathematics as a mechanical magician, but could never grasp how this fine and smooth machine worked or how to make it do its magic for me. I was forever stripping its gears, or, as Professor Murnaghan put it, "fudging the machine."

In his brogue the word "fudge" came out sounding like "foodge." When I made one of my frequent errors, he looked at my computations with alarm, then at me with pain before saying with sorrow, "You've foodged the machine, boy. You must never foodge the machine."

From the first day in calculus I did not understand a thing Professor Murnaghan was trying to teach. Physics left me equally baffled. Dr. Hubbard, the physics professor, was said to be just as brilliant about ergs and dynes as Dr. Murnaghan was about "the calcullus," and I believed it, because I was hopelessly lost in physics from his very first lecture. Dr. Hubbard's style was the opposite of Professor Murnaghan's. No Celtic flamboyance for Dr. Hubbard. He preferred the solemn, plodding, scholarly mumble. His sentences were thick, gray wool. Listening to them made minutes last for hours. His lectures, which began at the cruel hour of eight in the morning, affected me like chloroform. So did the textbook that was supposed to illuminate the lectures. Before the first week was out, I knew I was going to fail physics just as surely as I was going to fail calculus.

Neither course was required by the university. Taking them was my idea. I had picked up the notion, absurd as it turned out, that knowing physics and calculus would help my chances of becoming a navy pilot, which was my career ambition that summer. In the Battle of Midway, fought two weeks before I entered Hopkins, the navy's carrier-based pilots had not only crippled the Japanese fleet, but also fired me with desire to become a hero of aerial combat. That August I would turn seventeen, and at seventeen I could try to enlist for navy flight training. It was a demanding program and not easy to get into, so I had signed up for physics and calculus to give me an edge.

By my third week on campus I knew it was a terrible mistake. Hopkins was open-minded about such things. I could drop both courses and be free, but doing so would leave my academic schedule full of idle time. That was dangerous. The university had given me a full scholarship for the freshman year with notice that renewal for a second year would require a good academic showing. Without that scholarship I would have to quit college. Herb and my mother were well off, all right, but tuition for a school year at Hopkins was $450, and they were not rich enough to put up that kind of money. Also, since I was living at Marydell Road and riding the streetcar to college, carrying a brown-bag lunch my mother packed every day, I was already imposing on them for free room and board. Having to ask them for tuition money, too, would have been shameful.

I was walking across the campus agonizing about all this one sunny summer afternoon when I saw Charlie Sussman headed my way with a resolute look in his eye. Sussman had been my friend in high school. He was a man of limitless enthusiasms, a Renaissance man, as I thought of him, because he was interested in absolutely everything. The range of his enthusiasms was frightening. In high school when I was completely ignorant of politics, government, and diplomacy, Sussman was constantly trying to drag me off to meetings of the Current Events Club to hear discussions that would open my mind to the complexity of public affairs. When I was so illiterate about music that I couldn't understand why my friends were crazy about Benny Goodman, Sussman was urging me to listen to recordings of Kirsten Flagstad so that I might discover the glory of Wagnerian opera.

This day he had the usual gleam in his eye.

"Where you headed, Suss?"

On his way to learn newspaper writing, he said.

My head was filled with airplane fantasies and the agonies of physics lab, where my work on something called the torsion pendulum experiment was becoming a famous joke among my classmates. Newspaper writing? That crazy Sussman. What would he be into next?

Well, he said, he'd seen this notice on the bulletin board in Gilman Hall. The editors of the campus newspaper were going to give an hour talk on newswriting techniques. The session was open to all comers. Why didn't I join him?

My mind a confusion of airplanes and the torsion pendulum, I said I wasn't interested. This was a challenge to Sussman's conviction that everybody ought to be interested in everything.

"Oh come on," he said. "What else do you have to do?"

A good question. The answer was, "Nothing."

He led the way to a small sitting room with an upholstered couch and a few chairs. A half dozen other students drifted in and sat down. Then came two older, worldly-looking men who took chairs facing us. Hopkins did not regard journalism as an academic discipline worth the attention of a great university, so gave no courses in it and had no journalism instructors. It did, however, budget a little money for a weekly campus newspaper called the *News-Letter*. The aged and wise men who now faced us announced that they were editors of the *News-Letter*, and one started talking about how to write a news story.

"The first thing to understand is the Four W's . . ."

I listened with keen interest. Compared to physics and calculus, writing a news story seemed childishly simple. All you had to learn was Who, What, Where, and When, then write a sentence containing that information, and you were writing a newspaper story. It seemed irresistibly easy. Compared to the circulation end of journalism in which I'd toiled so long for Hearst, the reporting side of the business looked like picnicking on clean linen. It certainly seemed like more fun than calculus and the torsion pendulum. I decided I might give it a try.

The *News-Letter* appeared weekly if the editors were in the mood. Its office was a small room with a few battered wooden desks and a couple of arthritic typewriters in the basement of Levering Hall, which was the YMCA building. I wandered by a few days later, planning to tell the editor I had heard his talk about writing with the Four W's and thought I could do that if he gave me a tryout. The only people there were the editor and his deputy. They seemed even more awesome than I remembered them. Out of respect, I stood just inside the door waiting silently until they might choose to notice me.

They were mourning the loss of most of their staff to the war. They seemed especially upset about the loss of their feature writer. From their conversation, I gathered he was the finest feature writer in the history of *The Johns Hopkins News-Letter*. This meant little to me, since I was vague about what a feature writer did.

They finally broke off and I was beckoned forward to state my business.

"I wonder if there's any possibility you might need somebody to work for the paper."

The interview was cursory:

"Baker . . ."

"Freshman . . ."

"Sixteen, but I'll be seventeen in August. . . ."

"No, I never worked for the high-school paper. . . ."

The newspaper delivery route had required me to rush home as soon as school was out, so there had been no time for extracurricular activities, but I didn't go into that. Although innocent about many things, I knew William Randolph Hearst had an evil reputation with college men as a tyrant of yellow journalism, and it seemed unwise to let these polished men of the world know that I had worked as one of his agents.

They studied me with obvious despair. The deputy editor turned to the editor and said, "God has obviously sent us our next feature writer."

I did not miss the sarcasm.

"Do you write features?" asked the deputy, treating himself to a giggle, very pleased with his wit. I could see he thought me a hopeless case.

I said I didn't write features, just thought I might like to try out for something on the paper, and had been passing by, thought I might just drop in and ask . . .

The chief editor interrupted.

"Do you like to dance?" he asked.

"I can't dance," I confessed.

"Good," he said. "Neither can I," and sent me to interview a student who was planning a tea dance.

I tracked down this impresario in the campus cafeteria. He was an ancient twenty-year-old in a gray three-piece suit with a gold key on a chain dangling across the vest. Black horn-rimmed eyeglasses and meticulously combed black hair completed a portrait of campus power. He was, I later learned, a splendid specimen of the creature referred to in *News-Letter* headlines as a BMOC. Big man on campus. Over coffee in the cafeteria, I wrung out of him the details of his dance program and committed everything to paper. The *News-Letter* printed it the next week almost unchanged. I had finally cracked the door into the glamorous newsroom side of the business where Cousin Edwin dwelt.

*   *   *

When the war ended and the navy sent me back to civilian life after two peaceful years of flying over the American southland, I felt too grown-up to go back to school, so toward the end of 1945 I took a job in the post office. The pay was good, but the work made me feel doomed. Every day I rode the number 8 streetcar downtown to the central post office, where a manager assigned me to a filing case. This was a big wooden box with pigeonholes for each of Baltimore's three dozen branch post offices. A huge batch of incoming mail was dumped in front of me. My job was to scan the address on each letter, determine which branch office it should go to, and slide it into the proper pigeonhole.

Zip codes, which existed only in primitive two-digit form, were still not extensively used by letter writers. As a result, the job at first offered mental stimulation, since I had to learn the correct postal zone for each address that wasn't accompanied by a zip code. For this I could laboriously consult a booklet the management provided, or yell for help from the old-timers surrounding me.

"What's Catonsville?" I yelled.

"Twenty-eight," a voice replied.

"3100 block of North Charles Street," I shouted. "Is that twelve?"

And back came the reply, "No, it's eighteen."

The experienced help was cheerful about educating me, and for good reason. The boredom of the work was so mind numbing that they welcomed excuses to cry out. It was relief from deadly routine. Very quickly I learned Baltimore's street addresses well enough to make the letters fly into the pigeonholes, but no matter how quickly I cleared away one great pile, another was always immediately put before me. It was my first experience of being inhuman. I felt that I was nothing but a tiny fragment of a gigantic endless belt. The old-timers, seated on their high stools, peering through thick eyeglasses, shoulders rounded by years of boredom, slapping envelopes into pigeonholes hour after hour, day after day, made me wonder if a job with good pay was really all I wanted of life after all.

There was small relief on days the magazines arrived. Because of their size, they had to be filed in huge cases six feet high. For this labor the floor manager chose four or five men younger than most, since the work meant standing for hours and moving hundreds of pounds of printed matter. It was a chance to stand upright, to move around, and chat while we worked. It was a lovely break from the silent, mindless, hunched-over grind of the letter cases.

The great backbreaker was *Life* magazine. Every Baltimorean with a mailbox seemed to subscribe. Once every week trucks dumped tons of *Life* onto the unloading platforms. Those were good days. We could be on our feet most of the day, moving, talking, keeping our minds from going to dust. Our talk was not stimulating, just mind-saving chatter and poor jokes, just enough like conversation to remind us we were human. We heaved *Life*s and talked about nothing.

"You can have that Sinatra kid. He can't touch Crosby."

"I can't stand either one of them. They don't sing, they just breathe into the microphone."

"What are you, one of those opera lovers?"

"Give me Vaughn Monroe any day."

As a joke we always pronounced Monroe's first name as "Vawjin"; it was not work that cultivated high wit.

"Vawjin Monroe! You're kidding."

"Vawjin can't sing. He yells everything."

"That's what I like about him. I like a singer who opens his mouth when he sings."

Change of subject:

"I went out to Carlin's last night to see the wrestling."

"That's not wrestling. That's show business."

"Some of it's real though."

"You're crazy."

"No, some of it's real wrestling. How about Jim Londos, did you ever see Jim Londos wrestle? Are you going to say Jim Londos isn't a real wrestler?"

"The Golden Greek?"

"If Londos was a real wrestler, he wouldn't have to go around calling himself the Golden Greek."

When the Christmas mail rush ended I was ready to go back to college. Thanks to the G.I. Bill of Rights for veterans, which paid tuition and a small living allowance, the old problem of how to meet the bills no longer existed. This was another blessing for which I thanked President Roosevelt, and it confirmed my Depression-born faith in the New Deal and the Democratic party.

Returning to Hopkins that February, I soon drifted back to the *News-Letter* office. It looked the same as it had back in the summer of 1942, a little grimier maybe, the same old typewriters sitting on the same worn-out old desks. I went there looking for the company of people who liked to write.

Devoted to the classical university disciplines, Hopkins offered no writing program. If you had literary notions, you majored in English literature, which at Hopkins was assumed to have ceased in 1882 with the death of Dante Gabriel Rossetti. So students interested in writing, having no place else to turn, gravitated toward the *News-Letter* office, looking for others who had read the latest Hemingway and Faulkner novels and debated whether Scott Fitzgerald was truly first-rate and if it was childish to admire Thomas Wolfe. Most of us who turned up in the *News-Letter* office that February had little interest in journalism. All we wanted was to write something that we could afterward see in print.

Like all the newspaper offices I would later know, the *News-Letter*'s attracted people whose minds were open and interesting, people who were curious instead of preachy, people who distrusted people who had all the answers, people with a taste for the raffish, people who wanted life to be interesting rather than safe. They were mostly war veterans in their middle to late twenties and could talk authoritatively of an exotic world that extended from the shrines of Kyoto to the whorehouses of Naples. When I was weary of professors and library dust, and hungered for entertainment, the *News-Letter* office was the place to go.

There I found Wishmeyer, married and a veteran of the Italian campaign, scolding the entire staff for their ignorance of the Spanish philosopher Miguel de Unamuno. Leo Flashman, the editor, was an infantry veteran and a driven man, determined to get out a paper on schedule once a week in spite of a staff that considered the work essentially childish and treated the office as a literary salon.

"Could you postpone the usual Unamuno lecture," he asked Wishmeyer, "while we try to find some copy to take to the printer?"

Bill Gresham was the office radical. He was short, going bald, and bore a pronounced facial resemblance to the actor Edward G. Robinson, who was famous for "Little Caesar" and other movie gangster roles. He chain-smoked cigarettes and spoke authoritatively on everything, often exhaling powerful streams of smoke all over his audience while doing so, as if to show how little he thought of them.

In the war Gresham had been a gunner in a B-24 flying bombing missions for the Eighth Air Force over Germany, belted into the big bomber's open waist, swinging the .50-caliber machine gun at the Messerschmidts and Focke-Wulfs swooping out of the sun with hammering guns. The damage showed in the trembling of his hands. Watching him light a cigarette or lift a cup of coffee to his mouth was a suspense-packed drama. Wishmeyer made a joke of these tremors.

"Tell us again about the flak over Frankfurt," he said as Gresham's quivering hand lifted a too full cup and splashed coffee over a textbook. I was shocked until I saw that Bill enjoyed being teased in this way. Wishmeyer, I saw, was using this cruel tone as a subtle way of reminding us veterans of the bloodless stateside war that being waist-gunner in a B-24 over Germany was not the frolic Hollywood made it out to be.

At first I disliked everything about Gresham: the way he looked, the way he dressed, the know-it-all way he talked, the assault-and-battery way he smoked his cigarettes, and, finally, the way he wrote in blunt, graceless sentences and paragraphs that made no music but seemed to be written with a sledgehammer.

Soon he became a good friend, and much later he became godfather to my first child, and long after that he became a trial and a tragedy, but that was in a future far distant from the time I am now speaking of, when the war had just had its happy ending and all prospects were bright for once poor boys who thought that the worst was behind them and they could never be corrupted.

Though I was younger and more inexperienced at war than most of the *News-Letter* crowd, they accepted me in the inner circle, probably because I could write campus-newspaper prose more rapidly and fluently than any of them. This was because I did not take it seriously. To me, working on the *News-Letter* was like playing newspaper. As a newsboy, I had spent too many years reading and studying real newspapers. In those years I had absorbed an instinctive sense of how the real thing was written and how to tell the real from the fake. A front page dominated by news of the senior prom could only be kiddie journalism to a man who had grown up on Hearst front pages packed with corpse-filled trunks, heiresses' love nests, and international bank heists.

Thinking of the *News-Letter* as play, I did not strain at the writing, but went at it in a relaxed, offhand, playful spirit. It wasn't serious, it certainly wasn't work, and I did it for the pleasure and fun of it, which made it easy, often spoofing the stories shamelessly in a way that would have got me kicked out of any journalism school. I became a tireless writer of sophomore humor, then discovered the higher sport of parody. Soon I was handing the editor stories written in the baroque style of early *Time* magazine:

"Strode last week did receding-hairlined, lacrosse-playing Student Councilman Merle Debuskey into the Christian dullness of Levering Hall . . ."

Leo took journalism seriously, and patiently handed back my best thigh-slappers with a polite request that I tone them down. Poor Leo. He wanted terribly to be a newspaperman and knew he would never have the chance. After college he was going to take charge of his family's furniture store. That was what his parents wanted, and Leo, who was the best of sons, could not bear to disappoint them, though it was newspaper work, not retail furniture, that he loved. Aware that his editorship of the *News-Letter* was the only newspaper career he would ever have, Leo was determined to do the job like a professional. He kept the worst of my horseplay out of the *News-Letter,* but since my skill at parody enabled me also to write a flawlessly dull news story in the style of the flawlessly dull *Baltimore Sun,* I quickly acquired a reputation as both a fancy and useful staff writer.

To keep me from losing interest, Leo, the editor in chief, cunningly invented the elegant and meaningless title of "managing editor" and gave it to me. Managing editor. It was the title that had haunted me since childhood. I understood what Leo was up to, and knew the title was meaningless, but nevertheless it affected me, and I took it more seriously than it deserved.

At Marydell Road I could not resist telling my mother: "You've now got another managing editor in the family."

She was pleased and I was immodest enough to refrain from belittling this splendid title, so did not tell her the *News-Letter* was only a play newspaper and my title was a kind of joke. Joke it might be, but I now bore the same title as Cousin Edwin.

But of course I wasn't really interested anymore in newspaper work, and my mother knew it. When I let her think my meaningless title carried weight, she said something like, "Now that you're managing editor of the *News-Letter*, maybe you'll start thinking again about a newspaper job when you graduate."

I was thinking nothing of the sort. Journalism was not serious work. It was fun. Writing novels was serious work, and people who wrote them could be taken seriously, like scientists and mathematicians. Any sophomoric wise guy could write journalism, but it took an artist to write great novels. My ambition was to become a novelist, preferably a great novelist. I wanted to be the new Hemingway.

5

Mr. Dorsey

The *Baltimore Sun* needed a police reporter that spring. The managing editor mentioned it to an editorial writer who lectured at Hopkins, and the editorial writer mentioned it to a professor, who mentioned it to me and gave me a telephone number to call at the *Sun*. I was to ask for a Mr. Dorsey.

On the phone I talked to a woman with a deep, snobby, go-to-hell voice, and she told me to come in for an interview a few days later. I took my only suit to the cleaner for the high-priced overnight clean-and-press job, asked my mother to iron my best shirt, and polished my shoes for the first time in weeks. It wasn't that I especially wanted to work for a newspaper. I was simply desperate for a job. Any job.

A few days later, looking unusually spiffy, I presented myself at the *Sun* building. This was not just a building. It was a pronunciamento in stone. Unlike the *News-Post*'s shabby newspaper factory, which I had visited with Deems so long ago, the *Sun* building was as stately as a monument, as grave as a temple to the god of truth, which the *Sun*, with "Light For All" as its motto, purported to serve. Gray and massive, it announced its importance with trimmings that included two dozen huge Greek columns, each two stories high, and three gigantic circular clocks set high into the stone walls and towering above the level of the top floor. To emphasize the point for anyone still uncertain about the *Sun*'s position in Baltimore, the building was situated at the geographical center of the city, the intersection of Charles and Baltimore streets. It was designed to make all who entered feel humble, and, in my case, it succeeded.

I went in through the front door. The receptionist guarding the elevator had apparently been hired to make visitors feel not only humble but also unworthy. I was still young enough to be intimidated by such gorgons, and when she examined me with an expression that said I simply wouldn't do, I felt apologetic rather than insulted.

"Can I help you?"

I said I was there to see Mr. Dorsey.

"Do you have an appointment?"

I did. Oh yes, indeed, I had an appointment. I wouldn't dream of disturbing her about seeing Mr. Dorsey if I didn't have an appointment.

"Yes, I have an appointment," I said, and, because that seemed inadequate, added, "I have an appointment to see Mister Dorsey at one o'clock."

"You are early," she said, and motioned for me to stand back from her desk while she dealt with a smartly dressed man who had come in behind me.

"May I help you?"

She sounded almost polite. Maybe it took fancy tailoring to make her behave.

"Mister Erskine of the *New York Herald Tribune* to see Myles Wolff," the smartly dressed man said in an authoritative voice.

She lifted a telephone.

"Mister Erskine of the *New York Herald Tribune* is here to see Mister Wolff." she said. Then: "Go right up, Mister Erskine. Mister Wolff is expecting you."

This episode impressed me even more than the building. For all its elegant airs, the *Baltimore Sun* was still just a hometown paper, but the *New York Herald Tribune* was a legend. True, I didn't know what the legend was, but I was aware that there was some magic attached to the *Herald Tribune,* just as there was to *The New York Times.* Those were great newspapers. I could sense some of the *Herald Tribune*'s greatness in the no-nonsense, big-town style with which Mr. Erskine had handled the receptionist. The discovery that a great paper like the *New York Herald Tribune* called on people who worked for the *Baltimore Sun* raised my respect for the *Sun.*

During these reflections, I was also busy feeling like a fool. The receptionist apparently intended to keep me waiting at her desk until one o'clock. Since there were no chairs for waiting visitors, I had to stand against the wall, as if being punished by the teacher. Well, I might not be from the *New York Herald Tribune,* but I was, after all, managing editor of the *Johns Hopkins News-Letter,* not Caspar Milquetoast.

"I'm going out and get a cup of coffee," I told the receptionist. "I'll be back at one o'clock."

"Just a moment, please," she said. "I'll see if Mister Dorsey is in yet."

She used her telephone again and, lo, Mr. Dorsey was expecting me, I could go right up. I walked past her and stepped into the elevator for the short ride to the top floor.

My problem that afternoon was that the day of reckoning was getting close. Day of reckoning. That's what my mother called it.

"He who dances must pay the piper, sonny boy. The day of reckoning is coming," she told me. "And don't you forget it."

Her warnings—there had been several—were provoked by the lovesick indolence which sapped my energies during my senior year at Hopkins. I should have spent those final months trying to launch my career as a writer. Instead, I had wasted them on love. In idle afternoons and long nights when I should have been polishing my short stories and getting a novel started, I was, instead, courting an enchanting young woman named Mimi. Obsessed by the joys of love, I found the lonely labor of writing impossible. The stories I wrote seemed empty, false, lifeless, and filled with wooden, bloodless characters. I lost all interest in writing them, and even began to glimpse the truth: that they were not very good stories and, worse, that I had no gift for writing fiction.

I was powerless to confront this bleakness. It was so much more pleasant to be in love with Mimi and let the future tend to itself. Something was bound to turn up, I thought. Surely something would turn up. Living at home at Marydell Road, however, made life hard for a lover. There, my mother, with hawk-keen eye, saw me devoting so much time to romancing Mimi that I had none left for writing. In June I would graduate from Hopkins without plans or job prospects.

"He who dances must pay the piper, sonny boy," she said. "The day of reckoning is coming. And don't you forget it."

After graduation, aspiring writers in those days did not linger on in graduate school. Graduate schools were for students who wanted to become doctors, scientists, or professors. Anyhow, my claims to being a writer were unimpressive. I still hadn't got around to starting the novel I meant to write. Worse, I had no idea what it would be about when I did start it. The short stories I mailed to magazine fiction editors were always mailed right back without a word of encouragement. Calling myself a writer would be laughable.

"Amateur writer" was more like it, and in 1947 nobody was hiring amateur writers.

It was May before I finally forced myself to think about the future. Graduation, the day of reckoning, was only a month away. Piper-paying time was at hand. I started studying the help-wanted ads. There was a paper-box factory offering not bad pay for a vaguely defined job. I imagined working in a paper-box factory and felt sorry for myself: one of the nation's great undiscovered young writers toiling, lost and forgotten, in an inhuman paper-box assembly line.

Then the professor mentioned the *Sun,* and there I was, in the elevator, an appointment to see a Mr. Dorsey, not really interested in newspaper work but even less interested in making paper boxes. Well, some great novelists had started as newspapermen. Ernest Hemingway, for instance. That was the way I wanted to go. The Hemingway route. A great artist of the written word. Novelists could become artists, while newspaper people could never be much better than hacks. Still, they did write, didn't they? What's more, they got paid every week. I began to feel reality taking residence in my soul. On the way up in the elevator, I decided not to let Mr. Dorsey see how little respect I had for newspaper work.

"So you think you can be a newsman," were Mr. Dorsey's first words.

We were in an office with a wide picture window overlooking the newsroom. I sat in the rigor mortis posture of the eager-to-please job hunter. Mr. Dorsey leaned back in a swivel chair behind his desk, smug as a hanging judge, and stared at me without the trace of a smile. He was Hollywood's dream of a managing editor. Tall and lean. Iron-gray hair closely cropped. Eyes chilly gray, infinitely wise to the world. An imperious manner, and a way of holding his head

that suggested arrogance, impatience, maybe danger.
A dangerous man, I thought. Not a man to trifle with.
Not a man to tolerate fools. Though we were both
seated, he managed to make me feel that he was looking down on me from great height.

Still, when he said, "So you think you can be a
newsman," it didn't sound like a sneer. Yet, it wasn't
quite a question either, so for a long pause I didn't
know whether he expected an answer. While I hesi-
tated about what to say to this awesome man, his
phone rang.

"I've got to talk to the Washington bureau," he said
to me. "It'll only take a minute."

Those words, "the Washington bureau," had the
same intoxicating effect on me that "the *New York
Herald Tribune*" had produced a few minutes earlier.
This was the big time, and for a brief instant at least,
I was part of it.

"What the hell is Truman up to now?" Mr. Dorsey
was saying to the Washington bureau man on the
telephone.

My God! He was talking about the president of the
United States, and the Washington bureau at the other
end of the line was actually telling him what the president was up to. I was among people who really knew
what the president was up to. In the *News-Letter* office
we often talked about what Truman was up to, but it
was silly, of course, because none of us had the slightest idea of what he was really up to.

"What's your experience?" Mr. Dorsey was asking.

"I've worked on the *Johns Hopkins News-Letter*."

How ridiculous that sounded when spoken to a man
who had just talked to the Washington bureau.

"I'm the managing editor," I blurted.

Mr. Dorsey snorted noisily.

Very close to panic, I almost said, "My mother's
cousin is managing editor of *The New York Times*,"

but stifled the impulse. Managing editors probably all knew each other; suppose Mr. Dorsey telephoned Cousin Edwin and asked what he knew about me and found out Cousin Edwin knew nothing about me. I'd better leave him out of it.

"You realize you can never get rich in the newspaper business," Mr. Dorsey said.

I scoffed at the idea that I might dream of wealth. "Rich?" I tried to smile the smile of a man calmly resigned to a life of penury. "I never expect to make a lot of money."

"If you want money, the news business is the wrong line of work to get into," Mr. Dorsey said, and sent me away with a handshake and a loud snort.

A week later the phone rang while I was eating supper at Marydell Road.

"This is Dorsey. If you still want to work for me, you can start Sunday at thirty dollars a week."

I was flabbergasted. Thirty dollars a week. That was Depression pay. This was 1947. The price of coffee was up to fifty cents a pound and milk to twenty cents a quart. A pair of shoes cost $9. I'd been in New York a few weeks earlier, and the prices there were incredible. A theater ticket had cost me $1.50, the hotel was $4.50 a night, a sirloin steak dinner, $3.25. Thirty dollars a week was an insult to a college man.

"Well?" Mr. Dorsey asked.

"I'll take it," I replied.

I'd had very little competition for the *Sun* job. Two or three classmates at Hopkins had also talked to Mr. Dorsey. Why he picked me was a mystery. Maybe because of that empty title Leo had given me. None of my competitors could call himself a managing editor. Whatever the reason, the job was no prize. America was still a generation away from the glamorous and lushly paid Age of Media when the country's brightest

Charles H. Dorsey, Jr., managing editor of the *Sun*

college graduates would be willing to kill for a newspaper job.

In 1947 newspaper work was for life's losers. Men who dreamed of big money and rich wives went in for medicine, law, business, or engineering. Those like me, without talent for high-income work, might go to graduate school to become professors. Professors were poorly paid, but the social cachet was good. Newspapermen, by contrast, occupied the social pit. Respectable folks did not want their daughters to marry one. They were thought to be a vagabond crowd addicted to booze, vulgar language, bad manners, smelly wardrobes, heavy debt, and low company.

At Marydell Road we did not share this uptown view. The astounding success story of Cousin Edwin made journalism a glittering career in my mother's imagination. With her schoolteacher's respect for words, she would have been delighted if I had turned out to be a talented novelist, but a newspaper job was just as wonderful in her view. When I complained that the pay was insulting for a college man, she refused to sympathize with me.

"If you work hard at this job," she said, "maybe you can make something of it. Then they'll have to give you a raise."

It had been a long time since I considered myself in competition with Edwin, so the idea of "making something" of the *Sun* job was far from my mind. Now that the job problem was settled, my hopes of becoming a fiction writer revived. Maybe I'd been foolish to think I could sell stories while still just a college kid. I probably needed a little more experience of the world, a little more writing practice before I could turn out really first-rate fiction. For this, the newspaper job would be a blessing. It would give me some writing experience and tide me over financially until I sold my first novel. Then I would quit the *Sun* and move to New York. Being a successful novelist wouldn't be much fun in Baltimore.

I still had no idea what that successful novel would be about. Whenever I lifted my pen to start writing it, my mind began to drift, and drowsiness fell upon me so heavily that to keep awake I had to phone Mimi and suggest we go to a movie. Years later, after I had met hundreds of people who wanted to be writers but didn't want to write, I was finally able to diagnose my problem: I wanted to be a great novelist, but I didn't want to write novels.

My ignorance about journalism was as deep as my ignorance of the art of fiction. I knew, for instance, that the *Sun* was a morning paper, but I didn't realize this meant I would have to work nights.

I knew almost nothing about my new employer

except that it also published an afternoon paper, the *Evening Sun,* and that the *Sun* and *Evening Sun* collectively were called the "Sunpapers." I was surprised to learn they had separate staffs, separate newsrooms, and separate editors, and were intensely competitive.

I was surprised to learn that the awesome Mr. Dorsey, though managing editor of the *Sun,* was not the supreme law of the Sunpapers, but that the *Evening Sun* had an equally powerful managing editor.

I was surprised to learn that above these two giants towered an even more magnificent figure, a widely dreaded tyrant named Neil H. Swanson. Swanson held the grandiose title of "Executive Editor of the Sunpapers" and justified it by behaving sometimes like Louis the Sun King and others like Cecil B. De Mille directing a Hollywood epic for the silver screen. Oldtimers remembered Swanson on the night of his appointment as executive editor appearing in the newsroom shortly before midnight accompanied by his wife and another couple, all in formal dress, and led by two large Great Danes, which Mrs. Swanson held on a tight leash. Removing his dinner jacket, loosening his bow tie, and rolling up his shirt-sleeves, Swanson had said, "Now we'll start to get out a *newspaper!*" It was a message foretelling the style of management to come.

Another thing I didn't know was that a police reporter was the lowest form of life in the *Sun*'s universe. Titans like Swanson and Mr. Dorsey had no time for police reporters. Theirs was the world of foreign correspondents, war, diplomacy, global catastrophe, national politics, presidents. They dealt with the great reporters, men who could tell them what the hell Truman was up to now. What police reporters dealt with, I soon learned, were purse snatches, liquor-store holdups, traffic accidents, six-alarm fires, and lost pets. On rare occasions when our paths crossed, Mr.

Dorsey looked through me as though I were invisible. The dreaded Swanson was so remote that our paths simply never crossed.

My main contact with power was Clarence Caulfield. He was day city editor, which was not as important as being city editor. "Cauley," as everyone called him, came to work in the late morning, made early assignments, and left at six o'clock when the night city editor arrived to take charge of the city room through the busy night hours. It was Cauley I reported to on my first day at work. He was a red-haired, blue-eyed, freckled, genial, nervous wreck. He wore steel-rimmed glasses and scratched constantly at imaginary itches around his rib cage.

It was midafternoon on a quiet summer Sunday, and the newsroom was quiet and uncluttered. A couple of older gents of the green-eyeshade variety were seated at the copy desk smoking philosophically and brooding silently about whiskey, racehorses, and commas. Two or three men who looked like they might be reporters chatted quietly on the far side of the room. The silence of it was surprising. Movie newsrooms had shaped my vision of the business, and I had expected uproar.

Caulfield seemed all right, though. He got up and shook my hand and smiled a shy, boyish smile when I introduced myself, then absently scratched the side of his rib cage. We exchanged small talk, and I waited for him to assign me to a desk.

"I'm going to send you out to the west side tonight with Hunter," he finally said. "It'll give you a chance to learn where the police stations are, and Hunter will show you what the go-around is."

After a little more talk about nothing much, I asked, "Where will I be sitting?"

"Sitting?"

"My desk, I mean. When I come in to write, where do you want me to sit?"

For the first time, Caulfield looked a little uneasy about me, gave his rib cage a vigorous scratching, and said, "You don't come in to write."

"I see. You mean I'll have to write in the police station."

"You don't do any writing," said Caulfield.

This was astounding news. No writing? One of the reasons for taking this job was the opportunity to get some writing experience.

"The rewrite men do the writing," Caulfield said. "When you get a story, you ask for the desk and give it to a rewrite man."

"Police reporters don't do any writing?"

That was the way the job worked, Caulfield said.

"You mean I won't really need a desk in the office?"

"Police reporters don't come into the office," said Caulfield.

"Never?"

"Well, they can come in if they want to visit now and then."

"I see."

"Of course, you come in every Friday to pick up your pay down at the cashier's window, but you don't have to come up to the office."

I was first amazed, then disappointed. Amazed because I hadn't known all along that police reporters didn't do any writing. Disappointed because the writing was the one side of newspaper work I had looked forward to. Reporting had never much interested me, and now I had stumbled into a job that was all reporting and no writing.

Caulfield saw I had lost some of my fizz. Later I learned he had been a schoolteacher, which probably accounted for his sensitivity toward the young. "Do you like to write?" he asked.

"A little," I said. I didn't want to let on that I wasn't crazy in love with reporting.

"If you do all right in the police districts," he said, "you'll get a chance to come inside and show what you can do on general assignments."

That would mean a desk of my own, writing my own stories, he said.

How much police reporting would I have to do to earn a prize like that? Caulfield, who wasn't authorized to discuss the future, scratched noncommittally and said, "Oh, you never know. A year or two, maybe, if you're still here. Sometimes faster."

A year or two, and I was already almost twenty-two years old, and not getting any younger. A year or two would be forever.

6

Uncle Gene

Uncle Gene was still just a boy when he was forty-five years old. My mother understood that and loved him a little more because of it, except when he was having one of his woman fits. In the power of a woman fit, Uncle Gene lost his boyish good humor and became snappish toward everybody in the house, glaring angrily at us for no reason at all and announcing loudly that he might "go downtown and get a woman."

"He's just having one of his woman fits," my mother said the first time I noticed Uncle Gene behaving curiously and asked her what was wrong.

Calling it "one of his woman fits" made it sound like a medical problem, which made his behavior seem almost excusable. She had been brought up the old-fashioned way, which taught that though men may lust for women, and a woman may sometimes even lust for a man, only heathens talked about it in the parlor. One cold evening when Uncle Gene had told everybody in the house, individually and en masse, that he intended to "go downtown and get a woman," my mother, all patience spent, cried, "I wish to God you'd go ahead and do it, and shut up about it!"

As though he had been waiting for permission, Uncle Gene dashed upstairs, put on his red plaid

Uncle Gene at Marydell Road in 1943

mackinaw, and bolted out of the house. He was back an hour later, just as surly as before he left. Where he went I couldn't guess, since the streetcar trip downtown and back would have taken the entire hour. A woman fit was usually over by the next day, and Uncle Gene returned to his normal behavior, which was lovable in a maddening way.

High-speed conversation was his forte. His normal speech rate must have been well over 250 words a minute, and he spoke in such an outlandish Tidewater Virginia accent that you had to practice listening to him before you could understand anything he said. When my sister Doris introduced him to Bruce Hoffman, one of our neighbors, Uncle Gene immediately took over the conversation. Afterward, Bruce took Doris aside and said, "I didn't know your uncle was French."

Uncle Gene was short with crinkly brown hair and

shoulders braced as stiffly as a West Point plebe. His face was ruddy and deeply lined, suggesting years of robust life in the sun. He was two years younger than my mother and slightly smaller. From the skin-and-bones look of him, I thought he couldn't possibly weigh more than ninety pounds, but he must have, because he was a regular army man. He had been in the peacetime army more than twenty years, had enlisted after the First World War because it was a job with regular pay, had served in the air corps in Billy Mitchell's time when real army men didn't believe in air power. He had been a private, then a corporal, then a sergeant, then a corporal, then a sergeant again. He was still a sergeant when he was discharged during World War Two with a medical disability: bleeding stomach ulcers.

A middle-aged bachelor whose only home was the army, he visited around with family, needing a place to light, finding polite but cool welcomes everywhere. Despite his gentle nature, he contained the power to drive people crazy. The childishness was part of it. Coping with a middle-aged child who constantly talked a blue streak was more than most people could handle.

"I don't see how you stand it, Lucy. He'd drive me crazy," Aunt Pat told my mother. Aunt Sally dreaded the possibility that the duty of housing Uncle Gene would fall to her if anything disabled my mother. He had been discharged in California, so went up to San Francisco to visit his older brother, my uncle Willie, who was divorced, childless, and lived alone. Uncle Willie had gently nudged him eastward. He turned up at Marydell Road one summer afternoon, immaculate in sharply pressed summer khakis, full of raucous laughter and loud military shouts.

"Pass the sidearms!" he shouted across the table when he wanted the salt and pepper. Bursting into a room where people were talking, he shouted, "At ease!" and smiled his big, happy, boy's smile as though he had just made an irresistible joke. Using a broom in place of a rifle, he often demonstrated parade-ground drill maneuvers in the living room, with cries of "Left shoulder—ARMS!" and "To the rear—MARCH!" roaring through the house.

Uncle Gene had arrived during the war while I was away in the navy, and was part of the family when I started working for the *Sun*. Doris sometimes threw up her hands and cried, "This place is a madhouse," and Uncle Gene would have been Exhibit A if she'd had to prove the case. It was more complicated than that, though, because the "madhouse" quality of our lives in that house had an underlying sweetness which was created by my mother's happiness in the bustle over which she presided.

Looking back on it long afterward, I realized that this was the happiest time of her life. With the arrival of the 1950s, her family began to break away and she was never so happy again. In those few years when we were all together at Marydell Road, however, she realized her old dream of having "a home of our own," and she was in full command of it. Now, running this complicated household that was like a zany little hotel, she relished her role as the person the rest of us all needed, the person who made everything work.

Taking in Uncle Gene had been a symbolic deed that put the seal on her authority to rule. In the bad old days of the Depression, she had been the desperate wanderer needing shelter, and had got it when Uncle Allen and Aunt Pat took her into their home in New Jersey, along with her children. Now she was the one strong enough to shelter a family wanderer.

She did sometimes regret that the sheltered wanderer had to be Uncle Gene.

"My God, Eugene, you'd try the patience of the Savior Himself," she shouted one day when she would rather have thrown something at him.

At first I was entertained by the commotions Uncle Gene created. Very quickly, though, his habit of telling the same stories again, and again, and again wore me down. He was incapable of talking on one subject for longer than thirty seconds and made wreckage of all efforts at conversation by those around him.

If my mother started telling the supper table about a man she had met at Aunt Sister's house, Uncle Gene interrupted to tell about a man he had met in California fifteen years ago. Everything reminded him of somebody or something he had once encountered in California.

"What do you think Stalin's up to in Eastern Europe?" I asked my mother, who kept up better than I did with world events.

"Stalin!" Uncle Gene immediately cried. "That reminds me of a fellow I used to know in the army. Big powerful fellow. Two-hundred pounds. Six feet tall. And strong! Strong as an ox."

He always threw in these weight and height statistics while destroying a conversation, for he was obsessed with physical fitness. He went to bed faithfully at ten every night, bounced out at six in the morning, and immediately did three dozen pushups. Now and then he went off for a week or two to a health hotel run by the health faddist and publisher Bernarr Macfadden in upstate New York. There, though he was already nothing but bone and a little fiber, he dieted on carrot juice and gritty substances said to improve the flow of the bodily juices and tone up the muscle tissue.

Uncle Gene was hard on grown-ups but a delight to children, once they learned to understand what he was saying. Nature had made him a perpetual child, and he enjoyed the company of children, as children enjoyed him. His favorite was Mary Leslie. She was still just a toddler when he came banging into the house one afternoon and announced he had bought her a pony. The idea of a little girl riding a pony in grim industrial Baltimore was so bizarre that I assumed he was joking. He wasn't. He had not only bought Mary Leslie a pony, but, displaying an organizational talent that astonished me, he had also arranged to have it boarded at the farm on the hill.

If Uncle Gene was the cymbal banger at Marydell Road, Herb was the bassoonist. As an "on-call" locomotive engineer for the B&O Railroad, Herb had no fixed work schedule. When the B&O needed an engineer they telephoned. The phone routed him out of bed at all hours. More often than not, it rang after midnight. At two, three, four o'clock in the morning, the insistent sound of the telephone was part of the Marydell Road night as the B&O summoned Herb to the big steam locomotives.

Whatever the hour, Herb rolled out of bed, and my mother too, and while he dressed she went down to the kitchen to make him a meal and pack his lunch bucket. Often, arriving home at 3:00 A.M. from my nightly tour of police stations, I found him sitting at the kitchen table in his railroader's overalls, sleepy-eyed, his big shoulders sagging with fatigue, getting ready to tuck into bacon, eggs, and coffee. He greeted me with an expression blending sadness, patience, and weariness. There was little warmth between us, for I never let him forget that he was only a stepfather, and our conversations were merely civil.

"You look tired, Herb. Did you get any rest?"

"Not much."

"What time's your call for?"

"Four-thirty."

"Going to Brunswick?"

"Just up to Mount Airy."

Then to my mother: "Betty, put an extra piece of that pie in with the sandwiches."

My mother was always "Betty" to Herb. Her name was Lucy Elizabeth, and her own family, including Uncle Gene, all called her "Lucy." She had wanted to be rid of "Lucy," however, when she left home as a young woman and moved to northern Virginia to take work teaching school. So she told everybody her name was "Elizabeth" and said they could call her "Betty." I never knew her reasons. Maybe she felt "Lucy" had been a failure and thought starting over fresh as "Betty" would change her luck. Whatever the case, Herb was one who had always known her as "Betty," and Gene's insistence on always calling out "Lucy" while Herb was calling "Betty" made it sound as if they were having a heated dispute about my mother's true identity.

The terrible lack of a regular work schedule kept Herb constantly tired. He might arrive home in early afternoon, but he could not know when the phone might toll for him again. And so he was forever trying to "get some rest," and rarely getting enough to erase the fatigue lines from his face.

"Betty, I've just got to get some rest," he said, arriving home from work at two o'clock on a beautiful summer afternoon and trudging upstairs to fall onto his bed.

An hour later a thunderous bang of the screen door announced Uncle Gene's return from a tour of the neighbors. His piercing voice rang through the house calling for my mother.

"Lucy! Lucy!"

He had just had a talk with old Mr. Simmons over in the park, and Mr. Simmons had told him something funny, and Uncle Gene was dying to tell it to my mother so she could have a good laugh, too.

"Lucy! Lucy!"

She was in the basement ironing.

Uncle Gene crossed the living room to shout upstairs.

"You up there, Lucy?"

No, she was in the basement, he soon discovered. Moving to the basement door, beaming merrily, he gave her a parade-ground order at the top of his lungs:

"Ten-shun! Private Robinson reporting to the basement, sir!"

By this time, the springs had creaked overhead in Herb's brass bed, and the slow tread of melancholy feet could be heard moving along the hall, then down the steps toward the living room. Could be heard by anybody but Uncle Gene, cocooned so deep in his own uproar.

From the basement my mother called, softly trying to tune down Uncle Gene.

"Not so loud, Gene. Herb's trying to get some rest."

She was too late. His rest shattered, Herb stood at the foot of the steps, not in the murderous rage most men might have directed at Uncle Gene, but in an attitude of silent accusation against the whole world. Just standing there in his white light-weight underwear on this warm summer afternoon, a portrait of silent, patient suffering and sorrow. Perhaps he yielded to fury sufficiently to give Uncle Gene a silent glare. Probably not. By now he knew that the subtleties of human communication were wasted on Uncle Gene.

Seeing Herb, Uncle Gene laughed his big laugh, then clapped his hand over his mouth, in a clownish gesture that said, "Oh oh, I've been a bad boy again."

"When did you get in?" he asked Herb at top volume.

Herb, low and somber: "An hour or so ago."

Then Herb, calling to my mother: "Betty! Betty!"

Sensing another crisis, she abandoned the iron and

rushed up the cellar steps and into the living room to find Herb looking like a man who wanted to sob. Uncle Gene, having already lost interest in the scene, had moved to the kitchen and was inspecting cabinets to see what groceries she might need from the store.

Too sensitive to shout at Uncle Gene, Herb raised his voice instead to my mother.

"I don't know, Betty. I just don't know."

"Why don't you go back upstairs and lie down. I'll send Gene to the store up in Irvington."

"A man just can't get any rest around here."

"I'll make you some iced tea. Then you can go back and lie down."

"Some people have it pretty good around here," said Herb, looking toward the kitchen and Uncle Gene so my mother would understand which people he was talking about.

"Don't get all worked up, or you won't be able to sleep. I'll make some iced tea."

"Never mind," Herb said, heading back up the steps. "I've just got to get some rest."

Compared to Herb's schedule, my upside-down day was easy for my mother to handle. I reported for work at either three-thirty or five-thirty in the afternoon and got off at either midnight or two in the morning. *Sun* parties rarely got going before midnight, and nights when there was no party I often joined other reporters at one of the East Baltimore Street strip joints to drink beer and watch the girls, who performed until the two o'clock closing. It was usually three in the morning before the number 8 streetcar deposited me at Marydell Road, and I normally got up for breakfast between eleven and noon.

This was usually a peaceful hour at Marydell Road. By that time my mother might have answered a 4:00 A.M. phone call from the B&O, got Herb off to work, and gone back to bed briefly before Uncle Gene popped up at six and started his pushups. Uncle Gene, nicely exercised, liked to go down to the kitchen and make his own breakfast, violating the dawn with a clatter of banging pans and crashing dishes unless my mother sprang out of bed and got downstairs ahead of him. She usually did, for I had the bedroom over the kitchen, and she didn't want him waking me in the middle of my night.

Her solicitude for me in such matters annoyed Doris, who felt that I was treated as the star tenant of the house, and in talking to Mary Leslie she sometimes referred to me as "her Jesus," though never in my hearing, of course.

After muting the worst of Uncle Gene's breakfast uproar, my mother then roused Doris, who had the household's one normal nine-to-five job, and Mary Leslie, whom she walked to school after breakfast. When I came down for breakfast shortly before noon she had already spent eight hours getting people started on their various days, and her own work, keeping that chaotic house in spotless working order, had scarcely begun.

Living at home was an awkward reminder that while I might be a working man I still couldn't support myself. I paid my mother part of my small salary for room and board, but knew I couldn't have rented a place of my own and bought food for such a trifling sum. This made me feel like an overaged child dependent on Herb's kindness, and in fact I was.

Being tied so closely to my mother was also irritating, because it licensed her to keep a critical eye on my life beyond Marydell Road. She disapproved of my relationship with Mimi, and let me know she disapproved, and I resented her claiming the right to disapprove. Yet I could not speak out because I was still essentially a child in her house, and because I loved her and knew her criticisms were part of her effort to help me to amount to something. In short, though I yearned for independence, I was a prisoner of the comforts of home.

While comfortably settled with my mother, Herb, Doris, Mary Leslie, and Uncle Gene, I dreamed of leading the kind of life we then called "Bohemian." This would involve liquor and cigarettes, wild partying, carousing with lewd women, romance by the light of candles stuck in wine bottles, and deep all-night conversations with sophisticated people about art, Freud, and the meaning of life. I was grown-up enough to realize there was something comic, even absurd, about all this, but I was also young enough to think it would be an enviable and exciting way to live. What was needed was a place to do it.

I had two close friends, George and Al, who shared my fancy for the life of glamorous debauchery. Both were doctors. I had known George since high school, Al since college. They were a study in the attraction of opposites. George was brash, noisy, florid, short; Al was subtle, soft-spoken, pale, tall. Both were talented in science, but whereas George was a brass band, Al was cool silk. I was walking with Al to his parked car late one night when we saw the car door open and someone rooting about inside. As we reached the car, the thief emerged carrying a bottle of whiskey Al had left on the floor. Al didn't even raise his voice, just snapped his fingers impatiently as though at a naughty child, extended his arm, and said, very calmly, "Here! Give me that bottle at once." The thief meekly handed it over and ran. Unruffled by what might have been a dangerous moment, Al started the car and, as we pulled away, said, "What gall."

At George's suggestion, the three of us decided to pool enough money to rent a downtown apartment where we could pursue the Bohemian life without family surveillance. George had got the idea from an older medical colleague named Norman Zinberg, who reveled in just such an apartment. Norman, said George, was a tireless seducer of women. Still, George pointed out, Norman could not do it without an apartment in which to exercise his fatal charm.

One Saturday night George finagled invitations for Al and me to join him at one of Norman's parties. Accompanied by Mimi, I went prepared to be impressed, and was not disappointed. Norman turned out to be a codger of twenty-six or twenty-seven, certainly old enough to be thoroughly steeped in vice, I thought. The party was a blast: people packed into a small dark humid space, everyone talking at top volume, men in business suits telling jokes, Norman himself managing somehow to dominate this tightly packed, low-yield riot with an ease and humor which awed me and enchanted Mimi.

Here was the life I yearned for. If only I had Norman's poise, *savoir-faire,* and sophistication. His smile was large, generous, and friendly. He asked if we would dare try some Silken Veils.

"Silken Veils?"

"I'd never heard of them either until last week," he said. "They're made with vodka and Dubonnet."

Vodka and Dubonnet! I had never drunk vodka, which was then still an uncommon drink in America, and didn't know what Dubonnet was. My ignorance of such exotic liquors made me realize how much I had to learn before I could become a man of the world. I left Norman's party full of Silken Veils and admiration for the wonderful life he had let me glimpse. I was irritated to see that Mimi had also been charmed by this suave sophisticate, but that was understandable. One day I would be equally worldly and women would find me enchanting, too.

After that, Al, George, and I wasted no time. For

fifty dollars a month we rented a basement apartment in a large, decaying house on Cathedral Street. A basement was more than we had hoped for. We associated basement apartments with Greenwich Village in New York, spiritual home of the Bohemian life. To heighten our sense of decadence, the place smelled of damp rot and was dark enough even at midday to justify lighting candles. The landlord had furnished it with a few sticks of pine, a bed of exhausted springs, an upholstered couch reeking of mildew, some cracked plates, and a worn-out refrigerator.

Al, whose taste was more delicate than George's and mine, thought the decadence was fine but needed a relieving touch of elegance to show guests that though we might be Bohemians, we were not barbarians. For this purpose he brought in a framed print of Vincent Van Gogh's "Starry Night" and nailed it over the mildewed couch.

We immediately invited people to drop in on Saturday night and "bring your own bottle." None of us could afford to be lavish with whiskey. Our first guests were mostly friends we had known in college. The favored drink was blended whiskey, something like Schenley or Four Roses, which were cheaper than bourbon and Scotch. The standard hangover was agonizing.

Soon our basement became so famous for good times that it was always packed on weekend nights. Even on afternoons, I rarely went there without finding a couple of visitors. Al, George, and I had discovered that Baltimore was swarming with young people as desperate to escape bourgeois family life as we were. With the crowds, the privacy essential to seduction was impossible, but a lot of liquor flowed in that basement, the cigarette smoke was often thick enough to overpower the mildew odor, and sophisticated conversation was incessant and intense.

I spent a night there only once. My aim was to experience what it would be like to get free of Marydell Road and have my own place. I chose a night in midweek when there would be no partying. Getting off work at midnight, I let myself into the apartment about one in the morning. There was nobody there, though there had been earlier in the evening. Dirty whiskey glasses were scattered around. Ashtrays were piled high with butts. I opened the refrigerator, got a whiff of something rotting, and slammed it shut. I sat on the collapsing couch to read the late edition of the paper, but the light was too poor. The smell of mildew and whiskey seemed, for the first time, unromantic, even unpleasant.

Marydell Road certainly smelled better. Also my mother might be up getting Herb off to work, so there would be coffee and my mother to talk to about my night's work. In the apartment I was engulfed by a depressing solitude. I went to the bedroom, rolled back the spread, and noticed for the first time that the sheets were gray. Though we had never laundered them, this surprised me. It hadn't occurred to me that sheets eventually got gray unless somebody occasionally washed them. I got into bed anyhow. I'd been aware when we rented the place that the springs were bad, but hadn't realized how terrible they would be to sleep on.

When the night finally ended, sometime shortly after dawn, I remembered that I hadn't brought toothbrush, razor, or shaving cream. The only towel in the bathroom hadn't been laundered any more recently than the bedsheets. Skipping all ablutions, I dressed rapidly and, feeling too dirty to enjoy breakfast, hurried down to Fayette Street, caught the number 8, and went home to Marydell Road's warm showers, clean towels, comfortable beds, and clean sheets.

My mother, who knew I had intended to spend the

night at the apartment, was surprised to see me out of bed so long before noon.

"Well how was it?" she asked.

I was too bitter about my miserable night to lie.

"Awful," I said.

"Will you be staying at the apartment again anytime soon?"

"Not unless you kick me out of the house," I said.

I had made a sad discovery: Down not too deep, I was a hopeless bourgeois. I might complain about hating to go home to mother, Herb, and Uncle Gene, but that was the life I was built for.

It was going to take Mimi and the *Baltimore Sun* a long time to get me off Marydell Road.

7

Murder

On my first night as a police reporter I was scooped on a murder. It was a Sunday. I worked from 3:30 until midnight covering east Baltimore police stations and got home around one in the morning. My mother was waiting up to hear all about the launching of my career, and we sat over coffee for an hour while I told her what police stations looked and felt and smelled like, and how dull the night had been.

I was grateful for that dullness. Riding the streetcar to work that afternoon, I had been worried. What would I do if a big story broke that night? Aware that I knew nothing about police reporting, I realized my incompetence could be disastrous if something newsworthy happened in east Baltimore before midnight. Luckily, it was a quiet night. I phoned the city desk with a few dim items culled from the police reports, and at midnight reported everything quiet in east Baltimore and got permission to go home.

I went to bed feeling lucky and was eating breakfast at 10:30 next morning when the phone rang. It was Mr. Caulfield, early man on the *Sun* city desk.

"Did you cover the east side last night?" was his first question.

"Didn't you notice that murder?" was his second.

Murder.

Instantly I knew calamity had struck.

"What murder?"

"Haven't you seen the afternoon papers?"

I was still eating breakfast.

"Take a look at them," Caulfield said. "Then come on into the office."

There were two afternoon papers, Hearst's *News-Post* and the *Evening Sun.* I was sickened by the huge headlines leaping off their front pages: MURDER IN EAST BALTIMORE. WOMAN BLUDGEONED TO DEATH. POLICE HOLD MAN IN SUNDAY SLAYING.

Sunday. East Baltimore. Murder.

Those monstrous headlines were jeers directed at me personally. "Some reporter!" was what they said to me. "Sunday in east Baltimore was your beat, and you couldn't even find out about this unspeakable murder."

Caulfield's command—"Come on into the office"— was ominous. He was the man who had told me police reporters weren't expected to come into the office. Somebody higher up, probably Mr. Dorsey, must have issued orders so severe that they could only be executed in the office. I dreaded to think what those orders might be. Mr. Dorsey might have decided that a man who could overlook a murder his first night on the job was too dim ever to be a newsman.

The humiliation I anticipated in the office was too painful to think about. One night during flight training in the navy, I had landed my plane without remembering to put the wheels down. Except for ruining the propeller, it was a beautiful landing that left me unscratched. When the plane finally skidded to a stop in showers of sparks, I stood up in the cockpit with spotlights playing over me while sirens screamed and fire trucks and ambulances roared to the scene. Standing there with my stupidity on brightly lit display before the entire squadron, I knew for the first time in my life what utter humiliation felt like. Going into the office to face Caulfield on this dreadful Monday would be even more painful. How could I face my mother and break the news that the next Edwin James had been fired after one day on the job?

I studied the murder story in the afternoon papers. It wasn't the sort of thing that would have interested a movie detective like Nick Charles or Perry Mason. There had been a sidewalk confrontation between a man and a woman, and he had hit her with a brick. Taken into the Johns Hopkins emergency room, she was pronounced dead. Later the police had picked up the man and had him locked up at the Northeastern Police Station.

Reading through these dreary details, I was horrified to realize that I had held the basic material of the story in my hand the night before and paid no attention to it. Part of the reporting routine involved flipping through each station's sheaf of daily reports the cops filed about the business they tended on their daily rounds: stickups, cats rescued from trees, purse snatches, fires, auto accidents, burglaries, pet owners warned to silence their barking dogs, assorted forms of violent death. Not all police reports were illiterate, but since becoming a Baltimore cop in those days depended on political connections rather than writing skill, most made heavy demands on the reader.

I had toiled through reports at Northeast and excavated a couple of routine items which I offered the city desk to show I was on the job. One of the many items I rejected was a barely legible document written in incomprehensible English. It seemed to concern a woman who had died at the Hopkins emergency room. No news there. People died in emergency rooms all over Baltimore every night. This particular woman, so far as I could make out from the report, had met a man on the street during her final day. I saw nothing unusual about that. The man had been carrying a brick. That was a bit odd, but hardly news, was it? The two of them had a discussion. That wasn't very newsy either. Two people meeting on the street often have discussions. The man had done something unintelligible with the brick, subsequent to which he walked away. After a while the woman was taken to the hospital.

Reading the afternoon papers, I cursed the cop who wrote that half-witted report. I also cursed the desk officer who'd been on duty at Northeast last night. Silently, I cursed him unprintably. Too late, I knew now that he had hated me when I pushed through the big oak doors, smiled at him as genially as I could, and introduced myself.

"New reporter for the *Sun* . . . Baker . . . how's the world treating you? . . . Anything happening out here tonight?"

He was a lieutenant, gold bars and silver hair, impassive face, an old-timer whose heart was not to be softened by a smile from a *Sun* reporter. My attempt to play the regular guy fell flat. He grunted once or twice in reply and shoved the docket to me. This was a record of everybody who had been arrested. It was routine stuff. A couple of men locked up for "disturbing the peace," another for not making his child-support payments. It was quiet, all right. There was one man listed as "held for investigation."

"What's he being investigated for?" I asked.

"I wasn't on duty when he came in," was all the lieutenant offered.

That was when a careful reporter would have got on the phone to the policeman who'd made the arrest, but I was not even a reporter, let alone a careful reporter. During my indoctrination, I'd been told that docket entries reading "held for investigation" were commonplace and that these investigations were usually small chaff—minor burglaries, hit-and-run accidents, things of no news value.

So when the lieutenant brushed off my question and handed me the day's file of police reports, I put the "held for investigation" entry out of mind instead of connecting it to the brick-toting man in the incomprehensible police report. As a result, I was now summoned to appear in the city room in shame and disgrace, a reporter scooped on a murder his first night on the job. Had any man in the whole history of journalism made such an inauspicious beginning?

Reporters used the small back elevator to the newsroom on the top floor. A central corridor divided the morning paper's city room from the *Evening Sun*'s. Big window panels afforded a sweeping view into the *Sun* city room. The city desk was situated toward the far end of the room, and just beyond the city desk was the managing editor's desk, which Mr. Dorsey used when not in his private office talking to the Washington bureau, interviewing job applicants, or doping the horses.

Through the windows I could see a half dozen reporters drifting around idly, the way reporters do when they have no assignment and are looking for trouble. Caulfield was sitting alone at the city desk, his back to the window. At the managing editor's desk sat fierce Mr. Dorsey in his shirt-sleeves, feet up on the desk, hands clasped behind his head, talking across the room to somebody on the copy desk.

I had not yet heard Lyndon Johnson say, "It's time to bite the bullet," but that's what time it was on that Monday afternoon. Standing outside the window, I collected myself as well as I could under the circumstances, opened the door, and went in, looking to neither left nor right, cheeks burning with shame, imagining that everybody in the room was staring at me, the pariah who had been scooped on a murder his first night out. Afterward, I realized that nobody could possibly have paid me the slightest attention, but that was long afterward, when I was wiser about newspaper life.

Caulfield didn't notice me at first. When he did he seemed puzzled about who I was and what I wanted. Then, recognizing me, he tilted back in his swivel chair and asked, "What happened last night?"

I made a determined effort not to look toward Mr. Dorsey. If he caught me looking at him he might call me over and fire me on the spot. Before ordering me out of the office, he would say something cruel like, "And you thought you could be a newsman. Hah!" Caulfield at least seemed gentle. He was looking at me calmly, even with the hint of a smile as he waited for my defense.

In straightforward fashion I tried to tell him how I had happened to overlook the murder. It was no use lying. Somebody later told me Caulfield had once taught high-school Latin, so he must have heard every conceivable excuse for failure. Now, however, peering over his steel-rimmed eyeglasses, he looked flabbergasted by my explanation for missing the murder story.

Yes, I confessed, I had seen the police report. But nobody could have made sense of it, the way it was written. It was hardly in English. I tried to reconstruct that constabulary prose for Caulfield, saying something like, "All it said was that a female expired consequential to injuries occurring during the course of a conversation with a man carrying a brick in the course of which the same did something unintelligible to her head with same, to wit, the brick."

Caulfield studied me as though he couldn't believe what he was hearing. "And that didn't seem to you

like something that might be worth looking into?"
Caulfield said.

"At no point in his report," I said, "did the cop
state that this was a murder."

"Didn't you talk to anybody at the station? Anybody at all?"

Of course I did. I talked to the desk lieutenant. I
asked him if there was any news, and he didn't even
mention there'd been a murder.

Caulfield studied me as he must have studied the
class dunce in his days teaching Cicero. His voice was
low, quiet.

"Nobody told you it was a murder," he said.

Absolutely not.

His voice became a little louder now.

"You saw a report saying a woman died of head
injuries—"

Exactly.

"—after a man with a brick did something in her
presence with that selfsame brick—"

That's right.

"—and it never crossed your mind that what he did
with the brick might just possibly have been an act of
violence, and if it was and the woman died, that it
might just possibly have been murder?"

I saw what he meant.

"I shouldn't have counted on the cops to tell me
they had a murder," I said, hoping I sounded sincerely
contrite instead of merely stupid.

Caulfield never used coarse language, so refrained
from cursing. Instead he lectured. A newspaper reporter, he explained, was supposed to be able to "add
two and two and get murder."

I said I understood that now.

"And you can't expect the police to tell you when
they've got news," he said. "The police hate having

news in the paper because news means the police might have to work harder."

This was the only lecture Caulfield ever gave me on newspaper work. Usually he was satisfied to do his job quietly and go home. His lecturing now was a good sign because if he was going to fire me he probably wouldn't be wasting his time trying to teach me something. This proved to be the fact when Caulfield said that Mr. Dorsey had ordered me to suffer a week of humiliation. I would not be trusted to undertake reporting duties again until next week. Until then I would have to tag along with the other police reporters and try to learn something about the work from watching what they did on their rounds.

There were worse things than being held up as a dolt before my fellow reporters. For instance, there was having to go home and tell my mother I'd been fired. With much unctuous groveling, I thanked Caulfield, promised always to use my head from here on, and assured him the *Sun* wouldn't be sorry about giving me another chance.

Out of the agony of this episode I learned one of the most important lessons every journalist needs to know about the craft of newspaper reporting; to wit, that only a fool expects the authorities to tell him what the news is.

There were other lessons. About newsless Monday, for example. Because Sundays produced little news, editors could not be finicky about how they filled their Monday papers. The murder that caused my troubles would have got little space any day but Monday; it lacked gore, mystery, melodrama, scandal, or sex, the elements that made murder stories juicy entertainment for the public. Except for being murdered on Sunday, the lady would probably have been buried "back in the truss ads," as reporters called the deep interior of newspapers. In fact, though editors of the evening papers splashed it in heavy ink in their early editions, they quickly busted the poor woman down to very small headlines as the day went on and the rising tempo of human activity churned up better stuff for later editions.

In newspaper terms, her death wasn't much of a murder, but on a newsless Monday morning it was better than no murder at all. As I soon learned, whether something was big news, small news, or no news at all depended on a complicated mixture of factors, including what day of the week it was. There were no written rules, you just had to get a feel for the relative value of events. Before my police days, I'd had the innocent notion that murder was murder, and it was all equally bad. As a police reporter, I learned better fast. The gravity of murder varied. There was quality murder and there was ho-hum murder. In the jargon of the *Sun* newsroom, there was the "terrific murder," the "good murder," and the "little murder." I soon learned to distinguish them so as not to waste the rewrite men's time on busy nights.

Phoning the desk, I might say, "I've got a little murder." To which the rewrite man might say, "Just give me enough for a couple of paragraphs. We've got a six-alarm fire on the harbor taking up most of the page."

Saying "I've got a good murder," however, got the city editor's attention. It meant a story worth prominent play even on a busy night. Any number of things could elevate a "little murder" into a "good murder." Was the victim "a prominent Baltimorean" or "a member of an old Maryland family"? If so, "good murder." Could the rewrite man justifiably describe the victim as "statuesque," the universally understood code word meaning "big breasts"? If so, "good murder," especially if the murderer was still unknown and the cops could be persuaded to hint at sexual motives behind the crime. Multiple murders were "good." So were murders of children.

The mass murderer, later to become a commonplace figure in American life, was unknown in Baltimore in those days. Now and then somebody with a pistol lost control of himself and killed two people in a single outburst, but the modern custom of killing strangers by the dozen as a deed of looney self-expression was still undreamed of.

The "terrific murder" was one so uniquely gory, so sex-drenched, so mysterious, or so diabolical as to be irresistible even to the *Sun*'s stodgy readership. Such murders featured dismembered corpses, "statuesque" women found dead in full nudity, husbands willing to kill to inherit a rich wife's fortune or to replace a cool wife with a warm mistress, and similar elements beloved by connoisseurs of barbershop magazines like *The Police Gazette* and *True Detective*. The "terrific murder" was so rare that as a police reporter I never had the pleasure of covering one. One of my major disappointments in journalism was the discovery that murder was almost always uninteresting.

This did not prevent the judges of Maryland from sentencing people to hang for it. The sprawling Gothic pile of the Maryland penitentiary with its death house and gallows was situated in a scrofulous section of Baltimore a mere five blocks from the elegance of Mount Vernon Place. Each newspaper traditionally provided one witness to its periodic midnight executions, and at the *Sun* this duty fell to the police reporters. I dreaded the night when my turn would come. Being squeamish about such things, I was afraid I might behave disgracefully. Reporters were supposed to be hardhearted men capable of watching the fall of a stripteaser's G-string or the drop of the condemned man's body with equal world weariness and a suitable wisecrack for each. The approved style was demonstrated in the oft-told tale of the reporter who, after watching a botched hanging, phoned the city desk to ask, "Do you want a feature or a straight noose story?"

I wasn't sure I could meet such high professional standards. Fortunately, there was a lull in the execution rate the summer I started at the *Sun,* so my test of manhood was put off for almost a year. In that time I tried to harden myself to the brutalities of life in Baltimore's lower depths, but only partly succeeded. Though I tried to pass for a regular guy among the cops, they saw that I was faking it, that I was a college boy with no sympathy for what the police had to put up with. Saw that I wasn't comfortable with policemen, that I didn't have the regular-guy touch, that I could probably not be trusted to keep their secrets.

All that was bad enough. To make my life harder, most cops disliked and feared the *Sun,* and some took pleasure in making things difficult for *Sun* reporters. Baltimore was as segregated racially as Johannesburg. Neighborhoods, schools, movie theaters, stores, everything was segregated. It was an all-white police force, and the *Sun* was an all-white newspaper. It hired no blacks except for housekeeping jobs and covered practically no black news. Murders of black people were not "little murders." They weren't murders at all, as I discovered early that summer on phoning the city desk with details of a man who had died of head injuries after being bludgeoned. "You can't hurt 'em by hitting 'em on the head," said the night editor, hanging up on me.

Many cops, nevertheless, suspected the *Sun* of being soft on black people and especially on the National Association for the Advancement of Colored People, an organization widely considered by policemen to be a Red conspiracy against the Republic. Police paranoia toward the *Sun* was rooted in a few editorials and some pieces in which H. L. Mencken had denounced people who took part in lynchings. Mencken's pieces had been written years before I got to the *Sun,* but the Baltimore policeman of the late 1940s enjoyed nourishing a grievance, and no amount of evidence that the *Sun* was just as racist as he was could persuade him to give it up.

After a year on the job, I knew I was never going to be a great police reporter. I disliked the brutality of the policeman's world, disliked the endless hours of idling in police stations, disliked the ignorance and prejudices of too many policemen. I felt sorry for the miserable, poverty-ridden black people whose troubles filled so much of the policeman's night, but among the cops I concealed my sorrow. If they suspected I was not zealous in my racism, they might brand me a "nigger lover." That could slam important police doors in my face, making the work even harder. All this made me dislike myself.

Yet there were gentlemen, princes, and men of wisdom among those policemen. My favorite was Inspector Koch, a small bundle of energy with a good deadpan cop face and a common-sense view of police work that was rare on the force in those days. At night, when he was often the man in charge of the entire department, he cruised the city in a limousine and could be a godsend if I was having trouble with some blockhead in one of the stations. One night a desk lieutenant at the Northern Police Station insisted he did not have a report on a shooting. I knew he did. Out on the street, the patrolman who wrote the report told me he'd turned it in at the station. The desk lieutenant's insistence that there wasn't any report infuriated me. I was yelling.

"You've got to have the report, damn it! The man on the beat told me you do!"

There was a bustle behind me, an opening door.

The desk lieutenant looked beyond me and abruptly stood up, very respectfully, coming to attention. Turning, I saw Inspector Koch in his civilian clothes. We exchanged nods of recognition. "What's the trouble here?" he asked.

Normally I wouldn't have gone over the lieutenant's head, but his oxlike stubbornness had infuriated me.

"I'm trying to get a report on a shooting, and the lieutenant says he doesn't have it," I said.

Inspector Koch spoke to the desk officer. "Do you have the report?"

The lieutenant nodded yes.

"Let me see it."

The lieutenant reached under the desk, drew out a single piece of paper, and handed it to the inspector. He scanned it quickly, then tossed it back on the desk.

"Give it to him," Inspector Koch said.

The lieutenant started to form a mild objection. "Are you sure we want it in the paper?"

"Give it to him," the inspector repeated, and then said something to the lieutenant that was wonderfully profound:

"It happened, didn't it?"

That was a sentence I was to use many times in years to come when dealing with desperate people who believed that terrible things didn't really happen unless they were reported in the newspaper. "It happened, didn't it? Keeping it out of the paper can't make it unhappen."

The Northern Police Station where Inspector Koch issued this observation was famous for its men's faith in the theory that almost everything ought to be kept out of the newspapers. Its territory housed a good percentage of Baltimore's rich and well-to-do and, hence, attracted the higher class of burglar looking for precious stones and metal. Occasionally some well-heeled burglary victim gossiped to some neighborly

Sun executive about her loss, and the *Sun* executive passed it on to Mr. Dorsey, who told the city desk to have a reporter look into it.

My friend John Wood got such a tip about a jewel burglary one night while covering Northern. Wood was told that since the tip came from Mr. Dorsey the story was a top priority assignment. Naturally nobody at Northern had heard of any jewel burglary up there in months and months. Wood had been given a bum tip, they said.

Wood was a gentlemanly but persistent young North Carolinian who, like me, had come to the *Sun* thinking it would open doors to a writing career and found that it meant nights struggling with the forces of unreason. Wood explained that he was not working on a bum tip. The tip came from the managing editor of the *Sun*. The managing editor, he said, had heard of the burglary from the woman whose jewels had been stolen. All he wanted, Wood went on, was to get the police version of events from the official police report.

Well, the desk man said, everybody would sure like to help, but nobody there had heard of any jewel burglaries.

Wood demanded to speak to Captain Lusby. That was a bold demand because police captains, though less eminent than inspectors, did not normally submit to conversation with young reporters. In Captain Lusby, however, the Northern district had a remarkably civilized commander, a man of considerable polish. Dealing with the swells, as a captain had to do in that territory, required someone sensible and polite. And so Captain Lusby emerged from his office and even listened sympathetically to Wood's plea.

When it was finished, Wood told us later, Captain Lusby replied with an absolutely persuasive explanation of why the report on that particular burglary could not yet be published in the paper without dreadful damage to the cause of law and order in Baltimore. Wood was persuaded, but Mr. Dorsey wanted the burglary story. Then Wood had a desperate idea.

"If I get Mister Dorsey on the phone," he asked Captain Lusby, "would you tell him what you've just told me?"

Mr. Dorsey? asked Captain Lusby. Who was Mr. Dorsey?

The managing editor of the *Sun,* said Wood.

Captain Lusby said he would gladly explain the situation to Mr. Dorsey.

Wood led Captain Lusby to the *Sun* phone in the back of the squad room, lifted the receiver, and asked the operator to put him through to Mr. Dorsey.

This was a deed of great courage on Wood's part, for Mr. Dorsey did not acknowledge the existence of police reporters, much less take telephone calls from them to discuss their work problems. It was not quite like an army private telephoning the Pentagon to talk shop with the Chief of Staff, but it was close. Wood was a man of courage, and when he found himself connected to Mr. Dorsey's desk his courage did not buckle.

"Dorsey here."

"Mister Dorsey, sir, this is John Wood up here at the Northern Police Station on that jewel burglary story you—"

Wood explained and explained while Mr. Dorsey listened, and finally Wood explained that he had with him at that very moment, right there at the telephone, Captain Lusby himself, who had kindly and humanely agreed to explain personally to Mr. Dorsey why publishing the story would do irreparable damage to law and order throughout Baltimore.

In finishing, Wood said, "I've got Captain Lusby

right here, and he wants to explain it to you. Will you talk to him?"

As Wood was passing the phone to Captain Lusby, he heard Mr. Dorsey saying, "Talk to him? Of course I won't talk to him. I wouldn't wipe my ass on a police captain."

After which, a click on the line left the captain holding a dead phone.

Wood told us the story late that night when we had all gathered downtown in the police headquarters pressroom for a midnight whack at the headquarters man's gin bottle. Wood had been so shocked he couldn't remember anything that happened after Mr. Dorsey had hung up.

All of us shuddered at the thought of how tough covering Northern was going to be from then on, and we cursed Mr. Dorsey for being callous to the plight of his police reporters, and while cursing him, also admired and envied him. How sweet it would be to treat those impossible cops with such rude contempt. That Mr. Dorsey. What a newspaperman.

8

Paying the Dues

A misfit at police reporting, I was getting nowhere in my fantasy of catching up with Cousin Edwin. Worse, after a year on the job I was falling behind at the *Sun*. While I rode trolleys month after month from police station to police station, new people were being hired, assigned to police coverage for a month or two, then moved inside.

"Moved inside." On the *Sun* those words were the stuff of police reporters' dreams. They meant having your own desk, being sent on fascinating general assignments, getting a chance to write, and never having to humor a policeman again.

Patrick Skene Catling was the first competitor jumped over me for promotion. Catling was handsome, red-haired, athletic, graceful, witty, and English by birth, early schooling, accent, tailoring, and instinct, though American by citizenship. Mr. Dorsey hired him three months after me. The police reporters did not greet Catling warmly, for the news that he was being paid a scandalously high salary of forty-five dollars a week poisoned our hearts against him.

It angered me, since his previous newspaper experience was no greater than mine, and I'd been started at only thirty dollars a week. I considered myself a victim of social discrimination. This was probably so.

Mr. Dorsey was notorious for loving everything English. "Dorsey is such an Anglophile," John Wood said, "that the only gin he'll drink in his martini is House of Lords."

Sulky about the forty-five-dollars-a-week rumor, I gave in to my radical instincts. This insufferably snotty uptown newspaper for north Baltimore swells could find forty-five dollars a week for Englishmen but only thirty dollars for a man from the blue-collar wasteland of southwest Baltimore, I told myself. The American Newspaper Guild was then struggling to bring *Sun* reporters into its union embrace. I signed up after hearing of Catling's astonishing salary and soon became a minor agitator and, in the eyes of the paper's conservative old-timers, I suppose, a pipsqueak Bolshevik.

After meeting Catling, it was hard to go on hating him despite the high British gloss. He was my age and I soon saw that, like me, he was a man on the make, though in a bigger hurry maybe to make something of himself and more likely to be ruthless about it than I was. We shared a sense of humor that was on the cruel side, and we both loathed police reporting. Catling could also be insolent in the rude English style. This was new to me then and seemed amusing when directed at some authoritative blockhead of a cop too dense to see he was being treated as contemptible. I quickly came to enjoy Catling's company, but when he was moved inside ahead of me I raged silently about the *Sun*'s injustice.

Then he was assigned one night to review a tired, roadshow production of *Oklahoma!* at Ford's Theater, and the next morning the review carried his by-line. I was outraged, and then I started to read, and outrage turned to wonder. The review was a beautiful piece of writing, quite different from the usual dusty prose of *Sun* reviews. Catling had done something extremely daring by newspaper standards of the time: He had made the review a small personal essay, using the forbidden pronoun "I," reminiscing about a moment during the war when he had been moved by hearing the music of *Oklahoma!* filtering through the short-wave radio aboard a bomber crossing the Atlantic. The piece sparkled, the writing so relaxed and entertaining, and not a cliché anywhere. It was completely alien to the *Sun* style, and yet they had published it. Catling had dared, had taken a risk, and they had not only published it but also rewarded him with a by-line.

I had to concede that Catling was not just a good writer, but obviously my superior. They had been right to move him inside ahead of me. I congratulated him on his writing and meant it, and continued cultivating him, hoping some of his skill might rub off. His *Oklahoma!* review left me with an important lesson about newspaper writing which I tucked away in my head for the day when my luck might change: Don't settle for writing it the way it's always been written; dare to write it differently, and maybe you will write it better than it's been written before.

Catling was the only reporter I ever knew to fight for his newspaper prose with his fists. After drinks one night, he came back to the office after two in the morning to read his night's story in the paper. Drink made him combative. Scanning his story in the paper, he spotted a printer's error and decided it spoiled the whole story. He confronted the late-night makeup man and said he wanted the error corrected. Impossible, said the makeup man. The final edition was running on the presses. Stopping a press run after 2:00 A.M. to correct a typo on a minor story inside the paper was just not done, he said.

Catling said, nevertheless, it would be done this time, and the makeup man again said no, it wouldn't. At that hour of the morning, with the paper pretty much shut down for the night, the city room was nearly abandoned. When Catling could no longer tolerate the makeup man's defiance, he stopped arguing and started punching. The makeup man was an aging gent who floated peaceably through life on a haze of alcohol and cigarette smoke. He was no match for inflamed youth as represented by Catling. The witnesses were a copy boy and ancient Mark Ritger, the lobster man, whose job was to doze at the city desk listening to police calls until dawn. They said the makeup man never landed a blow, and never even tried. Catling lost the battle, though. The typo in his story ran through all editions.

Others less flamboyant than Catling and less talented were hired and moved inside ahead of me, and as I moved through my second year without relief, it sometimes seemed I was destined to grow old and die among the cops. Gradually, I adapted to the squalor of the life, began finding it easier to talk with policemen, began liking a lot of them, and began understanding that the good ones were just as appalled as I was about the wretched underside of Baltimore that was their place of business. Gradually, I became skillful at collecting the sad details of the city's misery and started accumulating a pile of newspaper clippings whose headlines recorded the progress of my education:

MAN, 30, WAKES TO FIND ROOM IN FLAMES, DIES OF BURNS

MAN, 39, KILLED WHEN CAR ROLLS INTO STREAM

WIFE BEATER FINED $25

HOLDUP MAN GETS $25 FROM BARBER SHOP

BOILERMAKER BURGLAR GETS $29 FROM MUSIC STORE

BOY, 17, SHOPLIFTS PANTS, GETS 90 DAYS

TWO MEN JAILED FOR STEALING HAM IN LEXINGTON
MARKET
MAN, 42, PLEADS GUILTY TO THEFT OF CAR HE HAD
"AN URGE TO DRIVE"

Week after week, month after month, this tale of
humanity's sorrow unfolded ceaselessly, filling the
wads of cheap copy paper I stuffed in my pockets for
note-taking.

THREE RAILROAD MEN SERIOUSLY SCALDED IN
DERAILMENT
FIREMEN RESCUE GIRL, 2, FROM GRANDMOTHER'S
LOCKED BATHROOM
MAN, 64, BEATEN; SKULL FRACTURED BY THUG
WHO GETS $240
MAN, 34, BABY 22 MONTHS, DIE IN MOUNT AIRY
FIRE

The fire deaths were the most terrible if you had
the awful luck to get there in time to see the bodies
coming out. You were not supposed to get sick, and
I never did because I kept my distance from the
stretchers, but one night after a slum fire that killed
a black family of five, including three small children,
I saw the policeman who'd helped bring out the bodies
get sick.

WOMAN HIT, KILLED BY BUS
HUSBAND FINDS WIFE HANGING FROM CELLAR BEAM

I hadn't realized suicide was such a common part
of the city's daily routine. Every day brought one or
two. A high percentage of suicides were by hanging,
maybe because guns were not so common then. The
Sun rarely bothered with suicide stories, though there

were no instructions to hold them down. There were so many. Suicide just wasn't news.

SIXTEEN-YEAR-OLD STEALS 100 BARS OF SOAP FROM TRUCK
TWO BOYS, 14, ROB BOY, 18
MAN, 25, STRANGLES GIRL, 18
MOTHER SEES SON, 4, KILLED WHEN TRUCK HITS HIS WAGON

I rarely had to face mothers who had just seen their babies killed. That dreadful job was part of a policeman's duty. I could come along later and copy his report in the police station and maybe hunt down a witness or two to add an interesting detail. It was the cop who collected the emotional scars. Now and then, though, I blundered into scenes that destroyed my fine journalist's detachment.

One night I went to the South Baltimore General Hospital emergency room to check on a traffic accident and arrived a few moments ahead of the ambulance bringing the dead driver and his uninjured wife. As ambulance crew, cops, stretcher, dead husband, and surviving wife swept down upon me, I asked the closest policeman what he could tell me.

"Not now, not now," he growled, brushing me out of the way.

The dead man's wife, however, stopped, turned to me, and started pouring out a graphic account of the accident. Her face was chalky white and her eyes frantic. I wondered if she was in shock. I wanted to be away from her. It seemed obscene that I should be troubling her at such a time. I thought maybe she mistook me for an official she was obliged to talk to and didn't realize I was a reporter, so I said, "I'm from the *Sun.*"

That only made her talk more freely. She gave harrowing details of the collision, the truck sideswiping the driver's side of their car, what it sounded like, her husband's cry at the instant of impact, her certainty a moment later that he was dying . . .

She could not be stopped. It felt embarrassing to be an intruder on this singularly horrible moment in her life. Normally I didn't have to face the ragged, painful reality behind WIFE, 37, and DEAD HUSBAND, 40. When I did, there was always wonderful story material about pain, hysteria, despair, anger, and human breakdown in response to life's nightmare moments, but this was material for fiction writers. There was no place for such stuff in newspaper stories. Newspaper stories were supposed to keep the reader informed about the world, not to immerse him in its agony.

Reporting these stories every night, I instinctively learned to protect myself against the numbing awfulness of them by thinking of the people involved as faceless cyphers: DEAD MAN, 30. BOILERMAKER BURGLAR. BEATEN MAN, 64. DEAD SON, 4. CONDEMNED KILLER. WIFE HANGING.

Newspaper legends, created by entertainments like *The Front Page*, had promoted the fiction that police reporters were ruthlessly cynical about human misery. The fact was quite different. We affected the cynical style and turned grisly events into tasteless jokes because that was a way to maintain our emotional detachment, and staying emotionally detached from what you were seeing was a way of saving your life.

The legend also insisted that police reporters led lives of romantic gaiety and carefree independence, thumbing their noses merrily at the world's stuffed shirts, sassing mayors and managing editors, putting down whiskey by the gallon, and licking no man's boots. Most police reporters liked the romantic aura which this legend lent them, and struggled to live up to it. Few succeeded. I certainly didn't, though I wanted to. I found it impossible to make people think I was a romantic, carefree devil after they'd got a whiff of my clothes and recoiled from the smell of police stations and six-alarm fires.

Far more successful at it was Harry Riley, who worked for the *News-Post.* "Fire Alarm Riley" the cops called him, out of respect for the speed with which he arrived on the scene of whatever the story might be.

Riley cruised the city in an immense black Cadillac equipped with a police radio. At the first alarm signal he floored the gas pedal and roared through traffic at terrifying speed. The cops loved him. They took him aside and told him their secrets. Riley seemed to love the cops and love the work. He was a big, unkempt, red-faced man with black hair going to gray, big teeth, and a loud braying voice that sounded like the start of a riot. By baring his teeth and glaring wide-eyed at someone he wanted to disturb, Riley could make himself look like a dangerous maniac and enjoyed scaring strangers by doing so.

One Saturday afternoon when the *Sun* had sent a brand-new reporter over to the police headquarters pressroom, Riley burst into the room screaming, "I can't stand it anymore! I'm going to kill myself!"

Sprinting to the window two floors above the street, he threw up the sash and wriggled halfway out, continuing to scream that life was no longer bearable. The other reporters, long familiar with Riley, sat tight and smiled wanly at the performance, but not the new *Sun* man. Leaping from his chair, he ran to the window, seized the back of Riley's belt and, with mighty exertions, tugged Riley back into the pressroom. Feeling mildly heroic about saving Riley's life, he was naturally crestfallen to learn that he'd been made the butt of another of Riley's jokes.

No other police reporter could match the joy Riley

took in the work. Only a small boy could have done that. Riley had somewhere acquired a coffin and an old secondhand hearse that had clear glass panels on the sides. On Saturday nights, when the streets were busy, he liked to put a companion behind the steering wheel, then climb into the rear and stretch out flat on his back in the coffin, which was readily visible through the hearse's glass panels. The companion then drove the hearse into heavy traffic. When the traffic flow was stopped by a red light, giving motorists alongside a chance to study the hearse's somber contents, Harry rose slowly to a sitting position in his coffin and bared his huge teeth in a hideous grin at the cars around him.

I admired Riley's carefree spirit, but it signified a boyish delight in police reporting that I could never share. I wanted to be moved inside and to put police reporting behind me forever. For that I needed skills very different from Riley's. One skill I needed was mastery of newspaper lingo. As an English major in college, I knew that each discipline had its own language and that succeeding in your chosen line of work required you to learn to talk and write the appropriate form of English. Newspapers, for example, were not written in Shakespearean English, nor even in formal modern English. There was a distinctive lingo that made a newspaper story read differently from anything else, and I set about learning it from reading the paper intensely.

A big fire, I noted, was not just a fire, it was a "holocaust" or a "multimillion-dollar blaze." A young man holding up a gas station with a gun was not just an armed youth, he was a "bandit." If he panicked, squeezed the trigger, and killed somebody, he was a "slayer." Until arrested, he was "sought." Being sought, he was the "object of a manhunt."

This language was formal, unvarying, and trite.

Hailstones were "as big as golf balls." Heavy rainfall
was a "deluge." Thunderstorms "battered." Smoke
from million-dollar blazes "cast a pall." Gunfire
"erupted." People never jumped into the water to
prevent drownings, but always "plunged." People who
jumped from high places to kill themselves always
"leaped." Bodies of people murdered with a good bit
of bloodshed were found "lying in a pool of blood."

Working on the *News-Letter,* I'd discovered a large
talent for grasping newspaper clichés, and now intense
daily study of the paper persuaded me that, though I
might not be the prose writer Catling was, I could
write newspaper copy like a professional if the *Sun*
would only move me inside.

I studied newspaper writing under Paul Banker and
Jay Spry, the regular rewrite men who took the material I phoned from police stations and turned it into
news stories. By reading the paper next day to see
how they had turned my facts into stories, I slowly
learned the tricks of news writing: how to compress a
complicated story into a few paragraphs if space was
tight, how to expand a flimsy story into an entertaining tale when the city editor needed something to
brighten the back page, how to write hard news leads
and feature leads, how to use the short, telling quota-
tion for maximum effect, and a hundred other small
skills.

Banker was the finest writer on the local staff. Spry
was the most careful. They embodied what Mr. Dorsey meant when he told newcomers that learning the
business on the *Sun* would qualify them for a welcome
on any paper in the country. Banker and Spry were
as different as the *New York Herald Tribune* and *The
New York Times*. This difference extended even to
their dress and physical appearance.

Banker, a Yale graduate only four years older than
I, was as Ivy League as the *Herald Tribune* in his

Oxford shirts with button-down collars, soft tweed jackets, natty bow ties, loafers, and gray flannel slacks. He was tall and trim, broad-shouldered, with wide cheekbones and wide jaw, broad pleasant smile, voice low and pleasant, the picture of easy relaxation in a job that kept him constantly under heavy deadline pressure. He wore his hair in the fashionable close-cropped military style of the era, and, except for a cigarette habit, seemed as unflappable as it was possible to get in the newsroom of a big metropolitan daily during the pandemonium of an approaching deadline.

When I phoned with a story that was slight and unimportant, but funny and offbeat, I prayed to get Banker, whose wit and natural talent for writing might turn it into a small gem.

Jay Spry, though only thirty years old, had the old-timer's weary, seen-it-all look about him. His wardrobe was like mine: basic country-boy undistinguished. Baggy slacks, mismated shirt and necktie, and neither one much to look at. He had the kind of hair that won't stay combed. This, combined with a slight puffiness around the eyes, made him look as though he'd just got out of bed.

Banker and Spry worked at facing desks pushed up flush against the city editors' desks. They consulted constantly throughout the night with the city editor and with each other. Rewrite at the *Sun* was a position of power, and both could handle the city editor's job when he was absent, and sometimes did.

On rewrite, Jay was the man for eight-alarm fires, and you had better come to the phone with the correct identification of every fire company on the scene; the name of every fire chief, including middle initial; the identity, address, and job of the person who turned in the first alarm, what he was doing when he first noticed the fire, how many people he was doing it with, what part of the structure was burning when he noted it, and the time and method of sounding the alarm.

It wasn't enough to tell Spry that blazing shingles had fallen on a parked car. He would send you back to the scene to get the correct color of the car, its make, its model year, its owner's name, its price at time of purchase, how much the owner still owed on it, why it was parked at that particular location, whether blazing shingles had ever fallen on it in the past, whether it had previously suffered any similar battering whatsoever, be it from hailstones, lightning strikes, flowerpots accidentally pushed from third-floor windows . . .

Whining, as I sometimes did after being sent back for the fourth time with orders to find out if the car had white sidewall tires, was a grave error. Immediately Spry launched into an endless lecture on the urgency of thoroughness in journalism. It was garnished with long-winded anecdotes about famous news stories in which white sidewall tires played vital roles. You couldn't understand what the sidewalls of the tires had to do with the eight-alarm fire that was consuming the pants factory? Well, when you had a little experience of newspaper business you would know that writing a fire story requires a great many precise details. A reporter wasn't much good, was he? if he was sent to an eight-alarm fire and just stood there gazing at the spectacle for an hour, and then went to the phone with nothing to say except, "It was a big, spectacular, beautiful fire with lots of flames." A reporter had to get in the habit of noticing details, just like a good detective. And incidentally, while you're checking on those tires, find out if the car's front end is out of alignment, and . . .

That was Spry, a one-man school of journalism preaching the vacuum-cleaner philosophy of reporting then practiced by *The New York Times*, though not with the demanding exactitude Jay brought to it. His passion for thoroughness made him determined to study every page of every paper published every day in Baltimore and vicinity. Since he was usually a week or two behind in this labor of Hercules, he always traveled to and from the office with twenty-five pounds of old newspapers under one arm, hoping to catch up on his reading on the streetcar.

When he left the paper in 1952 for a public relations job, a mock edition of the *Sun* mourned his departure and suggested perpetuating his memory with "a mound of aged newspapers garlanded with wreathes woven from clippings of the 32,959 purse snatches he wrote during his long tenure on the city desk."

By 1948 it looked as if I would stay in the police districts long enough to cover 32,959 purse snatches. That summer Bill Gresham, my know-it-all pal from the *News-Letter,* had been taken onto the *Sun* staff. We were good friends by then, very good friends. I had introduced him to George, Al, and Mimi, and he had become a regular at the weekend parties and a hanger-on at the basement apartment. Despite friendship, however, I was prepared to throw a scene if the *Sun* moved Gresham inside ahead of me.

He was a natural at police reporting. Before he had been two weeks on the job he had established warm relationships with several of the most important lieutenants and sergeants on the force, including some I suspected of also being the most corrupt. Cops liked him. Maybe it was the Edward G. Robinson tough-guy face and the no-nonsense way he went at them when he wanted to know something. Maybe it was his self-assured air. He had the gift of speaking to people as though he were twice as smart as they were, so they'd better level with him because he didn't intend to put up with any foolishness.

A later generation would have called him "a take-charge guy." When he arrived on the scene of the crime, exhaling great clouds of cigarette smoke, mouth set in a firm straight line, demanding to know who was in charge and what was going on, even the crustiest cops greeted him as a colleague. He was the police reporter as tough guy *par excellence*. He had no patience with my tentative, polite style of dealing with cops.

"You're wasting your time being nice to those bastards," he told me. "They just think you're soft if you treat them like gentlemen."

Bill's grating style irritated other reporters, and he made enemies freely. I took him with me to dinner one Saturday night to meet Catling, whose indifference to the American convention of artificial politeness I thought might appeal to Bill. It was a disaster. Catling, who had money to squander that night, ordered a fine sherry before going on to a lavish meal that must have cost him four dollars. The sight of such capitalistic self-indulgence outraged the old-fashioned radical that was part of Gresham's complicated soul. The fact that Gresham could afford only hamburger and coffee intensified his anger.

As each course of Catling's meal arrived, Gresham greeted it with an offensive comment. When the sherry was served, Bill said he considered sherry an odd drink for reporters, who ought to be content with beer. The soup smelled unappetizing to him. When it gave way to the roast beef, Gresham announced that it didn't look worth the vast price Catling was paying for it. Through all this, Catling ate with unruffled aplomb. After the beef came a plate of salad. The ingredients included several black olives.

"What is that mess?" asked Gresham, pointing a fork at Catling's salad and wrinkling his nose in distaste.

"This," said Catling with the faintest of smiles while

spearing an olive on his fork, "happens to be a plate of sour grapes."

At this time Maryland's wheels of justice began to activate the gallows at the penitentiary again. There was a midnight execution, and Caulfield was talking shop to me on the phone later that day when he said, oh, by the way, "You can have the next hanging."

I had dreaded this since learning that the police reporters took turns at the duty of witnessing executions. I knew I could beg off by telling Caulfield that the idea of watching the state kill a man was so repugnant to me that I couldn't bear to watch it. This would have been only partly true. Of more immediate concern to me was fear that the horror of the thing would make me behave badly in the execution chamber and that I would embarrass myself. Reporters were supposed to take such stuff in stride, all in a night's work.

If I begged off, Cauley would understand and not hold it against me. I had got to know him as a gentle, civilized spirit incapable of malice. Still, word would pass through the city room that instead of exulting in my chance to see an execution, I had actually turned it down. When this got back to Mr. Dorsey, he would surely snort, mutter something like, "He'll never be a newsman," and doom me forever to the backwaters of journalism.

So when Cauley said I could have the next hanging, I suppressed an urge to cry, "Absolutely not!" and said something like, "Great," and tried to put it out of mind.

Then I had an inspired idea. Who was the toughest, rough-and-readiest police reporter in all of Baltimore? The one man who would relish the opportunity to watch a hanging? Hah!

Bill Gresham and I were having our evening meal at an East Baltimore Street cafeteria that had good fried eggplant.

"I'm at the head of the line to cover the next hanging," I told him, hoping I made it sound as if I thought myself the luckiest guy alive.

He bit.

This barbaric form of punishment, I said, was becoming so rare that in a few years it might not be practiced anywhere in the world. Being one of the last people able to say I'd seen a hanging would be a distinction. Dreary though police reporting might be, it had a few rewards and this extraordinary opportunity to watch an execution was one of the best.

Bill thought I was too young, too unfamiliar with violent death to do well at a hanging. His experience in the war, seeing the big bombers explode in the air around him, killing his comrades in an instant, had qualified him to gaze without flinching on any horror man could contrive. In short, he wanted me to let him take my turn at the death house.

After that I had only to play Tom Sawyer whitewashing the fence. There was no chance, I said, that I would pass up my crack at a hanging, even out of the deep friendship I shared with Bill. And so on until I reluctantly surrendered.

When the summons to death-house duty came, I told Caulfield that Gresham had pleaded for it so movingly that I couldn't deny him the right to go in my stead. Caulfield didn't care. Hangings didn't make much of a story. The *Sun* gave them only a few colorless paragraphs for the record, unless some remarkably gaudy killer was involved.

Gresham went in the spirit of artistic inquiry. He wanted to experience American society at its most savage. He was in for an unusual demonstration of it, for that night there was to be a rare group execution. There were three men to be hanged, and it would be done consecutively, one after another.

From talking to reporters who had gone through it,

I had an inkling of what it would be like. A handful of people assembled at midnight in a small, harrowingly intimate whitewashed space deep inside the penitentiary walls. The room would be high. A door opening on a platform at the second-floor level. The door would open, some men would appear on the platform. There might be a few words. Sometimes somebody said, "Good-bye" to a cop who had put him there. Then, all very quickly, the black hood, the noose, a nerve-rattling clap as the trapdoor opened, the body twitching and dangling at witnesses' eye level. Sometimes it was over quickly. Other times it did not work as it was supposed to, and instead of breaking the neck, the rope worked only as a slow strangling device until the doctor, applying his stethoscope, finally announced that the sentence had been executed.

Baltimore Sun police reporter's press pass

The night Bill took my place, with three to be hanged, it took a long time. Bill managed to get out on the street before he started to vomit. Afterward he was sick for days, and after that had nightmares for months.

Several years later, Bill became a close adviser to Theodore McKeldin, one of Maryland's most successful politicians. When McKeldin became governor, one of Bill's jobs was to review all death sentences for the governor's approval. As long as Bill held that job, McKeldin effectively abolished capital punishment in Maryland by simply commuting death sentences.

Not long after Bill's ordeal, Cauley got me on the phone at the Western Police Station one afternoon and said, "When you report to work tomorrow, come into the office."

"Is there something wrong?"

"You'll be working inside for a while."

He'd said the magic word: inside. I was finally being moved inside. After almost two years of my life out there in the lower depths, I was finally going to work inside. It was like the end of a long sentence to hard labor. Inside. I was being moved inside. I felt as Edmond Dantès must have felt when he finally escaped the Château D'If. Caulfield was moving me inside. Caulfield was a wonderful editor.

9

Inside

It was one of life's great days. Instead of getting off at Pine Street for the Western Police Station, I rode the streetcar all the way down to Charles, walked two blocks to the Redwood Street entrance to the *Sun* building, and took the back elevator up to the city room.

"It's Al Quinn's day off, you can use his desk," Caulfield said, scratching absentmindedly at his ribs.

Sitting at Al Quinn's desk awed me a little. It made me realize how far I still had to go before I became a real newspaperman. As City Hall reporter, Al had one of the most important by-lines on the local staff. He was a large, robust, middle-aged man with bushy, ginger-colored hair and a full moustache in an age when moustaches were not worn by every Tom, Dick, and Harry. He had a booming voice and was on a first-name basis not just with city councilmen, but with the mayor and even the governor.

He was an important man. When the traffic cops found it was Al Quinn they had in custody, as they did once or twice when he took a drop too much, they phoned the *Sun* demanding that someone come at once and save him from having to sleep in a cell. In an age when newspaper work was supposed to be a hard-drinking business, Al was the hero of legendary

drinking tales, which added luster to his reputation in
my eyes. My awe at the chance to use his typewriter
was quickly dispelled when Caulfield came over with
a wad of mimeographed press releases.

"Give me some shorts out of this stuff," he said.
"And get in plenty of names."

Caulfield held to the ancient belief that names sell
newspapers. After giving instructions to reporters
about to go out on assignment, he rarely failed to add,
"Get plenty of names." Pat Catling, instructed one
day to "get plenty of names" into his story, wrote a
lead that said, "Baltimoreans include," and handed in
a page filled with names taken from the telephone
directory. Caulfield laughed politely at the joke, but
it didn't stop him from reminding Catling on his next
assignment to "get plenty of names."

Aware that I was just a rookie getting a tryout, I
was not tempted to spoof Caulfield's theories of journalism. I was too delighted about sitting inside the
office with a desk and a typewriter. After the police
stations, this was bliss. The handouts Caulfield gave
me might be trivial, but they offered a chance to write,
and in a moment I was doing just that. I was writing!
Writing news that would be printed in a few hours
and read throughout a city that still did not know I
existed. It would know soon enough now.

I had taught myself touch typing the previous summer, and now I made Al Quinn's typewriter rattle
with news of things to come:

"Hadassah To Meet."

"Moose To Meet."

"Knights Of Columbus To Meet."

"Dundalk American Legion Bull Roast Slated."

"Dodgers Head To Speak."

For a few days I drifted from desk to desk with the
flow of the day-off calendar. Before the month was
out, Caulfield had entrusted two or three graver

assignments to me. These took me out of the office to hotels and meeting halls to hear the utterances of important men and report them to the world. In a typical piece of work, appearing under the headline SCOUTS PRAISED BY DR. BOWMAN, I wrote, " 'Boys and girls are eternal,' Dr. Bowman said. 'To live in the heart of a boy or a girl is to make a deposit in the world that is eternal.' "

After-dinner speeches like this were known in the trade as "bromides." Living on starvation wages, *Sun* reporters covered them gladly because every after-dinner speech was preceded by a dinner, which meant the reporter got a free meal at the press table. Caulfield parceled out these assignments with an even hand to help the staff hold body and soul together. Unless under management orders to turn the after-dinner oratory into a news story, veteran reporters often walked out as soon as the dessert was finished. Not me. I stayed to cover everything and raced back to the office to write at length.

Since by-lines weren't put on this sort of humdrum, the people of Baltimore could not tell that I had written it, but I knew. After turning in the copy, I waited for the edition to come off the presses with my story, admired it quickly before racing for the streetcar, then studied it at length on the long trolley ride back to Marydell Road. Silently I congratulated the copy editor who had invented such an eye-catching headline:

ADVERTISING CLUB BANQUETS—
WITH NEVER A DULL MOMENT

Slowly I read the opening sentence of my story, weighing every word to test whether it made a contribution to the overall structure:

"From lounge lizard to political sachem with his ear

to the ground, the Advertising Club's annual banquet last night offered a little something for everybody."

I congratulated myself for writing such a racy and distinctive lead. "From lounge lizard to political sachem with his ear to the ground"—that was certainly peppier than the *Sun*'s usual writing.

If my mother was up when I got home, as she was this night, I showed her the story and suggested she might like to read it and give an opinion, meaning of course that I wanted her to praise it. Usually she did, but on the night of the Ad Club story something must have put her in an ungenerous mood.

"What's a political sachem, Russ?" was the first thing she wanted to know. The second was why one would have its ear to the ground if there was a lizard anywhere around. The truth was, I didn't really know what a sachem was. Something like an Indian chief or medicine man, I thought. But that didn't matter. As I told her, she was missing the point. "Political sachem," I explained, was a metaphor, meaning "a big shot in politics." And didn't political big shots always have their ears to the ground?

"I think it would have been better if you'd said 'big shots' instead of 'sachems,' " she insisted.

"You can't say 'big shots' in the *Sun*," I told her, rather testily. I wanted praise, not criticism. The worst of it was, she was right. All that about lounge lizards, political sachems, and ears to the ground was just noise and confusion, as though I were banging pans in the kitchen to call attention to myself. I was too much the beginner to know how strained and foolish such writing sounded, but she had instinctively put her finger on what was bad about the story. Afterward I consulted a dictionary, then resolved never again to use the term "political sachems" except when referring to the twelve governors of the Tammany Society of New York City.

Before long my mastery of newspaper English had so impressed Caulfield that he assigned me a desk of my own next to Amelia Muller. Miss Muller was seventy-five years old or so, wore her pure white hair in a Gibson Girl upsweep, and never got a challenging assignment. I didn't either at first, possibly because on the first assignment that gave me a chance to show off, as Catling had done with his *Oklahoma!* review, I had failed to sparkle. The assignment was to interview Evelyn Waugh.

Reporting to the city desk at 3:30 one afternoon, I was amused when Caulfield asked, "Do you know who Evelyn Waugh is?"

Of course I knew who Evelyn Waugh was. Wasn't literature my specialty? Evelyn Waugh was the famous English novelist. Made quite a splash not long ago with something. What was it? Yes, *Brideshead Revisited*. No, I hadn't read it yet. Come to think of it, though I didn't tell Caulfield, I had never read any of Waugh's books. However, I had certainly heard of Evelyn Waugh. That was what I emphasized to Caulfield.

Good, he said. Waugh was in Baltimore at that very moment. Staying at this house up in north Baltimore. He gave me a slip of paper with an address. Caulfield had just now learned that Waugh was there and had orders from higher up to get an interview in the paper.

"Get up there right away," he commanded.

Just a minute, now. What was Evelyn Waugh doing in Baltimore?

"I haven't heard. Why don't you ask him?" Caulfield replied. "Better take a taxi."

The *Sun's* local coverage was often planned with such slapdash insouciance. Caught short-handed for a job that justified giving a good feature writer a day to prepare for, Caulfield had to grab the first reporter who walked through the door. High authority had spoken: Get Waugh in tomorrow morning's paper, even if it costs us the price of a taxi ride. Caulfield's saying, "Better take a taxi" was the tip-off that this was a vital assignment. The *Sun* did not squander money on taxis unless the need was dire.

In a fearful stew, I sped northward by cab. Everything about this assignment spelled "big story." This could be my big chance to shine. But what, what, what in the world could I possibly ask this great author, this lion of modern English literature, of whose works, of whose life, even of whose purpose for visiting Baltimore I knew practically nothing?

Not a single idea came to me. Nothing. I could think of nothing that might make the interview succeed. My mind seemed frozen.

The cab arrived at the house all too soon. It was an elegant, well-bred house. A proper north Baltimore house. I had never got around to dressing the proper north Baltimore way: tweeds, leather patches, button-down Oxford shirts from Brooks Brothers, superfluous buckles, belts, and rings all over everything. Now I was aware of being dressed in the proletarian striver style of southwest Baltimore, everything plain, honest, and absolutely wrong. Everything. Shirt, suit, necktie, shoes. Wrong. All wrong. And now I was being ushered into the room with the great writer. Evelyn Waugh. A lion of modern English literature.

Three things, all alarming, struck me simultaneously. First was Evelyn Waugh's clothing. It looked more north Baltimore than north Baltimore. North Baltimore clothing was the style I later knew as "Ivy League expensively shabby," but at that time I thought it looked merely odd and rather funny. Waugh's English squire getup was in the same general style, but funnier, as though he'd chosen it to burlesque the north Baltimore style.

Second, he looked like an extremely disagreeable

man. The wide pink face did not quite scowl at me, but it was a face from which the last smile seemed to have faded years ago. He had the eyes of an angry bird. As I introduced myself, I thought I saw pure hostility in those eyes, but that may have been my fevered imagination at work. Hostile or not, this was clearly a man not likely to be charmed by bumbling, damn-fool questions from boy reporters.

Finally, to compound my misery, there was another reporter already present and comfortably seated. He was James Bready, one of the *Evening Sun*'s brilliant cadre of feature writers, all of whom I admired with a respect close to awe. Bready was major league. The imagination, wit, and graceful lilt of his writing made him one of the glories of the *Evening Sun*. He was the kind of newspaper writer I wanted to be, but until this moment I had never met him. Thin, pale, and as ascetic-looking as a metaphysical poet, he gave me a wide, impish smile. He probably meant it to be genial, but in my frantic state of mind it seemed satanic and malevolent, as though he relished this chance to watch me humiliate myself.

Near panic, I realized I had burst in on the two of them, Waugh and Bready, while Bready was in the midst of his interview. Maybe that explained Waugh's irritated look. Maybe my barging in had spoiled a civilized chat between fine writers. Bready was the picture of relaxed graciousness in his comfortable armchair. They had paused in their chat and now looked at me, waiting for me to get on with it. But with what?

Somewhere I had read that Evelyn Waugh was a recent convert to Catholicism. Was there something there to make me seem wiser than I felt? The Hungarian Communist government, at war with the Catholic Church, had just imprisoned Cardinal Mindszenty of Budapest. Desperate for subject matter, I asked

Waugh a how-do-you-feel question, the sure mark of the amateur at wit's end.

"How do you feel about the arrest of Cardinal Mindszenty?"

Waugh was outraged about it, and said so forcefully. The opportunity to say so seemed to improve his mood, for he answered two or three silly follow-up questions very civilly. I left with a printable story: FAMOUS WRITER DECLARES CARDINAL'S PERSECUTION MONSTROUS. It was also a totally inadequate story, considering that Evelyn Waugh was, among other things, one of the finest comic writers in the English language. The persecution of Cardinal Mindszenty had been thoroughly denounced around the world long before I got Evelyn Waugh to add his voice to the uproar. All I had was a feeble dog-bites-man story which failed to capture the slightest glint of Waugh's unique wit. Given a chance to sparkle, I had flopped with a dull thud.

Bready's story next afternoon showed how it was supposed to be done. He had taken the trouble to find out that Waugh's latest novel, *The Loved One,* was a satire on the garish burial customs of Hollywood. And so he was able to get behind Waugh's solemn Catholic façade and catch a glimpse of the mischief-maker within by referring to the bizarre funeral customs of Los Angeles and asking Waugh, "What do you want them to do with you when your time comes?"

"Just throw me over the side," Waugh replied.

Luckily for me, the *Sun*'s famously miserable pay had sent morale so low by 1949 that there was constant personnel turnover. Everybody seemed to be looking for jobs with better pay, and many were finding them. This left the paper perpetually short of experienced reporters. As a result, to get ahead you didn't have to be very good, you simply had to hang around. Being unmarried and living at home, I could get by on my *Sun* salary, which averaged fifty dollars a week in 1949, so could afford to hang around. Having taught myself to type, I had another advantage. Most reporters, even the old-timers, used hunt-and-peck systems of their own devising, which could be maddeningly slow for editors waiting for copy on deadline. Once they discovered I could type with all ten fingers, they began giving me jobs they wouldn't normally have entrusted to a new man.

It was my typing skill that got me working the rewrite desk after only a few months inside the office. On a night both Banker and Spry were off, crime and fire erupted all over Baltimore. Obviously desperate, the night editor spotted me sitting in the back of the city room, came over, and asked if I was "the one who can type." I was, and he moved me to the city desk and put me in charge of Jay Spry's typewriter. I had two assets for the job. My long education in the Banker & Spry School of Journalism had taught me how to write a police story. And I could make a typewriter jump.

After that I filled in regularly on rewrite when Banker and Spry were out. Getting to the rewrite desk so quickly after moving inside gave me a splendid opinion of myself, for a rewrite man held an exalted post in the *Sun* newsroom. There were only two. With the city editor and his assistant, they shared a block of four desks at the center of the newsroom. This center of power was known simply as "the desk." Once there, you could pick up the phone, call Dave Maulsby at police headquarters, and say, "This is the desk. Get me enough for a short on that Pratt Street shooting."

The desk was power. Besides directing the wretched police reporters, the rewrite men worked closely with the city editor. He asked their advice and sometimes took it. To arrive at this newsroom Everest so soon after escaping the police stations was intoxicating, though I was doing it only part time. It gave me something to boast about to Mimi.

"Tonight I am really quite exhausted," I wrote her at 2:30 on a May morning in 1949. "It's the rewrite routine that I'm not used to yet. Spry was no good at all tonight. He worked on one story from the time he came to work and was still working on it when I left. Meanwhile, I had to do everything else—phones, dictation, proofreading, cutlines, new leads, police stories and mark-ups."

This was a transparent attempt to show her how important I had become, but its catalog of skills I'd learned after a few months in the city room was also a revelation. It should have amazed me that this newspaper, where I had started less than two years ago knowing nothing, had taught me so much so quickly about so many aspects of the trade. On any other big metropolitan daily I might have grown old waiting for a chance to move up to the city desk. At the *Sun* the steady flight of experienced people in need of living wages offered a beginner astounding opportunities to climb.

Just three months after my miserable meeting with Evelyn Waugh, I had begun to think that catching up with Cousin Edwin might not be so wild a dream. Nights I wasn't needed on rewrite, Caulfield was giving me plum assignments. On deadline day for income tax filings, which was March 15 in those days, I did the story on long lines at the tax collector's office. I went to the University Club to hear Thomas Skeffington-Lodge, a Labour member of Parliament, defend British socialism. I went to the Outdoors Show at the Armory and reported on the logrolling competition.

I covered a fashion show and an Easter passion

play, and went to Annapolis to cover a naval academy production of *Arsenic and Old Lace*. I wrote about traffic snarls at Pennsylvania Station, reported on a lunar eclipse, and covered Mayor Thomas D'Alesandro at Druid Hill Park accepting a gift of two camels for the Baltimore Zoo.

I interviewed two foreign delegates to a peace conference who were critical of American "hysteria" about Russia. From Notre Dame College of Baltimore, I reported Professor Valentine de Balla's account of tortures "a reliable source" told him the Russians used:

"A great number of priests and nuns were packed into a huge room . . . and kept there for a couple of weeks. . . . Then they were put into cells where the air can be sucked out, and they were put through the agonies of suffocation. Then the air was pumped in again, and they were revived. Repeated suffocation broke down their nervous systems."

I went to the Preakness, covered Monsignor Fulton J. Sheen giving a commencement speech, and wrote about frost in May, a heat wave in April, and humidity in June. After six months inside, I had put Evelyn Waugh behind me, persuaded myself that there was nothing I couldn't do, and started to complain that my small salary showed the *Sun* didn't appreciate me. I no longer referred to the managing editor as "Mister Dorsey," but now, like the old-timers on the paper, called him "Buck Dorsey." Not to his face, of course, since I never had occasion to speak to him, nor he to me. Now and then when I was on rewrite he glanced in my direction, looking puzzled about who I was and what I was doing on the rewrite desk, but beyond that he ignored me, and that was fine with me.

I had recently become active in the American Newspaper Guild, whose attempt to unionize the *Sun* newsroom had created tensions that scared the more timid staff people. Too young to be timid, I had become an outspoken union man, not caring that this might brand me an office Bolshevik, but aware that displaying union sympathy was likely to irritate the *Sun*'s oldfashioned, paternalistic management.

Then, on June 21, a dread summons awaited me at the office. "Buck Dorsey wants to talk to you," said Caulfield.

This was serious. It had been two years since Buck Dorsey had hired me; he had not talked to me since. Maybe my guild activism had been noticed. Even if it hadn't, an order to appear before the managing editor would have unnerved me.

I stood before fierce Mrs. Mabel Johnston, his secretary and the terror of the office. She had not spoken to me for two years either.

"Does Mister Dorsey want to see me?"

"Yes, Mister Baker."

My God, she knew my name! That was unsettling. There was safety in being a nobody. It meant Neil Swanson, the ogre who reigned as executive editor, never thought of me. It meant Buck Dorsey looking through me, seeing nothing. Or had they known all along that I was there, grousing, agitating, fuming, sulking?

"I will call you when Mister Dorsey is free," Mrs. Johnston said in her most sinister baritone. Among other duties, Mrs. Johnston had the cruel task of informing reporters when Buck Dorsey had rejected their expense accounts, and was said to enjoy it. This and a parade-ground voice had given her an evil reputation in the newsroom. Through the plate-glass window of his sanctum, I could plainly see Buck Dorsey. He had both feet up on his desk, was reading a newspaper, and looked free to me, but Mrs. Johnston sent me away to suffer a few minutes more before waving me back. I went in prepared for the worst.

Buck Dorsey's gaze was cold. He looked you dead
in the eye. Not a blink. It was a frankly inquisitive
look that made no apology for staring. The eyes
seemed to widen, the better to examine your soul.
Trained on me now, this haughty gaze suggested he
disapproved heartily of what he was seeing.

As I took the chair in front of his desk, I suddenly
realized what a green, overconfident, and incompetent
reporter I was, and how foolish I was to be fighting
the hardhearted management philosophy of this great
paper with its century of tradition. Before I could
plead youthful stupidity and beg mercy, however,
Buck Dorsey was speaking to me in a soft, highly
cultivated voice.

"I want to talk to you about good taste," he was
saying.

He pressed on a minute or two before I grasped
what he was talking about. A story I'd covered the
previous night bothered him.

"Some things are not in good taste," he was saying.

I had expected to be thundered at and threatened,
and he was giving me a lecture on esthetics. And so
gentle and professorial he was. Fatherly almost. It was
as though he had been disappointed to find I was lacking good taste, and wanted to set me right.

The story that troubled him was about the fiftieth
reunion of a Baltimore high-school class. It was the
sort of assignment that made reporters groan. Thirteen old gents who had been boys in 1899 had sat
around a table at the University Club and reminisced
about pranks in the gaslight era. Fortunately, one of
them had turned out to be interesting. He was Dr.
Samuel Wolman, and I had built the story around
him, starting with his determination to tell the others
"what would have happened if I hadn't left Poland
when I was five."

What was strange was that I thought I'd made a

fairly good story out of what might have been no story at all, yet Buck Dorsey disapproved. In writing it, I had focused entirely on Dr. Wolman, who wanted to talk despite his old classmates who rather hoped he wouldn't. It was a short story, barely five hundred words long, and the crux of it was that after being cut off two or three times from saying what he wanted to say, Dr. Wolman interrupted to say, "I don't want to take over. I just want to tell you what would have happened to me if I hadn't left Poland when I was five."

"Now, look, Sam," said the group chairman, obviously uneasy.

Smiling, Dr. Wolman went on: "I just want to tell you that if I hadn't left Poland I would have been burned by Hitler and never been able to attend this reunion. Do you know that Hitler killed two out of every three Jews in Poland? That's a strange thing, after nineteen centuries of Christian civilization."

The one clergyman in the group said, "Come on, Sam. Don't blame that on Christianity."

Dr. Wolman laughed.

"I'm not blaming it on you," he said. "I know you wouldn't burn any Jews. You wouldn't even burn any Christians."

I was slow to understand why it was tasteless to report this. It had been the one moment of human emotion in an evening of excruciating dullness, and I now said so. Buck Dorsey heard me out, then explained that this was precisely why it was in bad taste. In ritual occasions, he said, boredom was the essence of the event. Reunions were ritual ceremonies, and ceremony was meant to be uneventful and unsurprising, to be pageant rather than drama. To intrude human emotion into ceremony violated the ritual code, and though this did often happen, good taste forbade civilized people to let it overwhelm the importance of the ceremony. By concentrating on Dr. Wolman's insistence on reminding his classmates of Hitler's human extermination program, my story had missed the essence of the occasion and spoiled an important ceremonial evening for a dozen old gentlemen.

I told Buck Dorsey I understood, but I didn't. I was baffled but too cowed to tell him he was talking nonsense. Also too ambitious. Despite all my grousing about its pay, the *Sun* was the only future I had.

Thinking later about this strange talk with Buck Dorsey, I was never able to decide whether he meant it. Maybe one of those old-timers with an important friend at the *Sun* had been angered by the story and made a phone call. This could have produced a call to Buck Dorsey from a very important person, who wanted the managing editor to do something. Things sometimes worked like that at the *Sun*. And Buck Dorsey, after all, had let me off easily. A lecture. Maybe it had been as embarrassing to him as it had been puzzling to me.

The episode, however, did provide me with another useful lesson in journalism. It was the first of many scoldings for bad taste that I was to hear from editors over the years. "Bad taste," as Buck Dorsey had illustrated in that first lecture, was almost always the excuse editors fell back on when they lacked a persuasive reason to suppress news they didn't want to print. Rather than say, "This is something I don't want in my paper," they suddenly became sensitive to esthetics and justified squelching the story by saying, "Bad taste."

The Dorsey lecture scared me a bit and deflated the unduly high opinion I had been developing of myself since Evelyn Waugh had taught me humility. It reminded me once again that Buck Dorsey was a formidable figure, and I resolved not to irritate him. I was, after all, only a part-time rewrite man, and had got that job only because I could type. It would not strike Buck Dorsey as a terrible loss to the paper if I were taken off rewrite and shunted to the back of the newsroom to write shorts, or even sent back to the police districts.

The loss of self-confidence turned me sulky and angry. Once I had been amused by my absurdly low salary; now I seized on it as something to be enraged about. After three years of courtship, Mimi was pressing me with questions about marriage. I had no intention of marrying Mimi or anyone else, but it suddenly infuriated me to realize that I couldn't afford to get married even if I wanted to.

I began to suffer fits of despair and started muttering about going elsewhere to work, even about getting out of the newspaper business. I wrote Mimi saying I was "thinking of going to New York" in search of work "if I can scrape up enough money for the journey," My despair was black. "What will become of me God knows, because I have no desire to continue in newspaper business and there seems nothing else I am fitted to do. I feel desperate about my situation. What I really need for a cure is a one hundred percent change of environment and outlook."

Thinking this over, I realized that I suffered from a weakness for pointless bluster, and I quickly added: "It is foolish to think that I will choose such a change, because it takes more strength of character than I have at this stage of things."

Mimi never wrote in this stormy heroic style. Her ambitions were more sensible than mine. That was one of the reasons I loved her. She stayed anchored to reality, to practical things. Like vacations, for example. That July Mimi and I planned to take a vacation.

10

Mimi

One of Mimi's happiest childhood memories was of vacationing in Ocean City, New Jersey. During a bad time in her life she had lived in a home for abandoned children in Camden. Every summer the children, eighteen or twenty of them, were taken to Ocean City for a one-week vacation. After the drabness of Camden and the home, the Atlantic seaside was paradise.

Mimi remembered it as a place of wonder with its boardwalk and big, white frame houses, its rolling surf, endless oceanic sky, and its huge merry-go-round. The children from the home got passes to ride free in the afternoon when paying customers were few. Now, in the summer of 1949, she wanted to revisit those memories with me. She had a job in Washington that entitled her to one week of vacation pay. I was entitled to two. Why didn't we take a week together in Ocean City? I would love it. The air so clean, the sea so beautiful, the nights so soft . . .

I was not enthusiastic. For one thing, someone had misinformed me about Ocean City, telling me the whole town was little more than a summer-long Christian revival meeting, and I was in a stage of life where I believed it was impossible to have a good time without engaging in sin.

The more serious consideration was my mother. This was the fourth year that Mimi and I had been going together, but my mother still had faint hopes that I might come to my senses and take up with a woman who would be a social asset to a man struggling to amount to something. Mimi, with her tenth-grade education and hard-knock wisdom about the world, was not a woman my mother could visualize presiding in elegant drawing rooms. If Mimi and I took a vacation together, my mother would give way to either despair or fury. Such were the agonies a grown man, almost twenty-four years old, had to endure as the price for living at home. My enthusiasm for Ocean City was low.

On the other hand . . .

There was always the other hand in this tension between Mimi and my mother. Was I grown-up or still a child? Once asked, the question could have only one answer. I told Mimi Ocean City was a wonderful idea, and we planned to go during the last week of July.

Then some old friends offered a chance to vacation at Provincetown on Cape Cod. George, now a psychiatric resident at Seton Institute in Baltimore, was the author of this plan. By pooling money, four of us could afford a two-week rental at Captain Jack's Wharf, a briny collection of apartments that was the Bohemian essence of Provincetown, George said. Leo Flashman, the former *News-Letter* editor who now worked in the family furniture store, would go, and so would Phil Lebovitz, a mutual friend of ours since high-school days. The beauty part was that Lebo, as Phil was universally known, could get his father's car. Besides eliminating the expense of bus and train tickets, this would also make it easier to pursue loose women once we were camped at Captain Jack's. I agreed to chip in for one week in Provincetown, then go down to New Jersey and spend the second week with Mimi.

Nobody had warned me against the seductive charms of Cape Cod. After three or four days, I was bewitched by the Provincetown life. Sunny days on the great beach, martinis at sundown listening to New York musicians play Rodgers and Hart in the roadhouses, lobster dinners, sleek girls everywhere looking so inviting, though they always turned out to be looking for men with more money and less innocence than we could offer.

The prospect of leaving the Cape after just one week angered me. Was I not a free and independent man? Why should I feel obliged to give up this vision of the artist's life and tramp off to a New Jersey resort infested with Christians in every conceivable stage of prayer? Oh yes, I was fond of Mimi, she was a nice girl, but perhaps my mother was right, and even if she wasn't, I had a right to lead my own life, didn't I?

On July 24, before Mimi could leave for Ocean City, I wrote to her in Washington.

"Darling, I've got so much to tell you that I hardly know where to begin.

"I've completely fallen in love with this place. I'm having a wonderful time doing practically nothing."

After this cheery opening, I shifted gears:

"I suppose I should tell you what to you will be— I hope—the bad news. I think I will stick out my whole vacation here instead of coming down to Ocean City at the end of the week. There are several reasons for that decision, but the most cogent is—"

I talked about "prohibitive costs," then assured her that I was sensitive to the disappointment my sudden change of plan would cause her.

"I can imagine perfectly well how this all strikes you, and I'm partly glad that you like me so much that it comes as a blow to you—but partly sad because you probably won't sympathize with me. First, let me say that I love you very much. . . ."

No, she surely would not sympathize with me. Maybe if I could make her understand my need for inner peace, she would not be too terribly angry.

"I don't know how to describe the sense of release and relief that has settled over me during this past week. It's as if all the anxieties, drives and urges that normally keep me on edge were shucked off. The whole idea of returning to Baltimore, the family and the *Sun* is completely abhorrent and here I feel a terrific independence—and, I admit, a terrific irresponsibility. I just sit in the sun and vegetate and eat and sleep and think. . . ."

This was becoming a very hard letter to write. But how could I tell Mimi that after the elegant pleasures of Provincetown the prospect of Ocean City with hymn-singing on the night air was intolerable. Maybe it was best simply to talk about love.

"I want to see you as soon as possible when I return. I need you in the worst way and have so much that I want to try to tell you."

That wasn't going to work either. She was going to be furious, no doubt about it.

"I hope you aren't angry with me for not dropping by O. City—though I suppose you will be momentarily. If you can restrain your hostile impulses for a few days, you can confront me with them and we can settle accounts—I love you—."

The letter went on for seven pages before I finally gave up and closed by saying, "I hope you enjoy your vacation as much as I am enjoying mine."

Ordinary people did not use the long-distance telephone casually in 1949, so I knew there was trouble when Mimi phoned from Washington. I expected her to attack me for breaking my promise and spoiling her vacation, so was startled when she began by saying she was phoning to say good-bye.

Quietly, she informed me the company she worked for was transferring her to Texas. Since she had to leave immediately, we would never see each other again. Before departing, she wanted to tell me one last time how deeply she loved me.

I was flabbergasted. The company she worked for was the Willmark Agency. Its operatives' work was mainly shopping, in the course of which they checked the quality of service in client stores and whether sales clerks were robbing the till. It was small-pay, minimum-skill labor. As I absorbed the shock of hearing about her departure, I slowly realized Willmark was unlikely to underwrite the cost of moving one of its shoppers from Washington to Texas when it could readily find thousands of Texans ready to take the job. I told her I didn't believe the Texas story, not for a minute. Why didn't she grow up and stop playing games? I urged her to go on to Ocean City and have a good vacation. We would see each other in a week and compare notes.

She asked how I could be so callous, so cold, so selfish. I said Texas or no Texas, selfish or unselfish, I was staying in Provincetown another week, and that was that. Asserting myself felt wonderful for perhaps five minutes. Then I was abruptly smitten with bad conscience. How could I have been so callous, so cold, so selfish? Overwhelmed with self-loathing and remorse, I immediately decided to sacrifice Provincetown and go through with our plan for Ocean City. I ran back to the telephone to tell her of her good luck, but the switchboard that took her messages said she was out of touch.

Headed for Washington, I left Provincetown hastily and got to New York in midafternoon. At Penn Station I phoned Provincetown to learn if Mimi had phoned again. Leo said she was there at that very moment, very tired, angry to find me gone, and puzzled about what to do next. I was equally puzzled, but Leo with his talent for being sensible suggested getting her on the afternoon boat to Boston. There she could get a train to New York. I should check into the Hotel Pennsylvania, adjacent to Penn Station, book a room for Mimi, who would be arriving exhausted long after midnight, then leave together next morning for Ocean City.

We did ride the train south together next day, but not to Ocean City. I had spent most of my vacation pay in Provincetown and on New York hotel rooms. Mimi had spent all hers on travel. So much for her Ocean City vacation. I got off the train in Baltimore, she went on to Washington.

People still communicated by mail in those days. It was the twilight of the letter-writing age. Soon the telephone would replace the mail as the means by which people spoke to each other when apart, and everything would be forgotten before it was half spoken. When people still wrote letters, however, forgetting could be hard; letters were a record for posterity. They could make you wince years later, could make you realize that youth was not all glory, but was also comical, cruel, and insufferable. My letter to Mimi the week after the vacation fiasco started generously:

"I feel pretty guilty about hurting you as badly as I did and about being so damned selfish with my own vacation that I ruined yours. You're right—I can't rationalize that behavior—it was rotten of me and I secretly feel very bad about it."

Two paragraphs later, tired of guilt, I criticized her "adolescent behavior" in the Ocean City affair and urged her to "bounce back a little bit older and wiser for the experience, a little bit more of a woman and a little bit less of a scatterbrained adolescent."

In my next week's letter I gave her more specific thoughts on how she might improve herself:

"I think it will be good experience for you to toughen yourself to self-reliance. Emerson has a fine essay by that very title, and you would do well to study it and apply yourself. Well, here I am giving you advice in a snotty tone of voice, which is not at all what I want to sound like. . . ."

After this, the letter became almost human, lapsing into small news of people she knew. It was the kind of letter people who felt close to each other used to write long ago to remain close when they were separated:

"This is Sunday night in the *Sun* office, concluding another week of exciting developments on the home, business and social fronts, and I must bring you up to date on what is happening here. I have just returned from covering a television broadcast upstairs. The story was about a radioactive frog, and it took the last ounce of my waning wit to think of a hundred words to pour into the news story mold. . . ."

Long afterward, when I tried to make sense of my bad behavior and those terrible letters of mine, I saw that Mimi and I, though we didn't realize it, were practicing being married. The broken promises, the angry scenes, the ultimatums, the patronizing lectures, the sudden onsets of panic about loss of freedom were all elements of what marriage would involve for people as young as we were. They were the routine stuff of Hollywood's romantic comedies on which we had both grown up.

Those movies always ended with Carole Lombard, Irene Dunne, Jean Arthur, Ginger Rogers, Claudette Colbert, Rosalind Russell, and Katharine Hepburn getting married to Clark Gable, Cary Grant, Fredric March, Robert Montgomery, Fred MacMurray, James Stewart, Fred Astaire, or Melvyn Douglas. What was happening between the two of us was basic Hollywood romantic comedy, which could have only one possible conclusion. Mimi and I had another adventure or two ahead of us before the plot was completed at the altar in the spring of 1950 when she was not quite twenty-three years old and I was twenty-four.

The altar was chosen by my mother. It was in a small, sedate Lutheran church near Marydell Road to which she was temporarily dedicated. Shortly after our wedding, the pastor began expressing views on trans-substantiation that outraged my mother, though I had never known her to have the smallest interest in the matter until then, and she went back to her beloved Papa's Methodists. In early 1950, though, her loyalty to Lutheranism was still strong enough to persuade the pastor to overlook Mimi's and my indifference to Lutheran creed and perform the marriage.

He asked only that Mimi and I come for a private chat before the ceremony. He was scarcely older than we were and probably far less experienced in romance and disillusion, considering that Mimi and I were starting the fifth year of our courtship.

Gingerly, he broached the subject of sex to point out that marriages were often imperiled because young people, innocent of the sexual mysteries, were psychologically unprepared for the complexities and difficulties of carnal love. Sex was not easily discussed among strangers in 1950. Stammering and blushing, but determined to do his duty, the young pastor seemed bent on leaving Mimi and me just as embarrassed as he was. Hoping to ease him into more comfortable waters, I told him I had read excellent books on the subject, and Mimi and I jointly assured him that we were fully aware of where babies came from.

We were married on a rain-drenched Saturday in March. Mimi had come over from Washington the night before and spent the night with Aunt Sister and Uncle Harold, who showed her the family snapshot album and entertained her with stories about the old-time Bakers of Morrisonville, Virginia, and about my father, who had died in 1930 when he was only thirty-three years old. Aunt Sister was the only daughter in that generation of thirteen children. She and her husband, Harold, had always been especially fond of my sister Doris and me, and had liked Mimi from their first meeting.

Mimi and I had both bought new suits to be married in. Hers was a beige gabardine with a tightly fitted jacket and narrow skirt. She wore a dark blue hat with pale pink flowers and a veil. What a lovely spectacle she was when I first saw her at the altar. I was probably not so dazzling, though I had tried. My new suit was a blue woolen double-breasted from The Hub, with heavily padded shoulders and lapels five inches wide.

After the ceremony we went back to Marydell Road for the reception my mother had prepared. Going all out to fulfill his duties as best man, George had borrowed his father's car and drove us to Penn Station to catch the train to New York, where we were booked into the Commodore Hotel for a four-day honeymoon that would just about exhaust our capital. All the way north we sat in the coach watching the rain beat against the window and studying the reflections of ourselves in our wedding finery.

When the train finally deposited us in the vast steel cavern of Penn Station in New York, I was shy about going immediately to the hotel and facing a desk clerk. Suppose he demanded proof that we were actually married. Though we had documentary evidence, it would reveal that we had just been married this very day, and he would recognize us as newlyweds. Of course I knew all this was silly, but silly things could be worrisome, too. So I suggested we have some railroad station food to strengthen ourselves for the journey to the hotel, and Mimi agreed. When we were seated in the Savarin restaurant, however, I was dismayed by the menu prices and suggested we limit ourselves to coffee and blueberry pie.

When the room clerk at the Commodore heard my name and called a bellboy to take us upstairs without further interrogation, waves of gratitude and relief washed through me. From there on, my fear of being humiliatingly exposed to all Manhattan as a newly married man gave way to another kind of despair: New York made me feel that I was hemorrhaging money. Mimi, whose free-spending ways were obviously going to create severe tests for our married happiness, insisted on going to the theater to see Ethel Waters in *The Member of the Wedding* and the Kurt Weill musical *Lost in the Stars.* I ruled out a third play as an extravagance, but agreed to the more modest costs of movie tickets for *The Third Man,* which was playing in Times Square.

Still, even though we avoided using room service and ate a lot of our meals in the hotel coffee shop, it was obvious that staying all four days would send us back to Baltimore bankrupt. Mimi was agreeable when I suggested we cut the honeymoon short by a day and use the money instead to help furnish our apartment back home.

The apartment was two rooms and a narrow kitchen in the second-floor rear of a stately gray stone house on West Monument Street, just a block off Mount Vernon Place. The rent was fifty-five dollars a month. With about two hundred dollars, which we had for furniture, Leo Flashman had provided two good armchairs, a daybed that could pass for a couch, two lamps, and a small rug. My mother, who was on the verge of buying new bedroom furniture for Marydell

Road, gave us a battered double bed and a table she had moved around with her since leaving New Jersey in 1937.

Since I didn't know how to drive, Bill Gresham, who boasted of great experience driving trucks, volunteered to move the furniture from Marydell Road to Monument Street in a rental pickup truck. He arrived with the truck and a brutal hangover, and I soon realized that the boasts about his truck-driving skills had been hollow bluster. With much jerking, stalling, and cursing of the clutch, he got the truck under way, and we roared along for a mile or so with bedsprings and frame bouncing up and down in the back. Then at the foot of West Baltimore Street, where there was a ninety-degree turn on a downhill grade, Bill decided that he could take the truck through it without wasting any energy by applying brakes.

The truck did not quite turn over, but the terrible clatter behind told me we had left a lot of bedding in the middle of West Baltimore Street. Bill, who was not hearing as well as I was, kept his foot on the gas pedal until I screamed for him to stop and back up. By then, oncoming traffic was already running over the bed boards.

All this had been done before the wedding, and our apartment was waiting when we returned from New York. The financial situation was even grimmer than I had realized. The *Sun* had recently boosted my salary to seventy dollars a week, but before the wedding cake had dried out, Mimi gave me crushing news. She had unpaid department store bills in Washington amounting to $451.17. These were spread among six stores, and each of the six had a credit manager who was demanding immediate payment as the price for not blackening our reputations throughout the capitalistic world.

Asking me to come up with $451.17 was comical.

They might as well have asked me to pay the European war debt. When Mimi mentioned the existence of these bills, I asked how she could bear to run up such astronomical debt without becoming depressed. Didn't she realize that on her Willmark salary she would never have been able to liquidate such debt? No, she said, that hadn't crossed her mind. She had thought that sooner or later something would turn up to help her pay them.

Like a poor, miserable, overworked husband who would have to devote the rest of his life to paying for her extravagant ways? I asked.

She urged me not to start feeling sorry for myself. Everybody had problems. Why let them get you down?

Why let them get you down? My whole life was now mortgaged to the demands of six vicious, bill-collecting credit managers, who were promising to destroy me, and I should not let that sort of thing get me down? What kind of life did she think I had led all my life anyhow? Did she think it was the wastrel's, ne'er-do-well, spendthrift life, easy come, easy go, Mama's rich and Papa don't care? Was that the kind of life she thought I had lived? Was it the kind of life she thought I proposed to live now that I was married? Well, if so, she had better have another think because . . .

So went our first quarrel, a model for a thousand to come, all of them about money, which was so terribly important to me, but so ridiculously unimportant to the *Sun*. We finally paid off all six department stores by doling out five dollars apiece some months and as much as ten dollars and fifteen dollars apiece toward the end of the year.

By that time, it was urgent to get the old bills paid because we were piling up new bills, including some I hadn't anticipated when we were having a zany time carrying on like crazy young things in Hollywood romances. After three months of marriage, Mimi was pregnant, and one year and five days after our wedding, we were parents and more desperately broke than ever.

11

Ed Young

The great ogre at the *Sun* was Neil H. Swanson. He bore the grand title of "Executive Editor of the Sunpapers," which since 1942 had made him supreme editorial boss of both morning and afternoon papers. After seven years in that exalted position, he had managed to make himself loathed and feared by almost everyone under him, except for the few yes-men who formed his entourage.

Now in his early fifties and on his fourth marriage, Swanson was tall and fleshy with blond hair going gray. He wore steel-rimmed eyeglasses, chain-smoked cigarettes, and behaved like a cross between General Douglas MacArthur and a movie producer's dream of a dynamic newspaperman.

The movie influence may have come from Cecil B. De Mille. Swanson had written a historical novel about the American frontier titled *Unconquered,* which De Mille converted into a colonists-and-Indians epic with Gary Cooper and Paulette Goddard. Swanson then signed a publisher's contract to write thirty historical novels, most of which were never written.

Among other extraordinary claims to singularity, Swanson boasted that at the age of twenty-two he had served as a World War One army officer on detached duty with a French outfit called the *chasseurs à pied.*

Neil H. Swanson as executive editor of the Sunpapers in 1953 (Wide World Photos)

Swanson's imperial military manner and boyish pleasure in pushing people around to show who was boss contributed to making him villain-in-chief of the *Sun*. On a paper that esteemed dignity, understatement, and the diffident manner, Swanson's theatrical antics and determination to make life a melodrama in which he was the star were bound to sour the atmosphere. Though competent enough about some parts of the news business, he seemed absurd, contemptible, and embarrassing to a staff that considered the *Sun* one of the country's great newspapers and thought it was demeaned by Swanson's show-biz personality.

As usual with self-absorbed executive whizbangs, Swanson was isolated from reality by his own tendency to surround himself with people whose incompetence was offset by eagerness to lick his hand while shelter-

ing him from simple truths. By 1949 this had given
him a dangerous sense of security, and he was a
supreme boss with a thoroughly intimidated staff that
yearned to see him destroyed.

One of the most prominent yearners was Edwin P.
Young, city editor of the *Evening Sun*. Young was
then in his early forties and had been with the paper
fifteen years. Among most *Sun* people, Young was as
beloved as Swanson was hated. Most thought him the
best editor the paper had, and some thought him the
best editor in the world. Among those who worked
for him, feelings ranged from admiration to utter
devotion.

This was bound to provoke Swanson's hostility.
Swanson may have been a poseur, but he was no fool,
and he was quick to sense that Ed Young was not
only a rival of sorts, but also one who did not regard
the Swanson way of governance with proper respect.

Thirty years afterward, when both men had been
long gone from the *Sun,* Ed Young, at my request,
wrote his reflections on the Swanson of 1949:

"I disliked Swanson from the outset, and, while I
wasn't so idiotic as to confront him, he knew what I
thought.

"Of course he was a complete fraud from a to
izzard, and how he sat astride a formerly great newspaper for fifteen years—or just long enough to ruin
it—might be described as a mystery, except that it has
happened, and is still happening, to newspapers all
over the lot. It really is a laugh that newspapers, which
make a fetish of investigating everyone else under the
sun, are so often in the hands of charlatans."

This was in reply to a letter in which I recalled
a vague memory of Swanson wearing puttees in the
newsroom and asked Young if I could possibly have
seen such a spectacle.

"You are completely correct about the image

[Swanson] was trying to project. You didn't see him in puttees. You saw him in a trench coat, with Sam Browne belts, buckles and more damned rings than a merry-go-round has, plus an expensive and entirely incongruous brown felt hat. . . . He often appeared on the news floor in this rig, and I always refrained with difficulty from busting out laughing. But, and to the point, the puttees *were* there, even though you didn't see—only sensed—them."

As for Swanson's detached duty with the *chasseurs à pied* in 1918: "Pure Swanson hokum. . . . The fact seems to be that Swanson never saw military service of any kind."

Though the dislike between Swanson and Young was to become a great blessing to me, in the summer of 1949 I knew neither except by reputation. I accepted the popular view that Swanson was an ogre to be avoided at all costs, but had still never laid eyes on him.

I was equally familiar with Ed Young's reputation for excellence and had seen plenty of evidence of it in the *Evening Sun*. He had developed a staff of talented writing reporters every bit as literate and clever, I thought, as the celebrated staff of the *New York Herald Tribune*. They included superb feature writers like Jacob Hay, John Goodspeed, and James Bready, whom I had met over Evelyn Waugh, and fine reporters like Bradford Jacobs, William Manchester, and Burke Davis, who not only had the gift of making every story seem special but also found time to write books.

Our city editor on the morning paper was a quiet, workmanlike man named Bill Wells whom Swanson had promoted from the sports department. Wells's policy was to do his job judiciously while keeping his lip buttoned and his head low. As a result, dullness was the overpowering characteristic of the morning paper's newsroom.

All this was about to change at the very time my private life was suffering through the great Ocean City fiasco.

Swanson had long intended to do something terrible to Ed Young and had often been about to strike, only to be distracted by more pressing business. Once he had the inspired idea of burying Young in an assistant editorship of the Sunday supplements, a job widely regarded as a fate not quite worse than death, but almost.

Before Swanson could execute this plan, H. L. Mencken got wind of the plot and intervened with Paul Patterson, the company's president and publisher. Patterson's power was even mightier than Swanson's, and Mencken was Patterson's old, old friend. As Ed Young heard the story, Mencken urged Patterson to stay Swanson's hand, arguing that "Young is a good man."

Swanson dared not defy Patterson, of course, so Young was temporarily saved. Then, indisputable justification for getting Young out as *Evening Sun* city editor:

Lee McCardell, one of the paper's finest reporters, was being brought home from Europe after a long and dazzling career. Swanson decided to honor him by making him city editor of the *Evening Sun*. No one could object despite McCardell's lack of editing experience. Ed Young would have to go.

Buck Dorsey, whose eye for picking talent I came to appreciate only later, said, in that case, why didn't he take Young as city editor of the morning paper?

It was not the happiest thing that could have happened to Young. He was losing the fine staff he had built on the *Evening Sun,* and would have to start over with the anonymous bunch that worked for Bill

Wells. The morning paper also meant night work, with hours from five in the afternoon to two in the morning, and the end of most social life. Still, it was an important job, and Young respected Buck Dorsey.

So it was that two weeks after I finished ruining Mimi's vacation that summer, my regular letter informed her of news more momentous for me than I yet knew:

"Bill Wells returned from his vacation Monday to learn that he was no longer city editor of the morning paper. In a series of swift moves General Swanson has shaken his swagger stick and heads have rolled. Lee McCardell is returning from Germany to become city editor of the *Evening Sun;* and Ed Young, erstwhile city editor of the evening paper, comes over to our side to fill Bill Wells's vacancy. Poor Bill is booted down to the position of makeup editor of the *Evening Sun.* So I have a new boss."

Ed Young made his first appearance in the newsroom a few nights later. He did not fit my notion of what a great editor should look like. He was stocky, had a big baritone voice, a penetrating gaze, and a bright red complexion, which, I later discovered, turned purple when he drank, which was often, though rarely on the job.

He wore three-piece, slightly threadbare Brooks Brothers suits that seemed a size or two too small for him, and since he always wore his collar and necktie blocked tightly under his chin and kept his vests and jackets buttoned, he looked like a man encased in painful corseting. There was a story that he inherited this wardrobe from his wife's brother and was too desperate for money not to wear it. I never knew whether this story was true, but I did know Ed was miserably paid.

For his first few nights on the job, I watched from my desk far back in the newsroom as he took charge of the city desk. All buttoned up inside those constricting suits, he seemed supercharged with energy. He was perpetual motion. The hands worked constantly. They fiddled with his jacket buttons and bits of copy paper, darted to the top of his head to straighten his hair, twisted a paper clip, toyed with a rubber band, readjusted the angle of his eyeglasses. Then he was up and headed off with quick, short, nervous strides to deal with the night managing editor or the copy desk or a reporter or just to get a drink from the water cooler.

In constant motion even when he was sitting down, he suffused the air with energy and a sense of urgency notably missing from the newsroom before his arrival. The old newspaper cliché about a man electrifying the atmosphere did not seem silly when you talked about Ed Young.

From his first night on the job, the *Sun* at last felt like a real newspaper.

Toward the end of his first week, those short, nervous steps brought him back to my desk. He extended his hand and introduced himself, at the same time saying, "Why didn't anybody tell me about you?"

I mumbled something in my fake, bashful-boy style, which he immediately cut through, saying, "From now on, you're going to be doing important things around here."

With that, he pulled up a chair, sat down, and asked me to talk about myself. I was surprised to find it was easy. It was like talking to a loving father, something I hadn't done since I was five years old. I dropped the bashful-boy act. This was a man I could trust, a man I could talk to honestly. I told him my tale of misery: the rotten salary, how I was so desperate for money that I was thinking of looking for work in Washington and New York.

He listened intently. He really cared, I thought.

This man really cared about me. During my recital, his face registered sympathy for my plight, anger at the way the *Sun* had treated me, and determination to get me payroll justice.

Finally, rising, looking me straight in the eye, he said, "I'm going to do something about this. Give me a little time, will you?"

Give him a little time? He could have all the time he wanted. In those few minutes of talk I had joined those who thought Ed Young was one of the marvels of American journalism. This was my kind of editor. I loved him instantly. Long afterward, I realized that I had been searching for a father since I was a child and that Ed Young was the first one I thought might fill the bill.

Somehow, Ed Young did get me a raise. It did take time, several months, and how he did it was a mystery, because he couldn't even get a raise for himself, but he did it, and by the end of the year I was making a gaudy seventy dollars a week. This was enough to get married on if you were young and foolish enough to believe in happy endings, which was precisely how young Mimi and I were, though I pretended to be a hard-bitten realist who expected nothing of the future but failure, poverty, and despair.

Ed also made good on his promise to provide more challenging jobs. By fall I was working rewrite almost as regularly as Banker and Spry. Working beside Young on the city desk taught me respect for journalism. Until then I had taken the wiseguy view that it was a trivial, second-rate business for boozers, incompetent romantics, and failed writers.

My ambition to outshine Cousin Edwin reflected these attitudes. Nothing could have been more arrogant or foolish than the notion that, without any special education or training, I could someday match

Ed Young under the mistletoe between Hans Marx and John Stees of the *Evening Sun*

Edwin's achievements. I didn't think of them as achievements but as adventures, as fun for grown-ups. That's how I thought of journalism before Ed Young: fun for grown-ups.

Serious men, I thought, wrote novels. Until Ed Young I clung to my college dream of becoming a great novelist, as opposed to the kind of hack who wrote for newspapers. After working with Ed Young, I grew up enough to smile at the childishness of this idea, and I finally put it aside forever. By then, at age twenty-four, I had tried enough fiction to know I had no talent for it. Worse, I did not even enjoy writing it. Though always bored by it, I had kept at it only because of conviction that it was the noble art that serious writers ought to pursue, while journalism was a raffish and unworthy pastime, like hanging out at the racetrack or running a burlesque theater.

Ed Young rarely lectured, so he never pointed out that for a man who enjoyed writing news and hated writing fiction, becoming a good journalist might be a happier goal than being a bad novelist. Everything about the way he did his job simply insisted that journalism was serious work for serious people.

Confronted with the morning paper's dispirited and underpaid staff, he refused to surrender to the anger and resentment he felt for Swanson, but set out to breathe life and fire into his new crew. It was a revelation to me. Obviously he thought the work was important, the way doctors, scientists, and novelists thought their work was important and deserved the best they could bring to it, however miserable their circumstances.

So he went scurrying around the city room with all cylinders pounding, doing his utmost to make all of us feel we were vital to an important enterprise.

"Why didn't anybody tell me about you? From now on, you're going to be doing important things around here."

He must have addressed half the staff with variations on this theme in those first days in the newsroom. When Jim Cannon, another reporter, turned in his first piece of copy to the new regime, Ed scanned it, popped up from his chair, hurried back to Cannon's desk, introduced himself, and, pointing to Cannon's copy, said, "Where have *you* been all my life? This is wonderful stuff."

Though badly paid and ill treated by the company, he had unflagging enthusiasm for the work and no patience with the reporter who didn't. One of the worst sins you could commit was not working at your assignment as if it were the most important story in the paper that night. After Pat Catling, a man Ed considered too frivolous about journalism, left the *Sun* and wrote a newspaper memoir titled "Better Than Working," Ed's comment was, "How would *he* know?"

Money and its lack were the curses of the staff Young inherited. Everybody had a tale of financial despair. John Carr, who had a big family, was so desperate for money that when his only belt broke he could not afford a new one. So he came to work with a necktie girding his waist to hold up his pants.

Carr, a witty and sassy New Yorker with the light touch of the natural feature writer, offended stuffier hands with his necktie belt. Never mind that Carr was simply too broke to buy a belt. They viewed it as an impertinent demonstration against the *Sun*'s sweatshop pay. Among faithful old *Sun* hands, poverty was something to be accepted gracefully, for not everyone was privileged to work for the *Sun.*

The skimpy pay, even for stars of the local staff, left reporters vulnerable to financial seduction by the politicians they covered. Keeping a good political reporter seemed impossible, with Maryland politicians luring them away with decent wages. One left to take work with Governor William Preston Lane. His successor quickly found better pay on Mayor D'Alesandro's payroll. Al Quinn, who was covering City Hall when Ed Young came, was soon to opt for the living wage offered him when Theodore McKeldin became governor.

My old college pal, Bill Gresham, now an intimate friend, got the juicy job of covering the Republican side of the scandalous senatorial campaign of 1950. It was a national sensation because of the way the Republicans contrived to defeat the veteran Millard Tydings with a handsome, dim-witted Baltimore lawyer named John Marshall Butler. The Republicans, heavily financed with money from Senator Joseph R. McCarthy's Red-hunting supporters, managed to sell Marylanders the comic fiction that Tydings, a conservative mossback loathed by all good liberals, was a secret pal of famous Communists.

It was a wonderful story, topped off by the irony that Maryland's Democratic liberals had been trying unsuccessfully to get rid of Tydings for a generation. How it finally took the Red hunters to do him in was a story Bill Gresham did not report in the *Sun,* though he told Mimi and me some of it privately over Saturday night drinks. Bill had the makings of a first-rate investigator, but at fifty dollars-a-week he was not inspired to do an aggressive reporting job on the sleazy Butler campaign.

Irony piled on irony here. Bill had been a celebrated campus radical at Hopkins and a great late-night singer of "Joe Hill." Now the world was turned upside down. He was meeting a lot of Republicans he liked. And finding that they liked him. What's more, they were treating him as a fellow who was clever about politics, a cunning man of the world who understood how things worked, which he was. He was as vulnerable as the next fifty dollars-a-week reporter, and maybe more, to the flattering attention of important men. In any case, he was picking up a lot of fascinating information he didn't feel free to print in the *Sun.*

After Butler's election surprised the *Sun*'s readers, Bill quit the paper and began what was to be a long career as a high-level factotum for fancy Republicans, including Governor Theodore McKeldin and Senator J. Glenn Beall.

Among the oldest employees, the pay was disgraceful. White-haired Miss Muller, well into her eighth decade, was getting sixty-five dollars a week. The paper's two oldest employees, Mark and Walter, who had been with the *Sun* since the gaslight era, were in the same pay class.

Too feeble for real work, they handled the "lobster trick." This was the silent time between the hour we put the morning paper to bed and the dawn when the first *Evening Sun* people started arriving at work. From two in the morning until dawn, Mark or Walter sat nodding at the city desk, monitoring the police radio, theoretically prepared to summon everyone back to work if the Second Coming should occur at Baltimore and Gay streets at four o'clock in the morning.

The company was rumored to have a retirement plan, but its details were secret, and it seemed to be applied only rarely. Ancient and faithful hands, like Mark and Walter, were simply kept on at token pay until they ran down. Emmett Kavanaugh, the business manager, justified their negligible salaries by calling them "aged incompetents."

I was working the rewrite desk the night ancient Walter was retired, so had a close view of the ceremonies. Harry Black, the principal owner of the paper, showed up. This was an immense honor for Walter, but it was hard to tell whether he appreciated it, because he seemed baffled about where he was and why, and who Harry Black was, and why he, Walter, was standing in the middle of the city room with people making speeches at him, instead of nodding over the police radio and dreaming about a time in 1892 when he worked at the first typewriter ever used in the *Sun* building.

Ed Young was at his desk beside mine that night, so we both had the same view of the ceremony taking place right in front of the city desk. When it was over and Walter had tottered off, Ed, looking unusually agitated, glanced at me, then grabbed a sheet of copy paper, wrote something on it with a grease pencil, folded it a couple of times for secrecy, and thrust it to me.

Since it was obviously meant to be private, I held it on my lap under the desk before opening it. It said: "Hurrah for the Guild!"

This was treason, bold, pure, and simple. The Newspaper Guild, which had recently unionized the news staff, was struggling with no success at all to lure the *Sun* into the twentieth century on things like money, sick pay, and retirement. The *Sun* ownership viewed the guild as a vicious Bolshevik apparatus whose members yearned to dance on the graves of men like Harry Black and Paul Patterson after filching their wealth and putting them to the guillotine.

As a management man, Ed Young was raising the clenched fist by committing his secret guild sympathies to paper. Not that he would have been punished much for it if I had handed the incriminating paper to Swanson. By then Swanson had made it clear that nothing good was ever going to be done for Ed Young again.

Still, it took courage, I thought, to put his sentiments on paper in that atmosphere, and I smiled at him, nodded agreement, tore the paper methodically into tiny bits, and dropped them in the trash can.

Not long afterward, I was surprised to discover that the newsroom editors had built up a sullen mass of resentment about their own salaries. When Jim Cannon, after long searching, found a job in New York with *Time* magazine, he came to the newsroom to say good-bye to old friends. When he got to Dan Meara, night managing editor and Buck Dorsey's chief assistant, Dan asked Jim if he minded telling him what *Time* was going to pay.

"Nine thousand dollars a year," Jim said.

Dan was visibly shaken.

"Good God!" he cried. "I never expect to make that much money as long as I live."

The strange thing was that almost all of us, even those who were driven away, loved that paper and believed it was a good paper and could even be a great paper if we did the best work we could for it. This was probably why so many of us gave our hearts to Ed Young. He embodied our conviction that we were doing something terribly important and ought to keep doing it well even though the people who owned it and ran it didn't seem to understand why we cared.

12

Money

I did not expect my mother to take it well when I told her Mimi was pregnant, and she didn't.

"Hostages to fortune," she said, staring past me toward something far, far away.

Please, not those old hostages to fortune again, I thought.

"When you decide to bring children into the world, Russell, you're giving hostages to fortune," she said.

I remembered when Doris and I were small and the grown-ups, sitting around chatting over the coffee cups after supper, talked about "hostages to fortune." They always became terribly somber when somebody said "hostages to fortune." It cropped up in sentences very much like the one my mother had just spoken:

"When you bring children into this old world, you give hostages to fortune," they said. Or, "When you give hostages to fortune you'd better be willing to pay the piper."

I knew what paying the piper meant—no fun without pain—but "hostages to fortune" had been a puzzle. A memorable phrase, but puzzling.

Now, though, when my mother dredged the famous words up out of the past, I knew very well what she was saying:

Children were serious, grown-up business. Parenthood meant my days of carefree independence were over. With children I would become a prisoner to the luck of the moment.

She was under the impression that I was a great success at the *Sun*, and probably feared that the duties of fatherhood at age twenty-five would handicap me in the competition with Cousin Edwin. I'm sure she also thought neither Mimi nor I was competent to rear children. Few people were, except her, as she saw it. Still, she loved children, the younger the better, and the prospect of having a brand-new baby to spoil quickly softened her attitude to the project. Our talk ended with her insisting that after the delivery Mimi and the baby must come stay at Marydell Road so she could care for them until Mimi recovered.

In breaking the happy news to my mother I was also preparing her for the possibility that I might need a loan, for the big new seventy dollar salary did not keep Mimi and me from being always desperate for money. It had not occurred to me that birth could bankrupt people until Mimi came back from the obstetrician with the price list.

The doctor alone wanted $100 for delivering the baby. What's more, the hospital wanted a $50 deposit right away. Whether this would pay all hospital costs seemed doubtful as I scanned its prices: $3 a day for the nursery, $15 for the delivery room, $9.50 a day for a private room. Mimi agreed to settle for the semi-private room at $7 a day.

And this was just the beginning. Alone at home one day, I was visited by a Baby-Tenda salesman. He told horrifying stories of babies accidentally killed because parents too cheap to buy Baby-Tendas had let their little ones sit in the deadly, old-fashioned high chair. The Baby-Tenda was a new kind of seat for baby, something like the old-fashioned high chair, only better, more stable, completely safe, not likely to tip over, causing baby's skull to fracture, incapable of strangling baby to death while father's back was turned.

I would have nothing else, even after he disclosed the price of a Baby-Tenda, which was breathtaking. When my mother learned of this, she was outraged and called me several varieties of fool. She still had the old-fashioned high chair that my baby sister Mary Leslie had used and intended to give it to us.

I told her it was unthinkable that I would let my baby's life be risked in a deadly, old-fashioned high chair just to save a few dollars.

"I've seen some prize fools in my time, Russell, but you take the cake," my mother replied. "If you believe that Baby-Tenda salesman, you'll believe the moon is made of green cheese."

She had sold magazine subscriptions door-to-door in the Depression and was contemptuous of people who had no sales resistance. With iron in my voice, I told her I was taking the Baby-Tenda anyhow, which gave her the cue for one of her favorite observations:

"A fool and his money are soon parted," she said.

Well, of course we also needed a bigger apartment. We found one in the corner building of a block of big brick row houses on Park Avenue. A nice neighborhood. Even a little hoity-toity, socially speaking. The rent was seventy dollars a month, a fifteen dollar increase over our first apartment.

"That's an awful rent to pay for a basement apartment," my mother observed.

"It's not a basement apartment, it's a ground-floor apartment," I said, adopting the landlord's terminology.

True, you did have to walk down a few steps to enter, and when you got inside and looked out the windows your line of sight was level with passing ankles. As my mother observed, there was nothing underneath us but Baltimore earth, and the furnace sat just outside our bedroom wall.

"Ground-floor apartment, my eye!" was her comment. "You're living in a cellar." In my mother's world, people who moved down to cellars were moving down in the world, not up, and paid less rent, not more.

The baby arrived at dawn on a raw March morning in 1951. We named her Kathleen Leland because we thought Kathleen sounded pretty, and because Leland was an old name in my mother's family, and because the two names together fell musically on the ear.

On the first day of her life I arrived at the hospital without a dazzling bouquet of red roses for Mimi. I wouldn't have noticed this deficiency except for the dazzling bouquet of red roses on Mimi's bedside table. They made me feel painfully empty-handed. I couldn't have afforded roses, of course. The *Sun* didn't pay rose salaries. But I should have brought something, though I didn't know what. I had never in my life bought flowers, but there must have been one flower a *Sun* man could afford.

This was my second grave failure of the day. The first occurred at 7:08 that morning, the sacred moment of my daughter's birth. At that moment I had been blissfully asleep in my bed at home. Mimi believed a father's duty at such times was to pace the hospital corridor. The latter-day notion that he should assist the doctor was still unheard of, but he was supposed to be present in the hospital, an absurd, comic, useless figure reading out-of-date magazines and chain-smoking cigarettes by the hour. My failure could not be forgiven just because the doctor had sent me home with assurances that the baby couldn't possibly arrive before breakfast. And now, the roses.

On first seeing them brought to her bedside, Mimi had forgiven me, had said to herself that I was offering these priceless blooms to atone for being asleep at the sacred moment, and had thought how sweet I was and how much she loved me. Then, lifting the card, she had seen that they were not from me. They were from Bill Gresham.

This destroyed my only defense, which was that the *Sun* kept me too broke to buy roses. As Mimi quickly pointed out when I tried it, Bill's pay was even worse than mine, yet he could afford roses.

"Sure," I said, "but Bill doesn't have to buy a Baby-Tenda, does he?"

Sometimes it seemed the *Sun* had mysterious powers to know precisely down to the last penny how much we needed to survive for another week. And that, knowing this, it paid me just a dollar less, so that with each passing week we sank just a slight bit deeper into the quicksand. Then just when it seemed that all was lost, that the gas and electricity and telephone were sure to be cut off, that my only suit could never be recovered from the dry cleaner, that I would have to get a second job if I wanted a new pair of shoes—at that point of utter despair there would come a small salary increase, and it became possible to survive a few more months.

For the pay hikes we had the Newspaper Guild to thank. Frail though the guild was, it had got the *Sun* to agree to a contract of sorts providing a top salary of one hundred dollars a week for reporters after seven years on the job. My three years was worth sixty-eight dollars, but with the added money Ed Young had finagled out of the *Sun*, I was making eighty-two dollars a week when Gresham's roses arrived. For a few months, Mimi was able to keep most of the bills paid up, and we could even afford Scotch and bourbon for Saturday night instead of the usual cheap blended whiskey that made you yearn for death if you took one too many.

Nobody at the *Sun* ever seemed too broke to buy whiskey. Poor people rarely are. Maybe alcohol is the luxury necessary to make poverty tolerable. We were not real paupers, however. Just miserably broke. We had no car and so little prospect of ever having one that neither Mimi nor I had even learned to drive. When we took the baby to visit Marydell Road, we rode the streetcar at ten cents apiece, babies free.

We had a radio with a secondhand phonograph attached to it by a couple of wires, but no television set, and no interest in buying one. They were prohibitively expensive, for one thing. For another, a world in which people sat silently in the parlor looking at a box that showed little moving pictures was so alien to our experience of the way people lived that it never occurred to us to want a television set.

There were signs, though, that television, like whiskey, was soon to become a consoling vice of the poor. On rewrite one night in 1951 I wrote a police story about a mother in an east Baltimore slum who was "shot to death while two small boys sat undisturbed in the next room with their attention glued to the televised gunplay of Hopalong Cassidy."

The comfortable eighty-two-dollar-a-week life ended when a rat invaded our ground-floor apartment on Park Avenue. It was a small apartment, so it was easy to discover there was a rat among us. The sight of a long rat tail sticking out from under the daybed was the conclusive proof.

I was semiheroic. Armed only with a broom, I closed the hall door leading to the baby's alcove, opened doors leading to the sidewalk and to the backyard, then suddenly yanked the daybed away from the wall while shouting fiercely for the rat to be gone. Faster than I could wave my broom, it fled out the door, across the sidewalk, and out of our lives.

Mimi moved almost as fast to find another apartment where an infant would be safer than in our ground-floor crib space. She found it on rustic, tree-shaded Evesham Avenue off York Road, in far north Baltimore. It had two bedrooms and a large living room, once a painter's studio, with a high beamed ceiling and a huge window to catch the northern light. It was lovely. It was devastating. The rent was ninety dollars a month.

Obsession with money, like the loathing for Neil Swanson, made it easy to recognize *Sun* people. Yet if we were sullen toward the company because of the shabby pay, it also made us work better. Doing a good job at the *Sun* was the way to get a good job on a more generous newspaper. As Buck Dorsey often said when hiring a new reporter, you would never get rich working for the *Sun*, but after learning the trade at the *Sun* you would be qualified to work for any newspaper in the country.

The *Sun* itself offered a few possibilities for glory. It had one of the biggest Washington bureaus in all of journalism, with a dozen glamorous reporters who got Page One by-lines every day and must, I thought, earn princely salaries.

For drudges on the local staff, the Washington bureau was paradise and those assigned to it, giants. I knew them only by reputation, for they rarely set foot in Baltimore except on election nights, when they invaded the city room and commandeered the best typewriters to fill the night's front page with the big national voting stories. Between editions they were given the freedom of a grand buffet and bar spread out for them in a room out of view to the local staff.

I was too worldly now to gawk at such gaudy stars, but with discreet inquiries I had each of them identified for me. There were Joseph Short, who knew presidents, and Philip Potter, who had covered the Chinese revolution and talked to Chou Enlai. There was Price Day, who wrote like a dream and had the Pulitzer Prize for his coverage of India. There were national political reporters like Dewey Fleming and Gerry Griffin, who traveled the country on lavish expense accounts, and trouble-shooting veterans like Tom O'Neill, who might be sent halfway around the world on an hour's notice to cover a story.

Tom O'Neill was the *Sun*'s legendary reporter, the man who could go anywhere, do anything, and do it better than anybody else, whether it was covering the Alger Hiss trials, exposing asininity and corruption in the Maryland legislature, covering a presidential election, or reporting the American attempt to undo the Iranian revolution and put the shah back in power.

I first glimpsed the majesty a *Sun* reporter could achieve during O'Neill's coverage of the Iran story. His daily copy from Tehran arrived in cable shorthand and had to be retyped, often by me, in form suitable for the printers. At the end of the very first cable I handled, O'Neill added a message to Buck Dorsey. It said: BUCK, SEND FIVE THOUSAND IMMEDIATELY.

The five thousand O'Neill wanted sent immediately were dollars. It was a staggering revelation. It made me dizzy to realize that a reporter, without ceremony, without apology, without explanation, could tell the managing editor to send him five thousand dollars. Immediately. Five thousand dollars was more than my salary for a whole year.

Typing another O'Neill cable ten days later I got a second shock from the concluding message:

BUCK, SEND ANOTHER FIVE THOUSAND, DON'T KNOW WHERE IT GOES BUT IT'S GONE.

Here was a vision of what a *Sun* reporter could be if he could slip the chains of the local staff and become one of its "correspondents" in Washington or overseas. So far as I could see, no expense was spared to keep these dandies happy. O'Neill, for instance. He dressed like a capitalist: elegantly cut suits from the finest shops, a spotless gray fedora, shirts with French cuffs. Each Saturday he luxuriated in the sybaritic pleasures of the Lord Baltimore Hotel barber shop, which kept his thin silvery hair meticulously trimmed and his fingernails gleaming from the manicurist's care. What's more, he looked like an important man. Short, lean, and dapper, he carried himself like a marine general, shoulders squared, chin tilted up. His face was thin and delicate in the highbred patrician style, and the impression that this was a man of importance, not to be trifled with, was heightened by its cool, unsmiling expression, the authoritative look of a man who never had to be eager to please anybody.

Chances of getting a foreign assignment were hopeless. Since the end of the war, the *Sun* had been closing its foreign offices and now had only the London bureau operating. This was one of the paper's prize plums and usually went to a creaky Washington veteran in reward for distinguished service.

The possibility of escaping into the glamorous world of correspondents never entered my mind. For one thing, I had little interest in government and politics and even less in the international scene. Aside from the big money that went with these jobs, the work didn't really interest me. My goal was to become good enough at the business on the local staff to qualify for a living wage on another paper.

My closest *Sun* friends at this time were Bill Gresham, Jim Cannon, and Ellis Baker, and each was dealing with the money problem in his own way. Bill was using the *Sun* to cultivate the politicians who later hired him. Ellis Baker—we were not related—was attacking the *Sun* frontally as leader of the Newspaper Guild. Jim Cannon, whose limitless supply of gumption and get-up-and-go would have warmed my moth-

Tom O'Neill in Tehran, 1951

er's heart, simply got up and went at the first
opportunity.

The opportunity was the Korean War. Cannon,
then thirty-two years old, had been on the *Sun* two
years, after getting his experience on a small paper in
far upstate New York. Tall, dark, socially poised, and
courteous in the formal southern manner, Jim was
from Alabama and had done war service in the O.S.S.
Ed Young took such a liking to him that he invited
Jim to join him on the train ride up to Philadelphia

for the Penn-Cornell football game. For Ed, a Cornell man, the game was a sacred ritual, and Jim got back heavily marinated in alcohol with "Far above Cayuga's waters" roaring endlessly in his memory. Now and then Ed suggested they slip down to the Gayety burlesque house for the matinee, justifying it with the excuse that H. L. Mencken could often be seen there. "Let's go see if Mencken's down there," he urged.

The Korean War broke out late on a June Saturday. Cannon desperately wanted to go. At work Monday, he told Ed Young, who said he would speak to Buck Dorsey. Cannon knew, however, that Dorsey was not the man to get him to Korea as a war correspondent. Only Swanson could do that, and Cannon knew it.

On an idiotic impulse, he marched out of the city room and right into the ogre's office. That was how he thought of it afterward: "an idiotic impulse." With two years' experience on the Gloversville (N.Y.) *Leader-Republican* and only two years on the *Sun*, you had to be a little unhinged to think of bracing Swanson for one of the most important assignments on the paper.

You didn't just walk in on the great man, of course. You had to get past Bill Perkinson, a Swanson factotum in a small front office. Confronting the Perkinson barrier, Cannon demonstrated the good reporter's gift for ingenuity.

He noticed that Swanson's office was separated from Perkinson's only by a cheap partition that did not go all the way to the ceiling. Thinking Swanson might be able to hear over the partition, Cannon started speaking to Perkinson as loud as he could without actually shouting,

"In this loud voice," he told me, "I said that I sure would like to go cover that war in Korea. I think I could do a great job, this is my dream, that's a great assignment, and so forth, speaking to be heard over this partition."

Perkinson said he'd tell Swanson, then sent Cannon back to the city room.

When Cannon was gone, Swanson emerged from his office and asked Perkinson, "Who was that?"

In the city room shortly afterward, Buck Dorsey summoned Cannon and said Swanson wanted to talk to him.

Within two weeks Cannon was off to war via London, Paris, Rome, and the Mediterranean, carrying a thousand dollars in cash and ten thousand in traveler's checks. Swanson had a hunch that the Korean invasion was just a feint directed from Moscow, and that the Soviets might launch a heavy assault elsewhere. Europe was the obvious bet, so Swanson started Jim to Korea by ordering him to fly east.

After five weeks of London, Paris, a luxury hotel on the Riviera, and at sea with the Mediterranean fleet, Cannon was ordered posthaste to Asia, a seven-day journey that took him via Rome, Athens, Istanbul, Damascus, Karachi, Delhi, Bangkok, Hong Kong, Taipei, and Tokyo.

Those of us who had lacked the gumption to march into Swanson's office and talk to Perkinson at the top of our lungs were in rages of envy. Cannon had done the inconceivable: With gall and cunning, he had broken free from the local staff and crossed over to the wondrous world of the correspondents, where giants had pockets stuffed with traveler's checks and fired off cables saying, BUCK, SEND FIVE THOUSAND IMMEDIATELY.

When he reached Japan, two of three other reporters Swanson had sent to cover the war had been wounded, one very seriously.

"Whatever you do, don't get killed," was the farewell advice the other offered from his hospital bed as Jim departed for Seoul.

Jim Cannon as *Sun* war correspondent in Korea

It was a good possibility. That winter he was traveling with a small unit of the First Marine Division near
the Chinese border when a small plane dropped an
urgent command for them to pull back immediately.
Mao Tze-tung had just committed his forces to the
war, and Cannon and the marines, totally ignorant of
the new situation, were barreling headlong toward
three divisions of the Chinese army situated scarcely
a mile away.

The Chinese onslaught began immediately and
turned into an American debacle. Cannon spent the
next three and a half days without sleep, running for
his life, desperately scuttling this way and that through
the snow-covered mountains of North Korea to escape
the encircling Chinese army. A year later he came
back to the *Sun* a hero.

Alas, heroism did not qualify you for an expense account in Baltimore. Abroad, Jim had been traveling first-class at the *Sun*'s expense. Nobody seemed to care how much you spent on expenses once you left the city limits. When you came back, though, it was chin up and make do on the same old *Sun* pay scale. Cannon, who wanted to get married, had not escaped the local staff, after all. He was getting ninety dollars a week. Soon he did get married and started looking for another job.

Ellis Baker was a more complicated piece of work. Where Jim set goals and moved toward them without guile under a full head of energy, Ellis seemed driven by motives so complicated that they baffled those who knew him best, and maybe even Ellis himself. Outwardly, he seemed as calm as a stone Buddha, yet he took risks that suggested there might be emotional fires seething underneath the serenity.

There was never an unlikelier labor agitator. For one thing, Ellis was good Baltimore society, than which there was nothing more conservative. Good Baltimore society was likely to think unionism intolerable not because it was Bolshevism pure and simple, but because union people didn't dress properly. It was impossible to have such a creature to dinner, much less marry your daughter.

Ellis, whose full name was Ellis Thompson Baker III, not only dressed like a proper north Baltimore toff, bow ties and button-down collars and seersuckers for summer heat; he also spoke in the prim and reasoned voice of the unimpassioned intellectual. He had been Phi Beta Kappa at Duke and was a writer of great subtlety. The thundering barn-burner rhetoric of the union hall was utterly beyond him. Outwardly he was the man of pure reason.

Nor did he look like an incendiary. Rotund without being fat, he moved at the stately pace of a contented monk strolling a monastery garden. His hands were small and delicate, and he had a thin man's face: thin lips, thin pointed nose. His hair was always cut within a half inch of the scalp in the standard military whiffle of World War Two. Surrounded by two-pack-a-day cigarette puffers, he was a cigar smoker. His social pleasures were gin and Dixieland jazz.

Strangest of all, early in his career, Ellis had been marked for future glory at the *Sun*. Everybody said he had a brilliant future there. He would move steadily up the executive ladder and, very likely, end up running the paper someday. He had all the requirements: remarkable talents for writing, reporting, and editing; superior intelligence; administrative ability; good roots in Baltimore society. That mattered at the *Sun* despite its frequent editorial insistence that America was a classless society. Baltimore, in fact, was sharply divided along class lines, and the *Sun* was patrician, heart-and-soul. Good roots in Baltimore society mattered.

They were also dangerous. The small, snobby society that produced Ellis might say of one of their own who crossed over to the labor crowd that he was a traitor to his class. This might make them more unforgiving, more ruthlessly determined to destroy him than they would be toward someone like, say, Swanson who was middle-class and vulgar. Jim Cannon, who liked Ellis and worried about him, was convinced that his brilliant future would be cut off before it began by the vengeance of the bluestockings who mattered at the *Sun*.

Ellis had come on the paper in 1940 right out of college. Heart trouble kept him out of the war, which gave him a chance to master most of the jobs on the paper. By the end of the decade, proof of the *Sun*'s esteem was his $125-a-week salary, which was in a class with editors' pay. Most *Sun* people assumed he would soon be made city editor.

He never was. Early in his career he had run afoul of Swanson. Swanson had asked him to move over from the morning paper to study the *Evening Sun* and recommend any necessary changes. Swanson was infuriated when Ellis reported vast room for improvement and proposed extensive changes. Ellis realized too late that what Swanson wanted was praise, not improvement. That was the beginning of the end for him with Swanson.

When I arrived in 1947, Ellis was leading the guild campaign to organize the newsroom, and the *Sun* ownership was resisting vigorously. Editorially the *Sun* had long been antilabor, but it did not seem to occur to Ellis that fomenting the cause of hateful unionism might destroy his brilliant future.

Or maybe it did, and maybe he willingly accepted the risk anyhow, because he wanted to do something for all the people who were groaning about the *Sun*'s sweatshop pay.

Or maybe he was so fired by inner anger about something or somebody at the *Sun* that he was willing to risk losing his brilliant future for the satisfaction of hitting out. He obviously detested Swanson. He also despised the paternalistic arrogance with which he thought the *Sun* treated the hired help. This was dramatically symbolized for him in a curious elevator ritual involving the publisher, Paul Patterson. Whenever Patterson boarded the elevator, its operator ignored all other passengers and sped it nonstop to Patterson's floor. It was doubly galling to Ellis that after boarding the elevator Patterson spoke to no one, not so much as a "Good morning" to the whole group.

Sometimes Ellis acted as though he thought the union struggle was a gentleman's game in which loser and winner would shake hands gracefully at the end

and walk together to the clubhouse. As embodied in
Swanson and Patterson, however, the *Sun* did not con-
fuse cash flow and good sportsmanship. They gave
their blessing to a company union intended to lure
newsroom people away from the troublesome mili-
tancy of the guild. One day Ellis noticed the office
mailbox stuffed with copies of a letter from the company union. In a playful mood, he wrote "Fink" on
each envelope.

Buck Dorsey's response was not playful. He told
Ellis he had "compromised" his position on the staff
and issued orders that he was no longer to work at
the city desk. This was especially ominous because
Buck Dorsey was on friendly terms with Ellis's family
and had always been fond of Ellis himself. If Ellis was
alarmed, his spirits must have improved when he was
assigned to Annapolis for the important job of covering a session of the legislature.

Then, on Easter weekend, with the legislature
ended, he came back to Baltimore and a grave sentence. He had been assigned to cover the Eastern
Avenue Easter Parade.

The Eastern Avenue Easter Parade! It was a glove
in his face.

The *Sun* traditionally covered two Easter parades.
Baltimore's highborn folk paraded their spring gar-
ments up and down Charles Street. Covering this was
a dreary chore commonly given to old-timers too worn
out to whine or youngsters too green to be bored by
anything.

Not to be outdone by the nobs, east Baltimore's
Bohemians and Poles held their own parade on Eastern Avenue, the blue-collar boulevard of the city's
ethnic proles. It was a small Easter footnote to the
main event on Charles Street. The Ellis Bakers of the
staff were not assigned to the Eastern Avenue Easter

Parade. Ellis took the assignment as notice that the *Sun* had declared war and that he was the enemy.

In a way, Ellis won that war. He got the votes that defeated the company union and entrenched the guild permanently at the paper. He also negotiated the first guild contract with the company. It wasn't much of a contract, but it was a first blow toward smashing the *Sun*'s nineteenth-century paternalism.

Then Ellis quit the *Sun,* walked away from the ruin of his brilliant future in journalism, and went to work as an organizer for the Newspaper Guild. The guild couldn't match the $125 a week he got from the *Sun,* so he started his new career by taking a pay cut.

In the end, the money struggle drove all three of them—Gresham, Cannon, and Ellis—away from the *Sun.* I lingered on, grousing, desperate about unpayable bills, threatening to go elsewhere despite my love for Ed Young, but never making the effort. I began seeing a future in which, like poor old Walter, I would finally be retired with a rocking chair because I was too old to stay awake through the lobster shift.

To persuade myself that I was not too timid to at least growl at the *Sun,* I said yes when Ellis Baker asked me to sit on the guild committee that would negotiate our second contract. I thought this would probably be the death of any future for me at the *Sun,* but could afford to be brave since the future I foresaw had a rocking chair in it.

Then there came a miracle.

13

Day Off

The telephone woke me around ten-thirty in the morning. I normally didn't get to bed until four, so it was still dawn on my personal clock, and I growled a sour hello which was meant to say, what's the idea of waking me up at this hour of the night, you idiot?

"This is Mrs. Johnston," said a voice of command and, to put me in a more humble mood, it added, "Mister Dorsey's secretary."

Gunfire in the next room couldn't have brought me wide awake faster. Neither Mrs. Johnston nor Buck Dorsey had ever telephoned me at home.

I sprang out of the sheets, sat at attention on the side of the bed waiting for something awful, and with great respect asked fierce Mrs. Johnston, "How are you?"

Without bothering to answer, she said, "Can you have lunch today with Mister Dorsey?"

It was not a question, of course. It was a command.

I said I thought I could have lunch with Mr. Dorsey, since it was my day off.

"Will Hasslinger's be all right?" she announced.

I said Hasslinger's would be fine.

Hasslinger's would actually be dreadful if I had to pay for my share of the lunch. It was one of Balti-

more's best restaurants and was priced accordingly. I
had never eaten there, never dreamed of eating there,
and never even wanted to eat there, not at those
prices.

Mrs. Johnston suggested a time.

I said it was a perfect time for me, and she said,
"Good-bye," and hung up.

I bolted a cup of coffee and spent a lot of time
trying to assemble a presentable wardrobe, in the
meantime worrying and wondering about what was
about to happen. And something was about to happen, no doubt about that. Buck Dorsey did not take
lunch with drones on the local staff. With Tom
O'Neill, yes. Maybe once in a while even with Ed
Young. With local reporters and rewrite men, never.
Something was up, possibly something bad, but I
couldn't think what that might be. I had been working
well lately and had made no disastrous mistakes to
endanger my job. In any case, Buck Dorsey wouldn't
take me to lunch to fire me, would he?

Working for the guild had given me a small reputation as an office sorehead, but certainly nobody could
consider me a menace in Ellis Baker's league. On the
guild's negotiating committee, I had been little more
than a warm body at the table, making almost no
contribution to the union cause. Still, was it possible
that Buck Dorsey wanted to caution me to mind my
step in the union department? Highly improbable. He
rarely acknowledged my existence in the office, surely
he wouldn't take me to lunch to lecture me on the
need to be discreet. Or would he? I remembered that
strange lecture he had once given me on good taste.

I took a taxi to Hasslinger's. The occasion was too
big to be approached by streetcar. I would probably
never lunch with Buck Dorsey again. I wanted to cut
a good figure. Suppose Buck Dorsey should see me
arriving at Hasslinger's. If he did, by God, he would

see me arriving by taxi, the way Tom O'Neill would arrive. Sometimes you had to squander money to keep your self-respect.

He did not see me arrive, but on getting out of the taxi I was far too excited to lament the dollar needlessly spent. I stepped out into a golden noon in November. Hasslinger's, occupying a corner on Charles Street one block from Pennsylvania Station, had big windows facing west and south. These were flooding the room with sunlight when I entered. It was a large, open room, rather plain and masculine, skillfully undecorated, and richer in feeling because of its simplicity, or maybe because of that soft golden sunlight suffusing it.

A man in formal black greeted me. I told him I was to meet Mr. Dorsey of the *Sun*.

Ah yes, of course. Mr. Dorsey.

Mr. Dorsey was clearly a familiar and important man here.

This way, please. And he led me toward what was obviously a choice table near the center of the room. Buck Dorsey was already there. I was late. I had kept Buck Dorsey waiting.

I didn't care. Amazingly, I simply didn't care. There was no explaining it. The man I'd been yesterday would have cared ridiculously, would have turned pink with embarrassment, would have apologized and apologized until Buck Dorsey was forced to say, "For heaven's sake, man, don't have a breakdown, you're not late, I just happened to get here a few minutes early."

Today I was not even mildly flustered. So I was late and had kept Buck Dorsey waiting, and it mattered not at all to me. Tom O'Neill couldn't have been cooler about it. When I reached the table, Buck Dorsey stood, waved me to the other chair, and said, "I happened to get here a few minutes early, so . . ."

So he had ordered a drink. It was a martini, and not on the rocks. The custom of serving a martini with ice cubes was still unborn. Buck Dorsey's was a clear, icy liquid in a stemmed glass with nothing to dilute its power. He waved. A waiter appeared.

"What do you want to drink?" Buck Dorsey asked.

For me it was breakfast time. I never drank at that time of day. I rarely drank anything stronger than a beer even in the evening, except weekends. Still—"I'll have a martini."

"Any preference about what kind of gin?"

Normally I would have said, "It doesn't matter," but in the nick of time I recalled what John Wood had once said about Buck Dorsey: "Such an Anglophile that the only gin he'll drink in his martini is House of Lords."

And now Buck Dorsey was asking did I have a preference about the gin for my martini.

"Yes," I said. "House of Lords."

We made conversation stiffly, but there was no sense of danger in the air. Buck Dorsey seemed relaxed, possibly even happy. My martini was brought. He watched with concern while I sipped it.

"Is it dry enough?" he asked.

"Yes, it's fine," I said, then wondered if that wasn't a mistake. Buck Dorsey, I realized, was finicky about the dryness of his martinis and probably sent many back to be made drier. Too late, I saw that he probably would have thought better of me if I'd said mine wasn't dry enough and sent it back for improvement.

"You sure?" he asked, while the waiter hovered. The waiter was probably used to taking back martinis from Mr. Dorsey's table.

Now, though, I knew I had missed the moment for sending it back. Having pronounced it fine, I would look indecisive if I changed my mind.

"It's just right," I said.

We began working on the martinis, with Buck Dorsey making small talk at first, then asking about my family. He had been well briefed and knew Mimi and I had a new baby, born a few days after the election.

It was amazing how cool I was, how quickly I sensed that Buck Dorsey intended to do something rewarding for me. The martini seemed to increase the calm self-confidence I had felt ever since walking into that streaming golden sunlight. Perhaps he was about to give me a significant raise, I thought. Now seemed the time to show how much I needed one.

Yes, it was our second baby, I said. Our first was a little girl. This one was a boy. We'd named him Allen after an uncle of mine who had been good and generous to my mother and my sister Doris and me back in the Depression when times had been so hard. Of course, trying to keep up with the bills nowadays, well, sometimes Mimi and I felt as if the Depression had never ended.

"What did you make of the election?" Buck Dorsey replied.

I took the hint and stopped talking about the hardships of life for a *Sun* man. I was not foolish enough to tell him how I felt about the election, however, because I had him figured as a plutocrat, therefore a Republican, therefore probably ecstatic about General Eisenhower's victory over Adlai Stevenson.

It was wiser to finesse political talk with anecdote, I thought, so told him about going with Mimi to vote just four days before Allen was born. The polling place was in a private house up two dozen steep cement steps, and Mimi so big she could hardly—

Buck Dorsey had signaled the waiter for a second martini. "You like another?" he asked.

I nodded yes and went on about election day.

—well, I knew Eisenhower was going to swamp Stevenson when I saw ambulances outside that polling place. They were bringing in people on stretchers to vote, and on the sidewalk there were old people in wheelchairs waiting to be carried up those steep cement steps to vote. I knew then it was Ike by a landslide because nobody who is happy with the status quo leaves the hospital to vote. I'd said to Mimi, this isn't an election, it's a murder, and she needn't feel she had to struggle up those steps to vote because whatever she did, Eisenhower had it locked up, and—

The fresh drinks were there. I wondered if I had been talking too much, but Buck Dorsey seemed to be giving me his full attention as we laced into the second round of martinis. Then he started talking about his plans for adapting the *Sun*'s news coverage to deal with a new government in Washington. I ought to have been amazed but wasn't, thanks no doubt to the gin, because he was discussing his managerial problems as openly as if he were discussing them with Neil Swanson.

There was nothing very startling or very interesting to me in these problems, which dealt chiefly with shifting assignments for famous by-lines in the Washington bureau, but I listened judiciously, nodded now and then, and clucked when it seemed appropriate, until, lifting my martini glass, I noticed it was empty. So was Buck Dorsey's. What a good time we were having, sitting in the golden sunlight at Hasslinger's, discussing high management policy while an obliging waiter brought us these marvelous drinks.

"Shall we have one more?" Buck Dorsey suggested, signaling for the waiter, who arrived with menus.

"Two martinis," said Buck Dorsey, waving the menus away. Then, to me: "Tell me what you think of the paper these days."

Under the sway of the gin, my calm self-confidence had become suicidal self-importance. So when Buck

Dorsey asked me what I thought of the paper I actually started telling him what I thought of the paper.

While I did, the new martinis arrived, as well as menus, so fortunately we both lost the thread of my criticisms in a lengthy discussion of food. When we had finally ordered, the third martini was pretty well gone, and Buck Dorsey said he thought he would have a beer with his lunch, and would I like one, too? I said I would, and Buck Dorsey said, "What beer do you like?" to which I said, "Whatever you're having is fine with me."

To which he said, "No, you choose the beer."

My mental wiring may have been fouled by the martinis, but my internal alarm system went off, and I instantly suspected that Buck Dorsey was testing me and that choosing the wrong beer could be disastrous for me. Maybe the gin had even given me new cunning. It took only a fraction of an instant to realize that choosing most of the local beers, beers like Gunther and Arrow, would be the end of me. I did not especially like beer, knew little about it, and drank it simply because I thought newspapermen ought to drink beer and because it was cheap. I vaguely knew there was a local beer that might be marginally acceptable to a connoisseur like Buck Dorsey, but couldn't remember which it was.

In the next fraction of an instant I realized that the way to score big with Buck Dorsey was to order an imported beer. The trouble was that I had never drunk an imported beer and could not think of the name of one. In 1952 imported beer was a rare, almost unknown commodity in America. A few European companies were just beginning to test the market. Occasionally one of them might run an ad in one of the higher-brow magazines. James Thurber, E. B. White, and S. J. Perelman had made me a devoted reader of *The New Yorker,* and now, with Buck Dorsey waiting for my decision, I remembered seeing way in the back of a *New Yorker* a small ad for an imported German beer I had never heard of. It was called Lowenbrau with an umlaut *o*.

"I'd like a Löwenbrau," I said, hoping my German pronunciation was right.

"Two Löwenbraus," Buck Dorsey said to the waiter, then smiled at me man-to-man—or was it like a father who was proud of his son?—and said, "I certainly admire your taste."

The food came, and the beer, and when we started to eat, Buck Dorsey said, "How old are you?"

I said I was twenty-seven.

"How would you like to go to London?" he asked.

The question was so preposterous that at first I did not absorb its implication. It was as though he had asked if I would like to go out to Cleveland for a few days and cover an Urban League convention. Well, I said, a little hesitant, we had just had a new baby, and I wasn't sure it was a good time to go off and leave Mimi alone.

"Could I think about it a little while?" I asked.

Buck Dorsey was looking at me very strangely, and as the full weight of the great announcement he had just uttered broke over me, I understood why. He was sending me to London. The managing editor of the *Sun* had invited me to lunch and spoken to me like an equal because he intended to send me to London, and instead of fainting with joy, I had asked if I could have time to think it over.

"I mean, how long would you want me to be away?" I said.

"Probably two years," he said. "That's the usual assignment for men we put in the London bureau."

The full wonder of it was now spreading through my gin-soaked sensibilities. He was making me the London correspondent. "Chief of the London Bureau," as the title had it.

"Of course, once you get there and find a place to live, you'd move your family over with you," he was saying.

In my shock I must have muttered something about not being able to afford to move my family to London because he laughed and said, "Don't worry about money. Uncle Abell will pay for everything."

"Uncle Abell?"

That was his private way of referring to the *Sun,* which was owned by a handful of wealthy Baltimoreans organized as the A. S. Abell Company.

"Everything?"

"Everything," he said.

I said if he was truly serious of course I would go, then resumed eating whatever it was the waiter had brought, trying to behave as though my whole world had not just been turned downside up. Buck Dorsey was talking about the coming coronation of young Queen Elizabeth, which would be the great story during my time in London, but I was now too excited to pay close attention. I was going to escape the drudgery of the local newsroom, after all. I was going to cross that chasm and pass into the glorious world where the correspondents saw their by-lines spread across the front page and sent cables saying, BUCK, SEND FIVE THOUSAND IMMEDIATELY.

It was the awesome, fearful, mysterious Buck Dorsey who had done all this for me. And all the time I had thought he hadn't even noticed my existence. What a lovely man he was. Just as great a newsman, I thought, as Ed Young, only in a different way. As we sat in the golden sunlight eating food I would never remember, he paused in his talk about the coronation, looked past me into the remote distance, and said, "I wish somebody had asked me to go to London when I was twenty-seven years old."

14

Fog

Thick winter fog had turned afternoon to twilight when the S.S. *United States* docked at Southampton. Then they wouldn't let me through Customs because my trunk was missing, and when the first boat train to London left without me, I began to unravel.

I was shocked to hear the train was leaving without me.

But I had a reservation on that train, I told a porter.

Don't worry, sir, they'll take you on the second train, he said.

Thank God, they had a second train. I hadn't known that. But where was my trunk? Could they have failed to put my trunk aboard in New York?

"Did you have it in the cabin, sir?"

No, it was stored in the hold.

Don't worry, sir. It takes a little longer to get luggage out of the hold. It'll be along presently.

We were in a cavernous shed. In the first excitement of getting off the boat, of actually setting foot in a foreign country, the shed had seemed a thrilling place, swarming with merrily chattering passengers, fast-stepping porters, and carts piled high with baggage. Now, though, with half the passengers gone, the other half drifting away, and the bustle reduced to a shuffle, my excitement was fading into dread.

It was dim and gray in that shed. The English being spoken by the porters and the Customs inspectors was not my English. Suppose my trunk was lost. What in the world would I do? But then, suppose it wasn't lost. I had four cartons of Chesterfields stored in that trunk, and English law forbade more than two. Suppose the Customs inspector commanded me to open the trunk and spied the illegal cigarettes. Surely they didn't send you back on the next boat, not for two cartons of Chesterfields. And yet, the Customs inspectors looked decidedly unfriendly. They were trained to distrust everyone, weren't they?

The shed was becoming sinister and hostile.

I was suffering an acute loss of nerve, and knew it, and told myself to get a grip on myself, and keep my chin up. I was an American, after all. We Americans were the twentieth-century Romans, weren't we? The Romans never showed fear. Tom O'Neill wouldn't whimper.

My loss of spirit was accelerated by the damp, wintry chill. It was January. Though I was wearing my new wool suit with vest and my new overcoat, bought especially for London, the cold passed easily through wool, cotton, flesh, and bone, settled into the marrow, then clamped the soul in frigid embrace.

From nowhere the missing trunk appeared on the low platform in front of the Customs man.

"Is this yours, sir?" he asked.

I nodded, and he made a chalk mark on the trunk and waved me into England smuggling twenty packs of illicit cigarettes. The porter led the way to the boat train and said he would put the trunk in the baggage car. I produced a fistful of English coins acquired aboard ship and gave him several of the heavier ones. He looked more than pleased, so I guessed it was a

decent tip and climbed on the train. The car was startlingly small and just as startlingly elegant. It contained eight small tables, four on either side of the
aisle. Each table was set for two with dazzling white
linen and the cups, saucers, plates, and silverware
required for serious eating. On each table a small,
silk-shaded lamp cast a warm orange glow. Armchairs
faced each other across each table, creating eight intimate conversational settings.

A white-jacketed porter put me at a table opposite
a well-dressed, middle-aged man whose tailoring, even
to my untutored eye, spelled Englishman. I had been
cautioned not to start idle chatter with travelers
because the British were tetchy about talking to
strangers, but in such close quarters it was impossible
to ignore him, so I nodded, smiled, and muttered an
innocuous greeting.

He did not smile back, nor speak. He simply glared
at me with undisguised dislike.

Good Lord! This man hates me!, I said to myself.

My spirits had risen a little on boarding the train,
but sank again at this sour greeting. To avoid having
to look at my dyspeptic companion, I took some blank
paper from my wallet and started making notes on my
welcome to England. Maybe he would become curious
and ask about my work, which would break the ice
and give me a chance to tell him I was an American
newspaperman. That ought to interest him. Head lowered, I made notes:

"Jan 19—arrival—bags fouled up—helpful porters—
very outgoing hotel [Claridge's] representative—didn't
tip him—bad? . . . . RR train—so small!—the odor
in car—medicinal—Pullman—2 armchairs facing a laid
table—orange-shaded lamp bulb, small open bulbs
overhead and along sides—cars look like all mahogany
paneled . . ."

At this point the porter asked, "D'ya want tea, sir?"

I said yes and was served the first cup of an ocean of tea destined to flow through me before I left England.

I made a note about the porter and the tea and wrote on:

"Pullman seats 16 people—with more private compartments at either end—great bustle of porters just prior to departure—'Scone, sir?'—'Yes, please'—So I get a buttered biscuit."

Now the train was pulling away from the pier. As it left the shelter of the dock siding, we could see that the fog was immense. Through the window I made out faint, blurry lights signifying that Southampton was out there, but nothing had form or outline, and then there was no light at all, just dark and impenetrable fog.

I had grown up on stories and movies set in prodigious English fogs, and I wanted England to be foggy, but this fog was not the gentle, romantic fog I had imagined. It was a fog with a dark heart, a fog that might never end, a fog that seemed to choke and smother the world. I jotted a few notes in this overwrought vein, then, having filled up the paper, had no choice but to tuck it away and deal with my tea and scone. As I did so, my companion stared directly into my eyes with such intensity that I must have raised my eyebrows in surprise, as if to say, "Yes?"

He spoke a simple, declarative sentence.

"America makes me sick," he said.

I smiled at him. I was too shaken by the quiet ferocity of his voice to give a spoken reply. If he had thrown his tea into my face I could hardly have been more shocked. The smile was the only retort I could muster. It was supposed to tell him he could be as rude as he pleased, but could never provoke me to anger because I was a gentleman, a man of the world too polished, too well-bred to kick his filthy shins under the table, as a less temperate man might do.

Finally I said something inane. Something like, "Well, we all have our prejudices and it's better having them out in the open than keeping them suppressed." I could get off banalities like that without thinking, and probably did so now because I was too rattled to say anything that needed thinking about.

The man talked on in a perfectly even conversational tone that did not carry to the other passengers. My mind took in the substance of it, but not the music. It seemed he despised everything about America. Its overfed people with their vacuous smiles and raucous voices. The stupidity of its policies in Europe. Its lack of history, its absence of culture, its vulgar belief that money could buy anything.

Why was he doing this? He did not look crazy. Was this the famous British eccentricity, which so titillated the travel-guide writers? Back home, I would never greet a perfect stranger from abroad by telling him that everything about his homeland disgusted me. Maybe this was the mysterious British sense of humor at work, perhaps the man was enjoying some bizarre practical joke at my expense. But no. No humorist ever burned with the fierce intensity that fired this man. This was a man who would cherish no mirth unless it was sour.

"This man hates me." I said it silently. *The first person I meet in England, and he hates me, and I am locked in with him at this table in this terrible fog, and will be, all the way to London.*

There was no guessing how many hours it would take to get to London. Gray foggy afternoon turned to black foggy night against the windows. Sometimes we passed station platforms with lights close enough to be visible through the window, and they slid past so slowly that the train scarcely seemed to be moving.

To cope with my hateful companion I fell back on reporter's reflexes, asking him questions and listening dispassionately to his answers. This way I tried to reduce him to just another of the crackpots who fill the newspaperman's life. The trick was to let them talk, keep an impassive face, pretend to be listening intently, then put them out of mind. This fellow was not so easily dismissed, however. Though I could pretend to listen to him while hearing nothing, he had already poisoned everything for me. I began sinking into despair, into total, black, terrifying despair.

I realized then that I had been deluding myself ever since that lunch with Buck Dorsey. I was utterly unqualified to be a London correspondent. I knew nothing about British politics, nothing about foreign policy, nothing about any of the complex economic or diplomatic matters that constituted the news from London. I didn't even know much English history. What was Dorsey thinking of when he picked me for this job? I was headed for humiliation and catastrophe.

Since coming down the gangplank in Southampton I had been sinking deeper and deeper into this living nightmare filled with symbols pointing to failure. The missing trunk, the train leaving without me, the awful penetrating cold. Then this fog. Such a fog. Not like any fog ever seen or imagined. A fog out of nightmares. Crawling through it in this bizarre little train, I felt like somebody in one of those plays about baffled travelers who slowly learn they are dead and headed for know-not-where. To complete the misery, destiny had seated me beside this prime British hater of everything American, including me, this spirit-crusher, this well-poisoner, this messenger of death and youthful sorrow.

Before the train was an hour out of Southampton, I was lonely, scared, and homesick.

The sailing from New York had been one of the great days in the history of our family. It looked to

Boarding the S.S. *United States* for London with Mimi carrying Kathy and Mother leading the way

Dining first class on the Atlantic with Ed Hughes upholding journalism's honor in a business suit

my mother as if I had finally made something of myself and was headed over the ocean to amount to something, and she was determined to be at the ship to make sure I didn't back out at the last minute.

She was entitled to enjoy the moment. She had driven, tugged, and hauled me a long way from Morrisonville, Virginia, since her bleak winter of 1930 when, bereft by my father's death and nearly destitute, she had taken us to New Jersey to live on the charity of her brother Allen and his wife, Pat.

Naturally she wanted Aunt Pat and Uncle Allen to come to the sailing, too. She couldn't have got me there without their help, so in some ways this historic day was as much theirs as hers. She thought they would surely want to be there, and she was right. We all spent a night at their house in Belleville, and next morning Uncle Allen crammed everybody and the baggage into his Plymouth and drove us across the Hudson to the pier at West Forty-sixth Street.

Mimi was not going yet. She and the children would cross in April after I had learned my way around London and found a place where a family could live. This was Buck Dorsey's command, and it made the historic day a glum occasion for Mimi, not only because we faced a three-month separation, but also because she was being left alone to cope with the children, put furniture in storage, find a new tenant to take our apartment lease, tend to bills and taxes, and do all the packing required to move a family overseas with two babies.

Nobody in our family had any experience of ship sailings, but we had all seen enough in movies to know the form: excited bustle in the stateroom, telegrams being delivered at the last minute, champagne flowing, ship's loudspeakers booming, "All ashore that's going ashore," then the last farewell kisses, the rush to gangplank and rail, the waving across the widening expanse of water as tugs nosed the great ocean liner out into the Hudson River. That's how it turned out, too, except for the champagne, which was omitted because my mother, Aunt Pat, and Uncle Allen were all teetotalers.

My mother was so exultant, even without champagne, that while exploring the cabin she managed to trip over a doorjamb and fall into the bathroom, but came up laughing and unhurt. Twice, stewards even brought in telegrams. They came from friends on the *Sun* and said, BON VOYAGE. Snapshots were taken. Everyone was smiling happy historic-day smiles except Mimi, who carried Kathy in her arms and looked morose.

At sailing time I went with them to the gangplank, then climbed to a top deck to wave at them down on the pier, but never found them in the crowd.

The next night Mimi wrote, "We raced along the entire pier yesterday trying to catch your eye as the boat pulled away, but you stood immobile as the Sphinx looking seaward."

The ship was the S.S. *United States,* fastest ocean liner in the world. Five days from New York to Southampton. It was like the world's best hotel if you went first-class, and first-class was the way I was going. The *Sun* expected it. Like some fairy-tale enchanter, Buck Dorsey had waved his magic martinis and turned me from a city-room serf into a prince of journalism. *Sun* princes traveled first cabin all the way and sent the bill to Uncle Abell.

Where would I stay in London until I could rent an apartment? *Sun* correspondents who knew the London go-around were unanimous. There was only one hotel where a *Sun* man could possibly stay: the Savoy. So I booked for an indefinite stay at the Savoy. I knew nothing about the Savoy, but noticed that people familiar with London looked at me with rising respect when they heard I would be staying at the Savoy for a month or two.

I was uneasy about this new license to spend lavishly. Until now I had never spent fifty cents for a cab ride without fearing the *Sun* would reprimand me for squandering money. Now I was being told to squander freely. In some embarrassment, I went to Buck Dorsey shortly after his enchanter's lunch and said I didn't have any luggage and couldn't afford to buy any.

"Get yourself a new suitcase and send the bill to Uncle Abell." He shrugged, as if to ask why I was troubling him with these piffling questions. Didn't I know that a prince of journalism had unlimited expense-account rights?

Taking Dorsey's advice, I bought a three-suiter of cordovan-brown leather. Even empty, it weighed a ton, and was supposed to. Heavy luggage was a symbol of power. It showed you didn't have to carry your own suitcases. In 1953 travel was still travel, not brutish transportation. Civilized people crossed the Atlantic in leisurely seaborne luxury, not like canned goods hurtling dementedly through the time zones. They bought their luggage heavy, and porters competed to carry it.

They dressed for dinner, too. Everybody said I would need a tuxedo to hold my head up in the first-class dining room, so I went to Hamburger's and bought the full regalia: jacket with glossy lapels, black suspenders, cuff links, shirt studs, shiny shoes, black bow tie, crisp white shirt. I bought a London suit, too. Dark gray with a thin pinstripe. Somber enough for an undertaker, it looked like London to me. I didn't have the nerve to bill the *Sun* for the clothes, though, so I spoke to my mother. She spoke to a lifelong acquaintance who was somebody in the savings-and-loan business, and he lent me two hundred dollars.

For five days on the North Atlantic, life was idyllic.

Because it was January, tourists were few and the passenger list short. Mostly they were business travelers and senior government people who, since the *United States* had been built with federal subsidies, traveled at discount.

With so few passengers to keep them busy, the stewards swamped us with services. I pushed a button in the cabin, and a few moments later someone was bringing me a tray of fresh fruit, a pot of steaming coffee with the pastry chef's latest confections, a pitcher of ice with bottles of Scotch and soda water, a new deck of cards, a full breakfast or lunch or dinner if I was too weary to ride the elevator to the dining room. After breakfast in the cabin and a leisurely bath and walking a mile around the promenade deck, there was the bar, where I could sit over a brandy milk punch and enjoy the sensuous roll of the ship riding gently in long oceanic swells.

In no time at all I had traveled light years beyond the shabby penury of our old Baltimore existence and was shamelessly devoted to the life of idle luxury.

"This is the third day out and the weather so far has been ideal," I wrote Mimi from the ship's library. "The first two days were like riding on a great placid lake. Shipboard life is very pleasant and not very exciting. The crowd is mostly very oldish—filled with the kind of women Helen Hokinson used to draw and very brisk old gentlemen who get up at sunrise and stride purposefully about the deck in—you guessed it—gentlemen's caps."

The people who looked "very oldish" to twenty-seven-year-old eyes were mostly in their forties and fifties. One passenger not "oldish" was Ed Hughes, *The Wall Street Journal*'s European correspondent, who sat with me at the chief purser's table in the dining room. The voyage was so empty of celebrities that the chief purser had to fill out his table with news-

papermen, and Hughes embarrassed the trade, I
thought at first, by coming to dinner in a business suit
instead of a tuxedo. When he did it a second time, I
was the one who felt embarrassed. It dawned on me
that a newspaperman who put on a fancy dress to eat
was probably ridiculous, particularly if he was so poor
he had to borrow from a savings-and-loan to pay for
it.

After that, I admired Hughes's cheek outrageously.
His was the common touch that no reporter should
ever lose, I thought. Nevertheless, on the third night
I again wore my fancy suit despite Hughes's example.
Dressing up for dinner not only provided a time-killing
amusement in an idle day, but also heightened my
delightful sense of luxurious living on shipboard.

Those five days at sea disconnected me so completely from the world that I ought to have been
decompressed before being allowed into the messy,
cold, foggy, and rude reality of England. My terrible
companion on the boat train had decompressed me all
the way down into deep depression long before the
porter announced we were arriving at Waterloo Station. I stepped out into a fog so dense that neither
end of the train was visible, nor the ceiling of the
station, if it had one, nor anything resembling a waiting room.

Desperate to put this nightmare day behind me, I
gave my bag to one of the porters swarming over the
platform and begged him to get a taxi and get me out
of there. I remembered my trunk going into the baggage car at Southampton, but had no idea how to get
it off, and didn't care. To hell with the trunk. Let the
railroad keep it. Close to panic, I was ready to drop
everything and run.

The porter put me into a cab. No doors for the
driver's seat. How antique it looked. It reminded me
of my father's Model T.

"Where to, sir?"

I said, "The Savoy Hotel," and sank back into the vast darkness of the backseat and let my mind race. My God, I had left my trunk back at the station. It was gone for good now. Stupid, stupid, stupid! One little bit of pressure and I had cracked completely. Some foreign correspondent. I had behaved shamefully, had humiliated myself because of that awful Englishman on the train. I had handled it as though I were a child, not a foreign correspondent, not a prince of journalism, not a colleague of Tom O'Neill's.

The taxi seemed barely to have gone around the corner before it pulled into a driveway.

"Here you are, sir."

A man in crisply tailored uniform was opening the cab door. Another was carrying my suitcase away.

How much was the fare?

The cab driver uttered some numbers that meant nothing to me. I had practiced English money at home with Mimi so I would understand it well enough to deal with porters and cab drivers. Twenty shillings to the pound, twelve pence to the shilling. Since the pound was worth $2.80, the shilling was fourteen cents, and the penny was a little more than the American cent.

I remembered none of it now with the cab driver waiting to be paid, so producing a one-pound note I asked if that was enough.

"Far too much, sir," said the cab driver.

I said why didn't he take out whatever I owed him and then take as much more for the tip as seemed fair and give me anything that was left.

What he gave back included some large heavy coins and a small brown paper note. It was startling to get so much change for my pound note, and though I couldn't tell how much it was, I knew instinctively that, given the invitation to rob me, the driver had

declined. That was the first happy thing that happened
to me in England.

Entering the hotel lobby, I was startled to find it
bustling with people. By then the day seemed to have
been a thousand hours long, and I'd had the vague
notion it must be long after midnight, so was amazed
to see that it was the cocktail hour.

Looking around the lobby, I noticed that it was full
of fog. Long wisps of it floated in ectoplasmic layers
just over people's heads, seven or eight feet from the
floor. It was black because, as I soon learned, it contained lethal quantities of poisonous soft-coal dust.
The lobby smelled strongly of coal gas, which was one
of the distinctive odors of London in the early 1950s.

While marveling that there should be layers of black
fog floating in London hotel lobbies, I was startled
again by the approach of a stately gentleman in
ambassadorial dress: tailcoat, striped pants, the full
rig. He seemed to work for the hotel.

Would I step over to the reception desk, please?

As I did, he accompanied me and stood at my elbow
while I signed documents and surrendered my pass-
port. Then he made a small gesture and uniformed
men came scurrying. One brought my expensive
suitcase.

Did I have any other baggage?

I confessed that I had once had a trunk, but had
abandoned it at the boat train in Waterloo Station.
The ambassadorial man made another small gesture,
and a uniformed man went scurrying off.

Then, carrying a key, and followed by a uniformed
man carrying my suitcase and a second carrying my
portable typewriter, he led the way to an elevator,
and all of us ascended in silent grandeur.

The room we entered was even bigger than the
immense bathroom that went with it. We were joined
by a funereal-looking man who announced that he was

the valet, started to open my suitcase, and became sulky when I insisted I didn't want it opened. Though I had never seen a valet in the flesh before, I had the impression that they were finicky men who might hold you in contempt if your wardrobe was not top drawer. I did not want this one discovering that my magnificent suitcase contained little but dirty laundry and a few frayed jackets and slacks, which had been good enough at the rewrite desk in Baltimore but would not pass muster at the Savoy.

Before I could get them all out of the room, in came another uniformed man wheeling the trunk I had expected never to see again. I was so overwhelmed with gratitude and awe at the efficiency of the Savoy's trunk-recovery squad that I almost forgave England for the awful man on the train and decided I would love it after all.

The phone rang. It was David Lampe, a Baltimorean who was trying to make a living as a free-lance writer in London. We had known each other years before in a writing class at Hopkins. On learning I was coming to London, he had written volunteering to help acquaint me with the city. As this bizarre day went on and on, it was good to hear an American accent on the telephone. Lampe offered to treat me to dinner, and I told him to come by and pick me up.

The phone went off again, and it was Joan Graham, the Englishwoman who was the second half of the *Sun* bureau. She was in the Savoy bar having a drink with a friend. I probably needed a drink by now; wouldn't I like to join them?

David was small and soft-spoken; Joan big and dynamic. By now I was too tired to notice much more about anybody. Still, when Lampe suggested we take the Underground to his place, where he could provide a decent dinner, I agreed, since it offered a chance to see a little of London and because I dreaded having to confront the mysteries of British restaurants alone that night. Many foods were rationed and hard to get, and most restaurants were supposed to be terrible by American standards.

In the dense, gassy fog, Lampe led me through Trafalgar Square and into Piccadilly Circus, where he showed me how easy it was to use the Underground, after which we rode an endless escalator down to a deep tube and took the train to his stop. He said we were near Regent's Park, but for me, lost in that fog in that immense sprawl of a city, it could have been the outskirts of Scotland. In the tiny kitchen of his tiny apartment, he quickly prepared a steak, which I ate with relish even though it did not quite taste like steak.

"How did you like it?" he asked when we were finishing over coffee.

"It was excellent," I said.

"It was horse," said Dave.

I must have looked baffled.

"Horsemeat," Lampe said. "It's not rationed and it's better than most of the meats that are."

Back at the Savoy before going to bed that night, I wrote to Mimi, omitting the more harrowing aspects of the day, though confessing, "I felt a little depressed when I arrived this evening." A postscript said:

"Got my first introduction to the rigors of British life tonight. Dave Lampe took me to his flat off Regent's Park and cooked me a fine horsemeat dinner—horsemeat filet—no kidding."

That same night in faraway Baltimore, Mimi opened her letter by writing:

"Darling: Your first day in London! Stomping at the Savoy! How exciting it all must be."

15

Innocent Abroad

Sleep and youth restored all my battered self-confidence during the night, and next morning I strode off down the Strand toward Fleet Street in love with London and with life. That morning I was a happy conqueror. There was nothing I could not do, and everything in London delighted me.

The traffic driving on the wrong side of the street delighted me. The big red double-decker buses delighted me. So did the people jumping on and off them, and the ritual cry of the conductors as the buses lumbered away.

"Hold very tight, please!"

The dense crowds hurrying along the Strand delighted me, especially the men with their black bowlers, black overcoats, and black umbrellas. A weak January sun tinted the foggy air a pale gold, which softened the weight of so many swirling blacknesses: black cars, black clothing, black taxicabs, black streaks in the walls of buildings where poisonous air was eating away layers of white Portland stone.

On an island in the Strand stood a bombed church. Just the shell of a church, really. Nothing left but walls and tower. Through open window holes, rubble was visible inside. It was my first view of what war had done to London: the ruined church of St. Clement Danes. As a newsboy for Deems and Mr. Hearst in 1940, I had read about the devastation of the London blitz in the papers I hauled up Lombard Street. That seemed a lifetime ago. Now I was standing in the very place where those German bombs had fallen, gazing on the ruin they had done. Being here was terrible, and thrilling, and delightful.

Looking down the turmoil of Fleet Street, I was startled to see a jumble of medieval turrets and spires on the skyline. What could it possibly be, I wondered, but a castle from the age of chivalry. Never mind that it was just the fake-medieval architecture of the Law Courts, built in the 1880s. On that first magical morning in London, my heart and spirit turned everything into delight.

London, London, London! I was in London! I had been imagining it all my life. At first it had been the fairy-tale city where the bridge was falling down and Dick Whittington's amazing cat made him a rich man. Later it became the sinister place where Fu Manchu hatched diabolical plots, Henry VIII chopped heads, and Jack the Ripper did unspeakable things to women in the night. Then, the city of the Mermaid Tavern where Shakespeare and Ben Jonson caroused, of the Tabard Inn where Chaucer joined a pilgrimage to Canterbury, and the Old Bailey where hard-drinking Sydney Carton first saw the woman for whose love he went to Paris, the guillotine, and a far, far better rest than he had ever known.

From my moviegoing days I knew Waterloo Bridge. There Robert Taylor had kissed Vivien Leigh farewell and gone to die in the trenches. I knew the elegant town houses of Belgravia and Mayfair, too, having seen Leslie Howard take Wendy Hiller to tea in them so she could practice talking like the nobs. I knew about gentlemen's digs in Marylebone from watching

Basil Rathbone of Baker Street instruct Doctor Watson in the science of deduction.

Now, passing into Fleet Street, I seemed to have known London all my life, and, heartened by this delusion, I went into a Lyons tea shop to get some breakfast. Trouble right away: It was impossible to understand the Cockney woman behind the counter until another customer, speaking impeccable Ronald Colman English, said, "She is asking if you wish to have milk in your coffee." ·

After that I didn't dare try ordering anything as complicated as food, but retreated to a distant table, nursed my coffee, lit one of my smuggled Chesterfields, and felt absolutely wonderful in spite of being unable to understand English.

My euphoria that morning was pure childish exuberance. Reality didn't justify it. I faced problems that would have sobered anybody less innocent than a twenty-seven-year-old with a fool's confidence that he could do anything he put his mind to. My being in London as a working newspaperman was absurd. Like D'Artagnan on his first day in Paris, I was the classic hick in the great metropolis, a country boy from Morrisonville, Virginia, a police-station sophisticate from Baltimore. True, I had taken a college course in English history, the one known on campus as "Wars and Whores," but the professor was a medievalist and lost interest after the Wars of the Roses.

I lacked every asset required of a foreign correspondent except curiosity and energy. I had little notion of how the British government worked, knew nothing about British politics, and knew less about the causes of Britain's economic despair, which was the big story out of London. Diplomatic issues like German reunification and the Austrian peace treaty didn't interest me. I was hopelessly untutored in such staples of the London news budget as the European Coal and Steel

Community and the European Defense Community. When I tried to overcome this ignorance by reading about them, my eyes got glassy and I nodded off.

I was a young man in need of the education London was prepared to give. Finishing coffee and cigarette, I walked out into Fleet Street, strode past Temple Bar, and started learning.

The *Sun* had two rooms on the fourth floor of the *Manchester Guardian*'s London offices at 40 Fleet Street. In the British style, the fourth floor was called the third floor. The elevator was small, slow and creaky, and was called the lift. When I stepped out of it and entered the office, Joan Graham was already there. She gave me a big welcoming smile and in a hearty voice said, "Watch your cock!"

I did my best not to look startled. Joan then started explaining the office routine in such colorless language that I figured her bawdy cry had been a standard London greeting which none of the guidebooks had warned me about. Later I learned that what she had actually said was, "Wotcher, cock?," a perfectly polite Cockney expression that could be roughly translated as "How's it going?" I was going to need English lessons.

The office was painted a chilly pale blue. Two big desks faced each other under fluorescent lights. There were two electric heaters and a gas-burning fireplace for warmth, some rickety bookshelves holding most of the volumes of an *Encyclopaedia Britannica* and Burke's *Landed Gentry,* two telephones, a Royal typewriter, a cheap radio, and a single file cabinet that was a model of disorganization. Two big windows looked down into Fleet Street. These provided a good northern light and the title for a weekly column, "From a Window in Fleet Street," in which the *Sun*'s London man could write about anything that struck his fancy. The windows overlooked the St. Julien Tobacco Shop, the Kardomah Exhibition Café, and the Protestant Truth Society. By stretching my neck, I could also see St. Dunstan-in-the-West, where John Donne had once preached.

Joan and I were the entire staff. She was tall, as tall as I was, and broad-shouldered, with carriage as stately as a duchess. Her hair was coppery red. Wide cheekbones, flawlessly straight nose, wide eyes, and thin lips heightened my impression of a formidable woman, which proved wrong. She was a few years older than I and had done some military service that showed her the horror of Warsaw after the war. She once told me that, for macabre entertainment, she and her friends would drive first-time visitors into the rubble of the ghetto at night, headlights off, then hear them gasp when the headlights suddenly went on to reveal carpets of swarming rats, rats everywhere, thousands and thousands of starving rats.

One of my predecessors had hired her for a job that was a little bit of everything. Secretary, office manager, and backup correspondent, Joan also wrote a weekly column about Paris. To get material she disappeared into France for a week every month or so for a bout of glorious eating and occasional dissipation. Though Joan and I were the entire staff, I held the title "Chief of the London Bureau," and from the first day on the job Joan insisted I bear the title proudly.

She began my first day of indoctrination by insisting I needed calling cards bearing my title. Being chief of such a paltry organization seemed comical to me, and I said calling cards would make me look more so. Joan insisted. A chief without a calling card was unthinkable. She looked very formidable that morning. Anyhow, what did I know about local customs? Titles obviously carried a lot of weight in London, even when they were meaningless.

Seeing that I was spineless on the calling-card issue, Joan immediately led me out of the office and up Fleet Street to Chancery Lane, where I watched as she ordered a hundred calling cards from a stationer. While we were out, she decided, I might as well meet the bankers, so I followed her up into Aldwych to a branch office of the Guaranty Trust Company of New York. There I shook hands with several banking types and signed a confusion of official papers.

Chieftainship empowered me to write checks on the *Sun*'s bank account at the Guaranty Trust. This gave me the right to deplete and replenish the office's petty-cash box and to write checks for important office entertainments and such other necessities as a chief might deem vital, whether they were necessary or not. I was also entitled to draw $250 a month above my salary as a cost-of-living allowance. Since the cost of living was cheaper in London than in Baltimore, this made me a rich man by my standards and by the standards of most Londoners. The dark side to my new financial blessings was the obligation to balance the bank book each month to Baltimore's satisfaction, no easy job if you hadn't grown up doing arithmetic in pounds, shillings, and pence.

Chieftainship meant people were dying to meet me instantly. Joan led me back to the office to meet the Western Union man and the Commercial Cables man. My first day on the job and there they were, the two of them, wearing their raincoats and looking like secret agents in a British spy movie, waiting in the office when we got back from the bank. They had thought about me crossing the stormy Atlantic and were happy to see I had made it safely and hoped I had had an enjoyable voyage. Hoped the fog wasn't causing me any inconvenience. It was a bit worse than usual, the fog, and they hoped I didn't mind it too much. They had just dropped by to say so, that's all, to let me know they had been thinking about me, and to tell me I could phone them at any hour, day or night, if I ran into any problem in London or anywhere in the British Isles, any problem at all.

They were irresistible in their gentlemanly salesmanship, and in time I came to think of them as good business friends and pleasant company. Cable companies in London competed hard for the transatlantic newspaper business. These customer calls were regular events intended to spread good will. Joan advised me to divide the business evenly between Western Union and Commercial Cables, so competition would keep them hustling, and it worked. Phoning either outfit, we could count on a courier picking up the copy under fifteen minutes and delivery in Baltimore without delay.

As we were packing them out the door, the phone rang with an invitation to lunch with Tony Cole, head of the Reuters news organization. He very much wanted to introduce me to his top editors at a lunch in the Reuters building. Would that be agreeable? And if so, would such and such a date be all right?

Of course it wasn't agreeable. It was horrifying. Lunch alone with Tony Cole, head of the whole Reuters news organization, would have been hard enough. But a boardroom meal at which all his top editors would be invited to see through me would be appalling. I could imagine the conversation, each editor skillfully exposing my total ignorance of diplomacy, politics, government, economics. . . .

Fortunately, it was Tony Cole's secretary on the telephone, not Tony Cole himself, and fortunately, she was talking to Joan, not to me.

"I can't do that," I said to Joan.

"Mister Baker would be delighted to come to lunch," Joan said to Tony Cole's secretary.

She was right, of course, as she explained. One

didn't say no when Tony Cole proposed top-level lunching. He was said to be a friend of Swanson's. Besides, the wine would be superb.

Next: Had anyone, she asked, told me about the bootlegger?

No, somebody in Baltimore had told me we had an account at Berry Brothers and Rudd where I could buy whiskey and excellent wines, but nobody had mentioned a bootlegger.

He bootlegged newspapers, not liquor, Joan said, and he was invaluable because you couldn't buy tomorrow morning's newspapers on the street tonight, as you could in most American cities. With ten newspapers in vicious competition, there was a natural reluctance to let the other players see your daily scoop while they still had time to duplicate it in their late editions. The "bootlegger" got early editions anyhow and, for a nice fee, delivered them to us around eleven each night. This would let me go home with the comforting assurance that I hadn't missed any earthshaking stories.

Now Harry came in to be introduced. He was the *Guardian*'s copy boy, though he was never so called. He was always simply "Harry." Harry was the precise opposite of the man on the train the previous afternoon. I knew at first glance that he liked me, probably because he indiscriminately liked almost everybody American. He was small and wiry, a man in his forties with a receding hairline and a broad smile showing big teeth. He always wore a suit on the job, but later I saw him stripped down to vest and shirt-sleeves a few times when temperatures soared into the seventies.

Harry was South London with all that implied: not much schooling, hard-working, fast-moving, canny about people, street smart, indomitably cheerful, outspoken, an urban democrat who liked a laugh at the nobs' expense. He was a page out of Dickens's *Pick-*

wick Papers, a Sam Weller in the service of journalism, and his speech of course was Cockney. He often discussed with me some story he had read in the "Dily Mile."

Harry was to prove indispensable to my survival. Throughout the night he made repeated trips up to my office bearing copy off the news-service wire, running accounts of developments in the House of Commons, and copies of the stories being turned in by the *Guardian* reporters. The *Sun*'s agreement with the *Guardian* gave us the right to use *Guardian* material, and without it I would often have been lost. If something unusual was breaking at night in London, I could rely on Harry bursting into the office to alert me, breathing hard from running up to the fourth floor with the bulletin.

That first day on the job, Harry played the tour guide of the *Guardian* office for me, introducing me to reporters like Francis Boyd, who covered the House of Commons; Richard Scott, who covered the Foreign Office; Mark Arnold-Forster, who covered Labour politics; and Philip Hope-Wallace, who reviewed theater and opera and whose airy writing style, sassy and light as a water strider skimming a pond, I was soon struggling, foolishly, to make my own.

About five that afternoon Dave Lampe came by the office and said I must come with him and meet Gerry Fay immediately.

I was tired of meeting people by this time. Another time, I told Lampe. Not today.

Dave Lampe had mastered the art of persisting through whispering. It wasn't a whisper, actually, that he spoke in, but a voice so low, and in such a monotone, that it had a hypnotically persuasive effect. It was a voice both boring and irresistible, and he began applying it to me.

Softly, so gently that I almost had to strain to hear

him, he began analyzing the strengths and weaknesses of the *Guardian* and its people, the very people with whom I would be working most closely in London. The London editor, he said, was John Beavan, but John Beavan was not suited for the job, did not do it well, was not much interested in it, and would soon go on to another job.

My interest in John Beavan, whoever he was, and in the office politics of the *Guardian* was nil, but I could not convey to David the true depth of my indifference. And he droned on, and on.

The number two man in the office should have been made London editor long ago, and would be soon. He was a marvelous newspaperman, a brilliant editor, an excellent writer. What's more, he liked Americans.

This paragon was named Gerard Fay, universally known as Gerry Fay, pronounced "Jerry." He was really more Irish than English, being descended from the Fays who established Dublin's Abbey Theatre, though his mother was . . .

Peace, David! Drone no more. Telephone this incomparable semi-Irishman downstairs and see if he has time to shake my hand.

No phone call was necessary, for the truth was, said David, that he had run into Gerry Fay downstairs, and Fay had issued strict orders to bring me down at once, and Lampe had said he would.

Incidentally, had I noticed the item in the *Guardian*'s "London Letter" today about my arrival? Gerry had written that.

Dave opened the *Guardian* and showed it to me. NEW "SUN" MAN, a small headline said.

"A new 'Baltimore Sun' man arrived in London tonight to replace Mr Rodney Crowther, who has returned to Washington to watch the new Administration coping with its fiscal problems and to write about what he sees. The new correspondent, Mr Russell W.

Gerard Fay, London editor of *The Manchester Guardian*

Baker, is the youngest 'Sun' man to come here in many years. . . ."

Three more sentences, all literate enough, but hardly lines of genius. I was startled about being news to the *Manchester Guardian,* but shouldn't have been. There had been a working relationship between the *Sun* and the *Guardian* since 1924. There had even been an agreement during the war that if Hitler should succeed in occupying Britain, the *Guardian* would continue to be published on the *Sun*'s presses in Baltimore.

So I let Lampe lead me down to the second floor, and there was the incomparable Fay seated behind a desk in the London editor's office. With outstretched arm and an imperious wave of his index finger, he silently directed us to the sofa where he wanted us to sit and continued his conversation.

Watching him, I judged he must be far more Dublin

than Manchester. Round face, bright red cheeks, chestnut hair rather thin on top, piercing blue eyes— the face was intelligent, aggressive, not a tired seen-it-all face like so many newspaper faces, but an interested, curious, receptive face. In theatrical contrast to the blackish grays I had seen all day on London males, he wore a sports jacket, a necktie of jaunty color, and a bright yellow tattersall vest.

Finishing the telephone business, he popped out of the chair and came briskly around the desk for Lampe's introductions. He was neither tall nor short. His presence was so intense that you didn't notice things like short or tall, and afterward, if asked, you could not have said because it didn't matter.

We exchanged handshakes, then, without further small talk, he said, "Come, we'll have a beer," and moved briskly out into the hall and started down the stairs while asking if I liked beer, then rapidly explaining that if I didn't they had Scotch at the Clachan though it was bloody expensive considering it was only seventy proof, we were lucky in America about the Scotch, they sent all the good stuff to the States, and it cost less there than the weak seventy proof Scotch cost in England, what did I think of Alistair Cooke, and how long was I going to go on living at the Savoy, I ought to get out of there as soon as possible, too many Americans living in luxury, and find a place of my own in a neighborhood where I could get the feel of living in London. Hampstead might be good for someone like me with small children, though it was a bit remote, he lived in Highgate himself, north London, good bus and Underground service though.

All this was calmly spoken in flawlessly constructed sentences without any of the verbal stuttering common to the casual conversation I was accustomed to at home, but the pieces came at me so rapidly that before I could think of a response to one subject he had moved on to another. The pace at which he spoke and his clarity of expression left me feeling slow-witted and clumsy of tongue, a sensation I was to suffer often during the early days in London before I learned to speed up my speaking rate.

By now we had got out of the building, walked a few doors down Fleet Street, and wedged ourselves into the human uproar of the Clachan in Mitre Court, favored pub of *Guardian* men for beer. For wine and whisky they went, like most of Fleet Street, to El Vino, a few yards farther down the street. Gerry intended to introduce me to the higher ceremony of El Vino soon enough, but realizing probably that he was dealing with a kindergartner, he decided to start me in a typical Fleet Street pub with the common drink of the trade.

Planting himself at the bar, he ordered a bitter for himself, and another for me, and another for Lampe after explaining that bitter was hardly more than improved water, without the unpleasant gassy quality of American beers, but if American beer was my preference I could get it in most pubs by asking for "lager." Then he said I must come to Sunday dinner at his house, and I thanked him for suggesting it and tried to catch up with his conversation by telling him what I thought of Alistair Cooke, just to show him I knew Alistair Cooke was the *Guardian*'s American correspondent, and he said, "Will Sunday after next do?"

Sunday after next?

For dinner at his house. I'd thought his mention of Sunday dinner was one of those meaningless politenesses people get off in idle conversation like the American line about having lunch sometime, but he had really meant it.

For Sunday dinner.

Yes, Sunday after next.

What was remarkable about it was that under the food-rationing program a British family's meat allotment provided meat for only one meal a week. Inviting a guest meant his own family would have to eat a little less. This man was determined to be my friend. Knowing me less than ten minutes, he was offering me one of the more precious gifts a Londoner could make. Though normally cautious about making friends, I was now a lonely stranger in a foreign city, and I accepted.

Our glasses were quickly emptied. The teacher again, Gerry said good pub form required each drinker to take his turn buying a round for his party.

"Three bitters here!" I shouted to the woman of the house, put down my mystifying coins, and lit one of my Chesterfields.

"Before lighting up, I'm afraid, you must also offer the cigarettes around," Gerry explained.

How innocent I was. So much to learn.

Back in the office late that night I wrote to Mimi:

"Good evening, darling,

"Well, here I sit, chief of the goddamn London Bureau, issuing orders and signing checks and not knowing the first—get this—bloody thing about what it's all about. I've been lounging around Fleet Street all day getting acquainted. The *Guardian*'s second man here, Gerry Fay, seems like a very nice guy and he introduced me to the local pub this evening for some British beer. Not half as bad as it's supposed to be, but a little bit watery. . . .

"I think you're going to like London. I saw a little bit more of it today. That's no joke about the men wearing black bowler derbies, either. Coming down Fleet Street today everybody stared at me as if to say, 'Why you damned bareheaded Yankee, where's your bowler?' Apparently I really look the American be-

cause I stopped in a small shop for coffee—terrible!—
this morning and the charwoman immediately asked
me if charwomen in the United States come up and
sweep around your table while you're eating. She then
proceeded to do just that. . . .

"I have been in a complete stew ever since I set
foot in England. Meeting this guy and that, fending
off cable-company representatives, being inspected by
critical English newspapermen, going over the office
accounts, trying to learn that this bogus-looking British currency is really more valuable than Monopoly
money, trying to force down this food and wishing I
had time to just sit down for a few hours and talk it
all over with you. . . .

"Well, it's elevenish here and the paper bootlegger
just came in with tomorrow's news. Not very exciting.
I find it very peculiar to think that now, as I'm preparing to go off to bed, it's only 6 P.M. in Baltimore,
Kathy is still up and romping round the house and
you are probably just getting dinner, but I suppose
you forget about the time difference after a while."

At about the same time my mother at Marydell
Road was writing, too:

"I've been thinking of you and wondering how
you're doing in the fog of London. I saw in the paper
yesterday that London had one of the worst fogs in
its history on Monday. Transportation was very bad,
it said, and many people were late for work. I thought
it would be a shame for you to be late for work on
your first day in the office."

This day, January 20, was also the first day on the
job for President Eisenhower, who was taking the
oath in Washington about the time I was being introduced to Gerry Fay. I was too absorbed in my own
problems and too uninterested in politics to remember
that it was also a momentous day in Washington. A
few days later Mimi's letter contained a postscript:

"According to the news broadcast on now, an amusing story is going around the Washington pubs. Last Thursday Eisenhower looked up from his desk and said, 'What day is this?' and one of his aides said, 'Thursday.' To which Ike replied, 'Good Lord, only two days. It seems like two years.' "

I knew exactly how he felt.

16

Buck

To meet Buck Dorsey at the London airport, Joan had rented a Daimler. I had suggested a Rolls-Royce. Nothing but the best for Buck Dorsey, I told Joan. Our futures might depend on making Buck Dorsey happy for the next seven days. Everything had to be better than best.

"That's why we're taking a Daimler, duckie," Joan said. "All the nobs ride around in Rolls-Royces, but a Daimler is special. Queen Mary's car is a Daimler."

That cinched it. Remembering Buck Dorsey's love for everything English, I knew he would be impressed by riding in the kind of car preferred by the queen dowager.

The chauffeur picked us up in Fleet Street. The Daimler was a gigantic machine. Distances inside seemed vast. We climbed up onto the backseat, and the chauffeur leaned in and spread a blanket across our laps, and off we headed toward Heathrow, the two of us enthroned like royalty high above the commoner run of traffic.

It was absurd yet wonderful to be renting a car fit for a queen when, just a few months ago, I could hardly afford a Baltimore taxi. Two months in London, however, had already begun to put me at ease with life in the grand style. I hadn't acquired the gran-

deur of Tom O'Neill yet, but maybe I was getting
there. The Daimler was a touch worthy of O'Neill.

It was astonishing how much could be learned in
two months, especially with Gerry Fay and his extraordinary band of *Guardian* reporters doing the teaching.
I could now write a sensible story about political
grandstanding in the House of Commons, a cold-war
diplomatic problem, or the passions and prejudices
that split the Labour party among academic socialists,
Marxist romantics, and labor unions. From the press
gallery of the House I had got accustomed to the
debating styles of the great men of the day: Winston
Churchill, Clement Attlee, Anthony Eden, and Aneu-
rin Bevan.

Education came from everywhere. At the American
embassy I had been hoodwinked into writing a preposterous story based on a "background briefing" by
John Foster Dulles, the new secretary of state. Thanks
to Dulles's skill, I suggested, the next ten weeks might
produce "a satisfactory formula" not only to create a
common European army, but also "to end forever"
the age-old hostility between France and Germany.
Only a very young reporter who had never heard a
self-serving diplomat torture the truth could have
believed that in ten weeks Western Europe would be
building a common army while France and Germany
embraced in brotherhood. I believed it. The *Sun* dis-
played my gullibility on the front page. And so Dulles
enriched me with a priceless skepticism I would never
lose toward everything spoken by great men "on
background."

On Saturday mornings at tables against El Vino's
back wall, Gerry Fay had instructed me in the pleasures of wine, and the evil of drinking Barsac before
lunch. Gerry had also taught me how to cover a flood
in England: Same way you cover it in America, jump
in the first car headed for the mouth of the Thames

and express your confusion with overwrought prose, using phrases like "lake of the dead." Not that he would have approved the overdone prose if he had seen it, which in the case of "lake of the dead" he did not. Gerry preferred precision, facts plainly stated, and if facts could not be learned, he did not mind saying so.

Far from the disciplines of home and editors, a young man could easily get careless about facts. In a feature story about tourism in London, I cruelly criticized the food served at the Cheshire Cheese, a Fleet Street restaurant famous because Dr. Samuel Johnson was supposed to have been a regular customer two hundred years ago. The criticism was based on a guidebook that advised tourists to stop for a beer but leave the food alone. Gerry, scanning the story at my request, asked, "Have you eaten at the Cheshire Cheese then?"

"No," I admitted, feeling myself go red with shame.

"Hm," was the only sound he made, but it was a shattering comment which I would recall forever after whenever I was tempted to fob off unchecked, second-hand information as my own.

Never had I had so many exotic experiences in such a short time. I had lunched at the House of Lords with a peer of the realm, weekended in a seventeenth-century Kentish country house with a young couple who worked hard to persuade me there was a ghost among us, seen Margot Fonteyn dance *Swan Lake* at Covent Garden, and spent an evening with several thousand Communists celebrating the twenty-third birthday of *The Daily Worker*.

The peer was Lord Winster, who wrote occasional pieces for the *Sun*. He invited me to lunch with William Manchester, another young, first-time foreign correspondent for the *Sun*, who was passing through London en route to India. Winster was that distinctively British curiosity, a socialist converted into a baron by the royal honors list.

"Winster is quite a lively old guy," I wrote Mimi. "He ticked off all sorts of little gossipy items about how this admiral ran and became a hero, and how this Lady at 52 married this Lord at 27 because of what she had in her purse and he had in his trousers. The House of Lords is very impressive. It looks like Yale. Bill Manchester and I were met at the door by a flunkey in bright red coat, tight black knickers, black hose and a Henry VIII chapeau. He led us through interminable halls, exquisitely paneled, set with beautiful stained glass. Up and down heavily carpeted stairs. Past long corridors with high vaulted ceilings lined with great, musty, leather-bound tomes. Past libraries and lounges, smoking chambers and guest rooms. When he found Winster, he said: M'lord, your guests. Winster fed us a martini, then took us to the dining room where more people M'lorded him and brought us roast duck, plum pudding and rich red wine."

I was equally impressed by the ghost claimed by my Kentish hosts, Patience and Henry Bayne-Powell.

"Henry is quite proud of this ghost," I wrote Mimi. "He insists that it's the ghost of Catherine Howard, one of Henry VIII's executed wives, and that she is very useful at such things as dusting the staircase railings. I was awakened in the small hours Sunday morning by the noise of a door being slammed somewhere in my wing of the house. I had my own wing, you see, all to myself. I listened a while and noticed that the door banging was repeated at regular intervals as if someone were coming along the hall, opening and slamming the doors.

"Well, I must admit that in the pitch blackness and otherwise dead silence this upset me a bit, so I got up and put on the light. Listening a while longer, I heard a very loud slam. My nerve failed completely at that point, and I slipped surreptitiously to my bedroom door and bolted it, feeling terribly ashamed of myself. Nevertheless, I slept easily after that, until the maid woke me next morning with coffee, eggs and toast."

"The Bayne-Powells are very fortunate in having Catherine Howard's ghost," Mimi replied. "She was supposed to have been a great beauty. Only I must say her ghost must be the busiest ghost in all England. There are several castles that are also said to be graced by her spirit."

The Baltimore friend who had engineered my weekend in the English countryside also deflated my pride in ghostly encounter. "Mimi reported that you spent a weekend with Patience and Henry and a ghost, which was certainly installed for your benefit, because there was no sign of it last fall," she wrote. "They will go to any lengths to entertain one."

The Communists had their enlightening moments, too, as they wore down a Sunday evening with interminable appeals for their big audience to come across with cash to keep *The Daily Worker* going. I had never been caught up in the Communist panic raging back home, but the *Daily Worker* evening left me reassured about the safety of capitalism. The selections by the Young Communists' Chorus persuaded me that the Reds were cursed with tin ears, which would prevent them from ever winning the hearts and dancing feet of Western youth. For example, "Go Home, Yankee," to the tune of "Tramp, Tramp, Tramp the Boys Are Marching":

Go home, Yankee; Yankee, go home!
We don't want you any more!
For the way of life you sell
Doesn't suit us very well
And you'll never make us fight a Yankee war.

My favorite, though, was a singing commercial for *The Daily Worker:*

> From the River Clyde at Greenock
> To the Thames at Charing Cross
> You must read the Daily Worker
> If you want to beat the boss.

Though I judged the Communists too dull, too lacking in subtle cunning to threaten the governing classes, in London for the first time I understood why many hated the West's ruling systems. I had become wiser about what true hardship was. After so much whining about our poverty in Baltimore, I quickly learned in London what hard times were really like.

My first week in Fleet Street, three *Guardian* reporters invited me to join them for afternoon tea at the Kardomah across the street. The bill for a pot of tea and two crumpets came to the British equivalent of twelve cents. To tip the waitress, I put down sixpence, a dime-size coin worth seven American pennies. The *Guardian* men scowled at me. Why was I tipping like a rich American? They ordered me to put the sixpence back in my pocket and leave a threepenny tip. Threepence, they said, was the proper tip to make the waitress smile, and they were right. It was sobering to realize that life here was so pinched that three pennies were real money to a workingwoman.

"I've been here only a week and I already regard America as an incredibly luxurious, wealthy land of milk-and-honey," I wrote Mimi.

"British 'austerity' is very much like what America went through in the Depression. In no time at all, I have become highly sensitive to the fact that a cigarette is a valuable thing. You smoke them until there's nothing left but ash, and if you don't have time to finish, you butt the cigarette and save it for later.

When you're drinking with a group, one man brings out his pack and it goes around ceremoniously with everyone taking one. Next time, it's your turn and you're expected to reciprocate. Even matches become valuable here. If someone has a lighter you consciously avoid pulling out your box of matches and, instead, take a free light from the benzine machine.

"A penny is a valuable coin. For two of them you get a nice long bus ride. For five, you get a real long bus ride. For one and a half you can buy a newspaper. This morning I ate breakfast at the Savoy—tomato juice, scrambled eggs, roll, butter, coffee—for slightly less than forty cents, and I was eating the most expensive breakfast on the menu. You don't go out and buy a candy bar when you get hungry. For candy you need a ration card.

"About what to bring with you: *Bring everything you can!* Especially all your heavy clothing, and don't worry about how drab it looks. Bring all the blankets and bedding we own. Bring Crisco, or its equivalent, as much as you can carry. It's invaluable here and you'll hoard it. Bring two cartons of cigarettes and two fifths of liquor—the maximum allowance. Bring everything linen that you might want while you're here. The local product looks like burlap. Bring as much chocolate as you're allowed. Bring book matches—can't find them here. I can't impress upon you enough that things you throw in the garbage at home would keep a family going in fine style here."

Buck Dorsey's plane was due at 9:45 that morning, but the fog was heavy again, and the airline announced a one-hour delay. The one hour became two and then three. The fog had thickened. It had been a historically bad winter for fog. Now there was a bleak announcement: the airport was closed. Nothing landing or taking off. How long before it would reopen?

The airline people shrugged. It would reopen when the fog lifted a bit, sir, that's all we can tell you just now, why not have a nice cup of tea and perhaps things will clear up shortly.

The thought of Buck Dorsey being bounced around somewhere over England waiting for the fog to lift a bit was not a happy one. I had it from confidential sources in Baltimore that Buck Dorsey had a bad case of flying fear. This was his first trip abroad, my informant said, and he was making it only because Swanson insisted.

He had resisted it for two very basic reasons. First, he hated traveling. Second, he loathed and feared flying. His fear was so deep that though his wife, Becky, was also making the European trip, he would not let her travel on the plane with him. They had a young son. Buck Dorsey did not want to leave him motherless as well as fatherless. To be doubly safe, he had sent Becky by sea aboard the *Queen Elizabeth*. He obviously faced the flight with dread. Shortly before departing Baltimore, he sent me an extraordinary note asking me to look out for his wife if anything should happen to him, and it did not have the ring of a man making a joke.

Now, circling somewhere over England in a monster fog, he probably felt that the end was near. I did not feel wonderful myself. When he did arrive, and I was sure he would arrive, somehow, somewhere, he was bound to be in a murderous state of mind, hating England and everything associated with it. I was associated with England. The glorious Daimler would be wasted on him now. He would probably see it as nothing more than an unjustifiable waste of money.

I cursed the fog. It wasn't even fog, and I cursed the English for pretending it was. It was a black, filthy, smelly, deadly smog compounded of poisons pumped into the English sky by millions of soft-coal fires. On days that passed for clear the sun at noon was dusty orange. A white shirt was black by evening. I washed face and hands ten times a day, and each time the water was filthy when I finished.

My mood became as black as my shirt as morning turned to afternoon. I had counted on being back in the office by now and should have been. Queen Mary, she who lent such distinction to the Daimler, was dying. Early morning medical bulletins left no doubt. Her death would be a big story. She had been the wife of one king and mother of two and was the grandmother of Queen Elizabeth. The *Sun* would want a long, well-written obituary. That meant I should be digging through bales of history to get some sense of her life instead of waiting for a fog to lift.

Then, an announcement: Buck Dorsey's plane was landing, but not at London. Far out on the southeast coast of England, it had found an airfield with enough visibility to land. Passengers would be brought to London by train. When they would arrive and where, nobody knew. We rode back to Fleet Street in the Daimler that was destined never to impress Buck Dorsey, paid off the driver, and started working the telephones to find out when a train bearing a planeload of Americans might arrive in London.

For the first two months in London, Buck Dorsey had left me free to cover what I wished and seemed satisfied with what he was getting. He had even sent one cable so flattering that I suspected he had taken a few martinis before writing it. Still, he was an unknown quantity to me, a haughty, somewhat imperious authority, and I was worried about my ability to please him, as a child might be anxious about pleasing a stern father.

Mimi had dealt with him back in Baltimore and found him anything but fierce. After my first week in England, she wrote, "I must confess that yesterday I was so worried about you that I called Buck Dorsey. Dorsey was very pleasant. I told him I hadn't heard from you, and all the grim stories yesterday's *Sun* carried about England upset me—thousands die in London smog—flu epidemic rages through Europe—also you had only one story in the paper this week.

"He said, 'Lady, don't you worry. He's all right.' He told me he didn't expect anything from you for several weeks as you would be busy finding your way around. He guessed the story you sent just fell into your lap and you cabled it in to get your name in the paper. He invited me to call him any time I need reassurance."

A few weeks later she wrote: "I was frightened out of my wits, to coin a phrase, tonight. Buck Dorsey called and said Quote Mrs. Baker, you called me a few weeks ago and asked if Russ was all right, you hadn't heard from him, etc. Unquote. At that point my knees were quaking, I was sure Buck was going to say you had been killed by a hard pitched beer bottle or something equally ghastly, but then dear old Buck went on to say Quote I just wanted to tell you that O'Neill, Swanson, Ed Young and I just sent Russ a cablegram telling him what a fine job he is doing. O'Neill and I think he is doing magnificent work. He is really going to make a name for himself over there. I knew Russ would do a great job. I was willing to stake my reputation on it. Unquote. I'll bet Buck had a few drinks under his belt, but 8 P.M., the time he called, is a little early to get soused."

Such a cable—"DELIGHTED WITH EVERYTHING YOU DOING"—did, in fact, arrive in Fleet Street. "OF COURSE COMMA IT COMES AS NO SURPRISE TO ONEILL AND ME," it concluded. Like Mimi, I attributed its enthusiasm to the cocktail hour in Baltimore. Newspaper people who constantly sent cables often got carried away by the fun of composing in cable-ese. The rockets they fired around the world were not always to be taken seriously. Still, Buck Dorsey had mentioned me in the same sentence with Tom O'Neill. That might be the highest praise I would ever get.

When Stalin, the century's other great monster tyrant, died in early March, the *Sun* had no correspondent in Moscow and only one other man anywhere in Europe. I immediately cabled Baltimore that I was applying for a visa for Moscow. This proved harder to do than I anticipated. Phoning the Soviet embassy in London, I got a Russian male voice out of a stage comedy about Soviet bungling.

Visa? Moscow? What did he know about visa? About Moscow? Nothing.

Could I please talk to someone who did know about visas, someone who handled visa applications?

Visa applications? What was applications?

Couldn't he just refer me to somebody . . . ?

Somebody? Absolutely not! Who did I think I was calling?

The Soviet embassy. I was calling the Soviet embassy. I wanted to speak to someone in the Soviet embassy about applying for a visa to Moscow.

"No one here now. Everybody gone. You call again tomorrow."

He hung up on me.

It was past the dinner hour. Maybe the place really had shut down for the night. First thing tomorrow morning I would appear at the embassy in person.

This proved unnecessary. Before the night was out I had a cable from Buck Dorsey with firm orders to stay in London and—NOT REPEAT NOT GO MOSCOW. It was signed, as all his cables were, LOVE STOP DORSEY.

"I spoke to Dorsey today," Mimi wrote. "He said, 'Do you know what that screwball husband of yours did?' Dorsey seemed quite delighted and bubbling over when he told me of your cablegram Quote

Applying for Russian visa to attend Stalin's funeral. Objection? Unquote. I am glad Dorsey instead of Swanson received it. You would probably be on your way by now. Dorsey says he doesn't want you going behind the Iron Curtain.''

I thought it strange that a paper as important as the *Sun* did not want a reporter in Moscow at that moment. Stalin's death, with the change in the Soviet government, was a great story. As events showed, the Soviets were not interested in having Western newspaper visitors just then, so the point was academic. My ignorance of everything Russian, from the language to the lunatic conspiracies of Stalin's rule, would have been crippling handicaps if I had got to Moscow. Still, just having someone on the scene describing what he saw at this historic moment would be valuable, I thought.

Buck Dorsey's talk with Mimi suggested he was afraid something terrible might happen if I put myself in Russian clutches. This seemed especially odd because, well, weren't newspapermen supposed to put themselves in harm's way when the news demanded? Anyhow, where was the danger? Did Baltimore expect Moscow to celebrate Stalin's death with a massacre of foreigners? In 1953, of course, Moscow was a dark, sinister cloud on America's horizon and seemed far more forbidding and dangerous than it did a year or two later when Stalin's terrible reign, like a dreadful nightmare, was receding slowly from American consciousness.

Despite the evidence that I was doing all right in Buck Dorsey's grade book, I was terrified by the prospect of having to keep him entertained for a week. I was an inexperienced youngster, green on the job, and anything but a man about London, yet to make the trip successful I would have to establish a social relationship with a boss who was twice my age, highly sophisticated, and had finicky tastes. Besides, Buck Dorsey was not your average, run-of-the-mill editor. As I wrote my mother.

"Dorsey is an odd gent. He is being forced to come to Europe against his will for a one-month tour. Swanson thinks it would broaden him since he's never been out of the country. I had one letter from him saying that his wife is coming by sea on the *Queen Elizabeth* and asking me to look out for her if anything should happen to him. I had written asking if he wanted me to arrange any appointments here for him and today he cabled back 'no arrangements for meeting outside people, for god's sake!' "

The breakdown in our greeting plans seemed disastrous, but I kept busy all afternoon working up Queen Mary's obituary. Outside the black daylight turned to black night. Finally, news: The train bringing everybody to London was due at Victoria Station at ten o'clock. I was on the platform, ready to smile, apologize for England, and put him in a taxi to Claridge's, where he was booked.

He emerged out of the fog looking like death, and no wonder after traveling through what must have looked like a twenty-four-hour night. Fatigued though he was, however, he was amused by something he had seen on the train.

"When they eat cheese and crackers here, they put butter on the cracker," he was saying as we got into a cab. The sight of an Englishman buttering a cracker before laying a slice of cheese on it struck him as comical. "It's like putting two kinds of jelly on a piece of toast," he said, and laughed softly to himself at the absurdity of British eating customs.

I got him checked in at Claridge's and said I had to get back to the office, check on the dying queen, and file my story if she had slipped away while I was at Victoria.

"You have time to have a drink first, don't you?" he said.

The bar looked closed, and he wanted to get up to his room anyhow, so I went up with him, and he telephoned room service and ordered three bottles of Scotch. At that time ordering three bottles of Scotch from room service at Claridge's was the kind of grand gesture associated with touring American movie stars and maharajahs who enjoyed flaunting their fortunes before their impoverished former rulers of the earth. I could imagine Tom O'Neill doing it, then cabling Baltimore to "send five thousand immediately," but I could never have done it. Watching Buck Dorsey do it now, however, would provide a memory to tell my grandchildren.

Remembering our lunch at the Chesapeake, I put the glass down after one drink, used the telephone to establish that Queen Mary had indeed died, and headed back to Fleet Street to file.

"When you finish, come on back, and we'll talk," Buck Dorsey said.

"We sat around until almost dawn discussing one thing or another," I wrote my mother a few days later. "He repeated what he had sent me by wire before, that everyone thought I am doing okay and he had no criticism, suggestions or orders. According to him I am just to go ahead doing the job as I see fit. He said he never knew of anyone having to take up a job under greater handicap than I did when I came into this one, and he was delighted at the way I had handled it so far. With that I poured him another drink and took a good stiff one myself."

Many years passed before I fully understood what was happening. He was a gambling man, a truly dedicated horseplayer, and, figuratively speaking, he had put a big bet down on me. It was Buck Dorsey, not Swanson, who had picked me for the London job.

Swanson must have been startled; he hardly knew who I was. Buck Dorsey was betting that his eye for newspaper talent was good enough to take an inexperienced man off the local staff who would do a bang-up job as a foreign correspondent. Swanson had to approve me, of course, and may have done so out of a sense of friendly competition with Buck Dorsey, hoping to see Buck Dorsey lose his bet.

This explained a great deal once I understood about the gambling instinct. Buck Dorsey's stake in having me do well in London was almost as big as my own, and he was using every opportunity to build my confidence. Before sunrise that morning in London we reached a state in our relations that was very close to friendship. For the first time, I began calling him "Buck." Not "Mister Dorsey," but "Buck," the same as Tom O'Neill called him.

Top of the world, Mimi! Just like Tom O'Neill! Wow!

17

Anglia Days

The *Sun*'s office car was a Ford Anglia. It had a twelve-horsepower engine, which made it a little sprightlier than a lawn mower. Before leaving Baltimore, I had finally learned to drive so I would be able to use it. The first time I took it out for a spin, the engine quit as it was coming off Vauxhall Bridge in the rush hour.

Nothing could get it started again, including the stare of the policeman directing the complicated pattern of traffic flowing off the bridge. At that hour Vauxhall was one of the busiest bridge crossings on the Thames. The tiny Anglia was starting a huge traffic jam. The policeman strode over. It was a bad moment: my first car solo in England, and the law was already on me.

What seems to be the trouble?

My long experience of American policemen prepared me for the worst, but he was surprisingly genial.

I told him the trouble. The thing just quit and wouldn't start again. See? I demonstrated by turning the ignition. Sure enough, again it wouldn't start.

"Perhaps it needs petrol," he said.

"Petrol?"

"That's right: petrol. It's probably just out of petrol," he said.

Petrol . . .

It came back to me now. That was what the English called gasoline.

"When did you last stop for petrol?" he asked.

I said something like, "I've never stopped for petrol." *No use lying,* I thought.

He seemed amused about me now. I imagined him thinking, "What fools these Americans are."

He was right about the petrol. The Anglia's tank was dry.

"Right there across the street," he said when I asked where I could get petrol, and pointed to a service station right before my eyes. While I went for a can of gasoline, he calmly directed the bridge traffic around the Anglia, and as I drove away waving at him, he laughed and waved back. London cops were soft. He'd let me escape without a ticket, or even a lecture about my stupidity.

The Anglia's gearshift stuck up out of the floor. This was the old-fashioned style. For an American, it increased the Anglia's quaintness. American cars had long since moved the gearshift from the floor to the steering wheel, and that's where it was when I learned driving in Baltimore. Having it on the floor gave me fits.

To make things worse, it had to be operated with the left hand. In America you shifted with the right hand. Americans drove on the right side of the road with gearshifts at the driver's right hand; the English drove on the left side and shifted with the left hand.

Blooded veterans of the American highway could probably have mastered the Anglia quickly, but I wasn't lying when telling the policeman I had never put gas in a car. At home I'd had only a few hours of instruction in a driving-school car. That was the totality of my motoring experience, though Jim Cannon did let me drive his car a few miles once so I

would know how it felt driving one without a second
steering wheel for the passenger's seat. After learning
to drive on the right side of the road with gearshift
on the right side of the steering column, I now had to
do it all backward—driving on the left side of the road
while using my left hand to work a gearshift sticking
out of the floor.

There was another problem. When turning a corner
the Anglia was disposed to come to a near dead stop.
To keep it moving with zest, you had to shift into a
lower gear by double-clutching.

"Double-clutch down," I had to think as the Anglia
started around a corner.

"Stay on the left side when coming out of the turn,"
I had to think.

"Remember, gearshift on the floor when you double-clutch!"

And "Left hand! Left hand! The gearshift's at your
left hand, not your right."

Double-clutching was hard, hard, hard, probably
because the driving teacher back in Baltimore hadn't
taught me how to do it. He hadn't even mentioned
double-clutching. I might never have known about it
except for a British army captain, an old tank man,
who taught me the art one Sunday morning en route
to a pub. The Anglia kept trying to die on the corners,
and the captain was afraid we wouldn't make the pub
by opening time. Since pubs were open only two and
a half hours on Sundays, losing a single minute of
drinking time was a terrible prospect. The captain
began shouting instructions on the corners.

"Shift down, Russ! Shift down! Double-clutch!
Double-clutch, Russ!"

By the time I got him home three hours later I was
double-clutching as readily as a Grand Prix driver, or
so I thought, such is the effect of two hours and a half
of tireless beer guzzling.

To navigate this alien city I needed a map, so expeditions in the Anglia involved furious mental activity in the driver's seat. While the Anglia puttered along at thirty miles an hour, I was struggling to remember how it worked, and which hand to use for the shift stick, and which side of the street to drive on, while simultaneously trying to find Hampstead Heath, the Old Kent Road, or Kensington High Street on a map twice as big as the windshield. Despite all this, sometimes I even had the Anglia under control.

The Anglia being studied by Russell at the wheel and admired from the balcony by Bill Gresham and Mimi

Since few people could afford to drive, I was not a serious menace on London Streets, as I would have been a generation later. Automobiles were still so uncommon that having one marked you as upper crust, and possibly rich. Even people who owned cars seldom drove to work. Gasoline was too costly. The car was reserved for weekend outings and holiday splurges. It was a luxury item or an expensive piece of sports equipment. Unlike Americans, Londoners did not take their cars for granted. One evening I attended the twenty-fifth birthday party for somebody's Bentley racer. We all stood around the car, drank wine, and made flattering remarks about how well it carried its age. There was a birthday cake with twenty-five lit candles, which the Bentley blew out with a blast of its exhaust pipe.

The shortage of automobiles gave London a great calmness. I often used the Anglia to drive friends home after late parties when the Underground had stopped running for the night. By midnight London was as quiet as a village on a Sunday in February, the emptiness of it dramatized by the hard glare of green and orange mercury-vapor streetlights, store windows dark, house lights out. We could drive through mile after mile of streets before seeing another car in motion. The night silence of London in those years was so wonderful and so eerie that I once tried to get it into words in a column composed for the *Sun* on a wintry midnight in Fleet Street:

"Across the office, the gas fire is sputtering drowsily, but except for this and the occasional rumble of a late bus echoing up off the dead building fronts, there is no audible proof that London is still alive.

"London, they always tell you, goes to bed early. This cliché is true, all right, but it conveys none of the loneliness or desolation, the mystery and the awesome dignity of London at sleep. . . .

"The night sound of London is the echo of leather heels off stone walls, the purr of a cat from the shadows, the murmur of the Thames running against the Embankment, the heavy stillness of fog coiled around a lamp post. . . ."

The Anglia made me an adventurer. With it, I could expose myself to experiences that helped me to learn a great deal very quickly at a time of my life when I needed to learn almost everything. With the Anglia, I could drive up to Scotland, and did. It took two days. Along the way, looking at the grim urban ruins created by an industry harnessed to greed, I learned why the socialist faith was so much stronger than the Church of England. Sherwood Forest was a ruined landscape, Robin Hood was a figure on a pub sign, and only the Sheriff of Nottingham lived on, in the Tory figure of Winston Churchill.

With the Anglia, I could take Mimi across the Channel and poke around in Normandy, then drive down to Paris and join the French national traffic jam around the Arch of Triumph. We took Dave Lampe, whose high-school French was better than mine, and drove from Dunkirk all the way to the D-Day invasion beaches and towns: Arromanches, Caen, St.-Lô, Bayeux, Port-en-Bessin, and Vierville and St.-Laurent, the tiny villages behind Omaha Beach.

"The whole north of France is one mass graveyard," I wrote my mother. "The dead of 1871; the dead of 1914–18; the dead of 1944. Cemetery after cemetery from Belgium to Omaha Beach which is a distance about as great as from New York to Baltimore. Along the roadsides, isolated tombstones to German soldiers whom the French refused to bury in their cemeteries. Every town and hamlet has its monument to those *'morts pour la patrie'*— who died for their country, or to their sons *'déportés, fusillés, victimes de la barbarie allemande'*—deported, shot, victims of German barbarism."

Standing in a German gun emplacement at Omaha Beach, I tried to imagine who might have been more terrified that morning: the German soldiers staring at that gigantic armada, or the American soldiers bobbing in the assault boats, knowing they would have to climb this terrible cliff, or suffer dreadful injury, or die.

In Paris with
Mimi, 1953

I had escaped combat in the war, and afterward had boyishly wished I hadn't. Now, looking down on this beach and imagining that morning ten years ago, for the first time in my life I was grateful about missing the great, bloody kill-or-be-killed romance of war. In this place the sense of war's agony was so overpowering that I could no longer believe in the fantasies of wartime heroism spun by popular entertainments and patriotic old men who send young men to die.

We stopped the Anglia overnight at Abbeville. Bill Gresham had told me about hating Abbeville in his waist-gunner days with the B-24s en route to Germany. There had been an especially deadly German fighter squadron based there, known among bomber crews as "the Abbeville boys." Mimi, David, and I had a more pleasant experience, and in a single night

I learned never to overdo Pernod and never, never to go on afterward to Calvados.

In Paris the Anglia took us safely past a thousand "Yankee Go Home" scrawls. As an English car, it was safe from the assaults of vandals carrying out a policy orchestrated in Moscow. The English had "won" the war, but in France, which had quit in 1940, the English looked like the losers. Britain was so broke that travelers were allowed to take only seventy dollars with them when going abroad. This made them the paupers of Europe. They were so poor that even dedicated Communists were ashamed to treat them rudely.

Aware of this advantage, Lampe and I both let our hair grow long in the English style and wore shabby tweeds with elbow patches, baggy-kneed pants, and threadbare neckties so we could pass as Englishmen. We stayed at the Hôtel Louisiane on the Left Bank because Henry Miller had mentioned it somewhere and Jean-Paul Sartre might have once stayed there. The Louisiane's walls were as thin as onion skin, and you could lie in bed and hear the couple next door make love in French. In the morning you woke to the sounds of haggling over prices of eggs and vegetables in the street market under the window.

In Paris I learned that all the wonderful things Americans said about Paris were true, provided you didn't stay too long. One evening in a noisy restaurant full of people almost as young as we were, we were joined by a young French diplomat home from Sweden for a few days. He was joining us, he said, for the express purpose of arranging a rendezvous with Mimi, and, having declared his intentions, turned his back to Lampe and me and gave Mimi a very passable idea of what it might be like to be courted by Charles Boyer with seduction in mind.

When he urged her to come to his house next day

at a time certain, I realized that he was entirely serious and became testy. I began interrupting their conversation with bibulous wisecracks that seemed devastatingly witty to me, but seemed only to alarm the diplomat-seducer. He counseled me not to behave like a middle-class boor, or words to that effect, and then, apparently fearing I might make a scene, rejoined his party. Not, however, before leaving his address and phone number with Mimi and urging her to phone next day.

Oh, those lovely Anglia days! They were as sweet for Mimi as they were for me.

In the golden English August of 1953, the Anglia took us out to the Welsh border for a weekend at Cefntilla Court, the seat of Lord Raglan in Monmouthshire. This was the work of Janetta Somerset, a young Englishwoman with whom we had become friendly in Baltimore. Janetta had held the London bureau job now done by Joan Graham, and was offered a reporting job on the *Sun* staff if she wanted to come to Baltimore.

Janetta was ecstatic about the idea. She loved the idea of America the way Buck loved the idea of England. She came in high, happy spirits, fascinated by America and disgusted with English acquaintances who talked about her departure for America, she wrote me, "as though I were going to take up permanent residence in a zoo."

She wrote me often in London, flattering me about my work, keeping me posted on office scandals, and fuming about the cheap reporting of America done by the popular British press. "A double-dyed toad" was her description of one famously cynical British correspondent "who has done more harm to Anglo-American relations than any man living, counting the New York Bureau of the *Express,* and the whole staff of the *Mirror.*"

Janetta was determined that Mimi and I should like England as much she liked America and in faraway Baltimore worked to put us in touch with the best of it. She instructed her parents to invite us for a weekend visit. They immediately obeyed. The invitation from Janetta's mother awaited me in London when I arrived in January.

Janetta's mother was the former Julia Hamilton and her father, FitzRoy Richard Somerset. The sensible thing, I suppose, would have been to dash off a note saying: "Dear Mrs. Somerset, We'd love to pop down for a visit after Mimi arrives from America." Instead, I froze over the stationery. Could I really write "Dear Mrs. Somerset" without being arrested?

The problem was that Janetta's father was not plain Mr. Somerset. He was The Right Honorable The Lord Raglan, a hereditary baron of England. This, I assumed, made Janetta's mother The Right Honorable The Lady Raglan, or maybe just Lady Raglan. Whatever it was, I was sure that a letter addressing her as "Dear Mrs. Somerset" would be a gaffe of international proportions.

I delved into a Debrett catalog of the peerage, looking for a clue but finding only family histories, which increased my worry: Lord Raglan descended from the fifth Duke of Beaufort; Lady Raglan was the daughter of the eleventh Lord Belhaven and Stenton. This was serious nobility. The wrong salutation on a handwritten note might forever mark me as an oaf throughout the drawing rooms of England.

Nothing I wrote down looked right. "Dear Lady Raglan" looked like the start of a demand for immediate payment of an overdue bill. "Dear Lady" and "My dear Lady" both sounded too much like Damon Runyon. I knew the English used "Honorable" a lot, but "Dear Honorable Lady Raglan" was surely all wrong.

In short, I never answered her note. Childish dread of making a social error paralyzed me, as it had years ago when I went to the newsboys' banquet in terror that Deems might catch me eating peas with the wrong fork. Growing up was so hard. Just when it seemed you had become a man of the world at last, you discovered you were still the prisoner of childhood fears.

Janetta persisted. That spring her younger brother Geoffrey phoned saying he had orders from Janetta to meet me. He understood I was immense good fun, and he was looking forward to it. Mimi was in London by then, and we had an apartment. I invited Geoffrey to come by. We were startled when a happily beaming, rosy-cheeked, bright-eyed youth, looking about thirteen years old but wearing a black bowler and a severe black suit, announced that he was Janetta's brother Geoffrey.

Geoffrey was the first person I'd met in London who made me feel grown-up. He had the aristocratic Wellington nose with accent and manners to match, and such enthusiasm for absolutely everything that he might have walked right out of an old Frank Merriwell story. He was not thirteen but twenty, and his somber wardrobe was standard civilian dress for an off-duty officer of the Grenadier Guards.

It was impossible not to be delighted by Geoffrey. He was every parent's dream of what a son should be. He could get down on the floor and play gracefully with the children, inoffensively offer hints to improve my bad driving, and sing most of the music of Gilbert and Sullivan.

One evening he had me dine with him in the Bank of England. Besides guarding Buckingham and St. James's palaces and the Tower of London, the Grenadiers also guarded the bank at night. The officer in charge could invite one guest for a dinner the bank traditionally served in the four-room apartment reserved for guards officers. We were permitted one glass of sherry each, a bottle of white wine, a bottle of port, and a large shot of whiskey apiece, and passed up nothing.

The guest had to be out of the building by eleven o'clock or spend the night locked in. It was Geoffrey's first night on this duty, the bank was a maze covering four acres of ground, and the quantities of wine we had downed complicated the tricky problem of finding the exit. Geoffrey managed it in the nick of time, though, thus denying me the chance to boast that I once spent a night in the Bank of England. Next day he phoned to confess that it had taken him forty minutes to find his way back to his bed.

Geoffrey brought us another invitation to weekend at Lord Raglan's. Since it could be answered orally, I told Geoffrey to tell his parents yes, and the three of us set off in the Anglia through the west of England.

Neither Mimi nor I understood the art of being a weekend guest. In the world we came from, when somebody invited you to come visit for a day or two, you showed up at the agreed time, they showed you where you'd sleep and wash up, then you went to the parlor to find out how they planned to keep you entertained. You expected to be entertained pretty constantly.

When this did not happen at Cefntilla Court, we were nervous. After unpacking, we descended to a handsomely furnished sitting room to hear what was in store for us. We stood there a while, rustling and stirring, hoping somebody would realize we were there and come tell us what was in store for us. Apparently, there was nothing in store for us, because nobody appeared.

There were women talking outside the window. Maybe we were supposed to go out. When we had rustled and stirred ourselves to exhaustion without getting results, we did go outside. Lady Raglan was there with her younger daughter and another woman, who might have helped operate the household. They were chatting casually and doing something with fresh vegetables. Mimi and I waited for instructions, but none came, though they now included us in the loose-limbed conversation. It was about weather and house-keeping and growing conditions and such. Apparently we could get involved in the vegetables if we liked, or just stand around and be pleasant, or wander else-where if we preferred.

We wandered to the front of the house. Sitting on the front steps in his shirt-sleeves was Lord Raglan. He was long and angular and trim. I knew a little about him now. He was sixty-seven years old. Educated at Eton and Sandhurst. Joined the Grenadier Guards when he was twenty, Geoffrey's present age. Rose to the rank of major. Served with the Egyptian army, served in Palestine in 1918, spent two years among the Arabs in Transjordan before succeeding his father as Lord Raglan in 1921. Lord Lieutenant of Monmouthshire.

His great-grandfather had fought with the Duke of Wellington in Spain, lost an arm at the Battle of Waterloo, and, forty years later, when commanding British forces in the Crimea, issued the misconstrued orders that sent the Light Brigade charging "into the jaws of death, into the mouth of Hell."

Lord Raglan was reading a newspaper when we appeared. Something had amused him.

"It has just been discovered that eating eggs will kill you," he said. "Listen to this. Does it seem plausible?"

He read from a news story. It sounded like a typical Fleet Street fraud. A scientist was quoted. He warned that a healthy breakfast of bacon and eggs could be deadly. Silly stories like this were always appearing in the British papers. Giant snow creatures unknown to science were discovered in the Himalayas in winter. Summer brought regular sightings of the Loch Ness monster in Scotland. Lord Raglan was reading one of the first stories about cholesterol and heart disease, and we all thought it funny. The great health obsession that was to terrorize the next generation had scarcely dawned in 1953, cholesterol was a word known only to laboratory scientists, and "a good healthy breakfast" still meant bacon and eggs. Lord Raglan's skepticism was reasonable.

Next afternoon everyone dressed for a lawn party at an estate several miles away. Not knowing the road, I needed a passenger in the Anglia who did. Lord Raglan's sense of a host's duty, I suppose, made him insist on riding with me, and in the backseat. It was unthinkable for Mimi to sit in the back, he said. It was even more unthinkable for Lord Raglan, but he did it. The Anglia was a two-door model. Getting to the backseat required acrobat's agility. Leg room was so tight the seat was suitable only for tots, contortionists, and youths as elastic as Geoffrey. Somehow Lord Raglan got back in there without losing dignity and seated himself in correct military posture. He was a Grenadier Guard, after all. A Grenadier Guard could endure agonies even worse than the Anglia's backseat without breaking.

Off we went, bumping up and down narrow rustic roads. Our destination must have been a mountaintop, because we went up several hills almost steep enough to exhaust the Anglia's twelve horses. By shifting down to the first gear, I nursed the Anglia to the top of each, where, quivering with exhaustion, it plunged gratefully into the downhill slope. Then I shifted it into top gear and floored the gas pedal, trying to build enough momentum to get us to the top of the next hill.

At the crest of the fourth or fifth hill, I looked ahead to the next and knew the Anglia was out of its league. So far, the hills had been merely steep; this one was vertical. It was like a ski jump. Even as the Anglia started its downhill run, I knew it would never make it to the top of this next monster. Mimi and Lord Raglan must have known it, too. Their silence was terrible as I floored the gas pedal to build maximum velocity on the downhill run.

The Anglia hit bottom and sped into the upward climb as though it intended to fly, and for a long time did not seem to lose momentum. We were almost halfway up, and still climbing boldly, and it seemed there might be miracles after all. Then I felt the Anglia's spirit fade and knew it was struggling, so I dropped into second gear, which helped a little, but only briefly, so I put it into bottom gear, and it dug in and fought that hill. Up, up, up it struggled, as if determined to prove it was a real car in spite of only twelve horsepower.

Mimi, Lord Raglan, and I—we all knew what had to happen now. It was as inevitable as the fate of the *Titanic* after the engineer inspected the damage, gave the captain a short lecture on physics, and said, "The ship must go down." The Anglia, it was obvious, must stall to a dead stop long before we reached the top of the hill.

It did. I felt humiliated. A lord of the realm had favored me by placing himself in my care. And not just any lord of the realm, but one in whom flowed the blood of a hero of Waterloo. And I had lacked the motoring know-how to get him to the top of a hill. It didn't matter whether the failure was the Anglia's or mine. We were dealing with a major of the Grenadier Guards. England expected every man to do his duty. Excuses were unacceptable.

We sat there dead on the hill for maybe two seconds

that felt like eternity. It was a narrow country road, bordered with trees and dense underbrush, no houses nearby, no humanity, no other traffic.

"I'll get out and walk up," Lord Raglan said, observing that decreasing the weight load should make it possible for the Anglia to resume uphill movement. Mimi said she would get out and walk with him, and he said, "That won't be necessary," and Mimi insisted she would do it anyhow, since she had to get out of the passenger's seat to set him free, and he said, well, people didn't do enough walking these days anyhow, and then I remembered something my Baltimore driving instructor had said:

"The most powerful gear in a car is reverse."

Nobody was getting out of the car yet, I said. I had an idea. Starting the engine, I backed to the bottom of the hill where the road widened enough to turn the Anglia around. Then, with the car in reverse and the back bumper aimed at the top of the hill, I gave it the gas.

The result was amazing. In reverse, the Anglia climbed with inexorable determination, never stuttering, faltering, or shuddering in exhaustion. Looking out the rear window to guide our forward progress, I couldn't avoid Lord Raglan's noble countenance, which peered calmly through the front windshield at the hill sloping away behind us. In his dark suit, his starched white shirt, black bowler set squarely on his head, he was the portrait of aristocratic imperturbability gazing calmly behind through the front windshield while being driven up the hill backward.

Later I felt responsible for a comic irony of history. The first Lord Raglan had produced the charge of the Light Brigade. Now here was his noble heir, not charging suicidally forward on a magnificent steed, but advancing backward slowly aboard the automotive equivalent of a swayback nag. For a long time I took this episode as an amusing metaphor for the decline of British glory.

Years later I discovered that Lord Raglan had been a provocative and respected amateur anthropologist whose books on war, incest, and myth disclosed a fastidious, contentious thinker, dissenter, iconoclast, and despiser of cant and conventional thought. Pondering the nature of international peace-keeping organizations, for example, in 1933 he wrote of the League of Nations:

". . . the League of Nations does not object to war, but only to a particular sort of war, that is to say, a war to alter the *status quo*. All existing frontiers, mandates, spheres of influence, by whatever process of violence or treachery they may have been arrived at, are sacred. What has been won by war the League will defend, and it regards the defence of stolen property as a sacred cause."

Discovering his books many years after taking him uphill backward, I realized that the dumbness of myself when young had kept me from being able to talk sensibly to this remarkable man in the backseat and, so, had kept me from learning what an original mind could do with an absurdity encountered while motoring. All mine could come up with was another banality about the decline of empire.

Among the Anglia's many blessings was my acquaintance with Henry Fairlie. He was writing editorials for *The Times* of London and being praised as one of the brilliant new men of British journalism when I arrived in London. He was drinking at the Clachan one evening when I was there with Gerry Fay and the rest of the *Guardian* crowd, and we were introduced. He was my age, perhaps a year or two older, tall, and darkly handsome with a smile that could only be called devilish. Unlike the *Guardian* men, whose wardrobes tended toward the gaudy or the seedy, Henry affected the formidable City of London look. The bowler, the dark suit, the white shirt. It was the uniform of bank men, lawyers, off-duty army officers, and, I assumed, *Times* of London men.

I was immediately impressed. He spoke with fluent ease about subjects that were far beyond me and conveyed a sense of self-confidence which I envied. Conversation came out of him in fully formed paragraphs ready to be sent to the printer without editing. It was witty, well informed, and more clever than anything I had ever heard in Baltimore. I had heard conversation like this from other Oxford and Cambridge men. Oxford and Cambridge seemed to turn out ambulatory books instead of mere scholars. I had never heard one, though, as impressive as Henry. Perhaps it was the slightly insolent drawl with which he spoke. This heightened the impression of mischievous impudence he conveyed. Hoping I might get to know him better, I was careful not to say anything that evening that might disclose the depth of my own foolishness.

The talk turned to housekeeping matters. The Labour party would soon hold its annual conference at Margate, a seaside resort on the southeast coast. I had reserved a hotel room and intended to drive down in the Anglia. Fairlie mentioned that he intended to go, but said he had not yet thought about the transportation problem. He could ride down with me, if he wished, I said, though warning him that the Anglia was small and uncomfortable. That was very kind of me, he said, and on the agreed date we set out from London together.

Henry seemed anything but sociable. He had a thick stack of newspapers and started to read them after our first exchange of greetings. I had counted on him to help direct me through the maze of London south of the Thames, but it was soon obvious that he had no enthusiasm for guide duty, for he insisted he was just as lost in the south of London as I was, and concentrated on his newspapers while I grappled with the street map and the clutch.

The fog came in thick when we finally broke out into the countryside, and visibility shrank down to a few yards ahead of the radiator cap. It was obviously going to be a long day's journey, but just as obviously there was not going to be much conversation to lighten the passing hours.

As we poked along cautiously in what might be farmland down in Kent, Henry tranquilly reading, I hunched over the wheel looking for dangerous intersections, the Anglia decided it had had enough and rolled to a stop. Henry's attention shifted from his newspapers to me.

"What's the matter?"

This time I knew.

"We're out of petrol," I said.

I had intended to gas up on the way out of London, but map-reading duties had distracted me, and then the fog had descended and hidden any filling stations that lay along the route. So now we were sitting in dense fog someplace out in the vast unknown without gasoline. Well, fortunately I wasn't alone. I had been getting irritated by Henry's newspapers. I had expected an opportunity to start a friendship, and Henry had been treating me like a chauffeur. Now, though, I was happy to have him. It was comforting having someone to help.

"What do you think we should do?" I asked Henry.

He looked at me as though stunned by the stupidity of the question. Wasn't the answer obvious?

"Get some petrol," he replied.

"But where?"

"Oh, just walk along the road a mile or so. You'll find a place," he said, and went back to his newspapers.

I knew I should be outraged, but the gall of him

was so breathtaking that outrage would only amuse him. Without another word, I got out and started walking into the fog. Afterward I knew what I should have done. I should have kept walking until I came to a bus stop or a town with a taxi stand and gone off to Margate, leaving Henry Fairlie sitting in the befogged Anglia with his newspapers. Henry would have enjoyed that and admired me for it, but I hadn't the courage required for such a swashbuckling gesture.

After walking a mile or two in the fog, sure enough, I found a place, bought gasoline, and lugged it back to the Anglia. Henry was still reading as I filled the tank. We got to Margate without much more conversation, and after that I didn't see much more of Henry. I owed the Anglia gratitude, however, for introducing me to an aspect of the English character that was important for an American to be aware of. Many, many years later in other lives, Henry and I met again and discovered, I think, that we liked each other, but by then we had aged beyond the point where new friendships are possible, so it didn't much matter.

After London was far behind me, and I thought of what a happy time it had been in my life and how much I had learned so quickly there and how it had changed me, the Anglia seemed to be a vital part of that wonderful time. Maybe it was because the Anglia, by forcing me at the age of twenty-seven to start driving through the world, finally turned me into a complete American: that mobile creature who travels, learns, lives, and loves, and often dies, on wheels.

One of the things I learned was that the highbred classes may suffer social uncertainty just as intense as the hayseed worried about how to address a Right Honorable Person. In the process, I also had a demonstration of how to reprimand a barbarian without abandoning civility. These came in the form of what

Janetta called "a plea" embodied in a long letter about many other things, which she sent after our visit to Cefntilla Court.

"Please, please, write to my mama, for she has not heard from you and thinks you did not enjoy your stay," Janetta wrote. "She and Daddy apparently are wondering what they did wrong, and are quite unhappy. FYI, and intending no offense, it is more than customary, it is compulsory to write thank you notes in England. A note, after you have spent a night or more with anyone, is a law of the Medes and the Persians. . . . I thought you would like to know and put my poor parents out of their pain."

18

The Crown

I rose at four-thirty that morning and started dressing in white tie and tails. It was still pitch black outside, and heavy rain was beating against the window. The rain had been falling like that all night, drenching a million people camped in the streets. What should have been a rosy June morning looked like the start of a wet, black nightmare.

Before long I was going to have to walk out into that downpour in fancy dress because I had been too stupid to apply for a permit to take a car up to Westminster Abbey. His Grace, the Duke of Norfolk, Earl Marshal of England, in charge of arrangements, had offered that choice. If I had filled out the forms, authoritative windshield stickers would have been issued, and I could have ridden to the Abbey in the splendor of the Dorsey Daimler.

I had laughed at the idea. An absurd fuss, a preposterous waste of car-rental money, I told Joan. Living within a short walk of the Abbey, I could easily stroll up there on a lovely June morning. It wasn't just chintziness that impelled me to walk. The American in me was tickled by the idea of walking to a coronation instead of being chauffeured by a lackey in royal Daimler glory. Thomas Jefferson walked to the Capitol for his first inauguration. Let the English see how Americans did these things.

Dressed for a walk to the Coronation at Westminster Abbey

Watching the rain stream against the bedroom window made me curse my foolishness. That short walk up to the Abbey seemed short only because I had never walked it in pouring rain. Actually, it was at least a mile. And in top hat, white tie, tails . . .

The earl marshal's instructions had been firm about dress. People not entitled to wear ermine, coronet, full dress uniform, court dress, levee dress coat with white knee breeches, kilt, robe of rank or office, or tribal dress must wear white tie and tails, with medals.

I didn't have medals. Since I didn't have a dressy suit either, I rented the full rig from Moss Bros., famous among the haberdashery-wise throughout the empire and always pronounced "Moss Bross." Knowing there would be a coronation run on Moss Bros., I went early and got a fairly decent fit. Because I'd never worn tails before, I got up a little earlier than necessary this morning against the possibility I might have a breakdown getting into the thing.

Mimi fixed a big breakfast. It was going to be a long day. I had to be in position inside the Abbey by seven-thirty and wouldn't get out until four in the afternoon. The rain let up while we were eating. Mimi got the camera and, while Kathy and Allen watched, took snapshots of Daddy wearing his coronation suit so there would be a record of this great day for them to show their grandchildren.

Whatever gods may be, they were all with me this day. The rain faded to a weak drizzle, then stopped altogether just when it was time to start for the Abbey. No, I would gamble and leave the raincoat home. Walking to the Abbey in top hat, white tie, and tails could be a great gesture only if it was done right. Wrapping up in a dirty raincoat would make it comical.

Mimi was going to Gerry Fay's house to watch the day's events on television. There weren't a lot of television sets in London yet, but Gerry's house had one, and his wife, Alice, had invited several disadvantaged families like mine to come see the show. Because it was a big day for me, as well as for the queen, I kissed Mimi and the children good-bye, said, "Wish me luck," stepped out into Lower Belgrave Street, and headed toward Victoria Station.

Not a soul in sight from Eaton Square all the way to Victoria. In thundering silence, I strolled briskly along through the heavy, wet air, getting used to the feel of the high silk hat on my head, happy to discover that it was not going to tip and fall off. In my hip pocket I had a half-pint flask of brandy to keep me awake during the long day. In my hand I carried a brown-paper bag containing two sandwiches and three or four chunks of yellow cheese. In my pockets I had a sheaf of official cards issued by the earl marshal, conveying the queen's command that policemen pass me safely through all barricades and instructing me which church entrance to use, how to conduct myself while eating during the ceremony (discreetly), and where to find toilet facilities in the Abbey.

Rounding Victoria Station, I heard the hum of a great, damp concentration of humanity and saw the broad avenue leading to Westminster packed from curb to building line on both sides. All along the six-mile route of the coronation procession, people had spent the rain-soaked night on the sidewalks. How many there were I didn't try to guess. The papers said millions, overstating it a bit, as newspapers usually do when writing of crowds. Still, there were plenty.

I had walked among them the night before. They were bedded down in sleeping bags and soggy quilts, under raincoats, and makeshift oilskin tents. Many had brought camp stools, portable stoves, knapsacks, picnic baskets, knitting bags, radios. They brewed tea on the sidewalk, they read, they slept, they sang, they sat stoically in the rain with only a felt hat against the downpour, they dozed with heads pillowed against tree trunks and lamppost standards.

During the war Londoners' ability to "take it," no matter how much punishment the Luftwaffe gave them, became such a cliché that it later turned into a small joke. On this cold, bitter, rainy night, with those good-natured hordes cheerfully camped on rainswept concrete, I had a glimpse of that peculiar British fortitude, dogged and indomitable in the face of adversity, which made them so formidable to Hitler.

At the morning's soggy dawn, in my top hat and tails and graced, I hoped, with some of the elegance Fred Astaire brought to the uniform, I presented my credentials to the police guarding the barricades on the route to the Abbey. Miracle of miracles! The police recognized them, passed me through, waved me into the broad empty avenue called Victoria, flanked on both sides by thousands waiting for a glimpse of history. The avenue ran straight to Westminster Abbey. I prayed I could make it before the skies opened again and stepped out as rapidly as I could without losing dignity before the damp mob staring at me.

And, yes, now applauding me. A smattering of applause came off the sidewalks as I strode along. They had been waiting so long for something wonderful to appear. Now here was the first sign that wonders would indeed pass before their eyes this day. I fancied myself a vision for them out of a Fred Astaire movie, a suave, graceful gentleman in top hat, white tie, and tails, signaling the start of a momentous event.

Not a vehicle moved from one end of Victoria to the other. It had been completely cleared to await the procession. At that moment, I was the procession. The applause grew as I stepped along. Having always prided myself on shyness, modesty, and distaste for theatrics, I was surprised to find I was not only enjoying my big moment, but also, here and there where the applause seemed especially enthusiastic, tipping my silk hat to the audience.

It wasn't until I got within a block or two of the Abbey that I understood what was truly happening. There I noticed a man in the crowd talking to a companion and pointing to my hand that held the brown bag with my lunch. At this, his companion laughed, then applauded vigorously, and the light broke upon me. What delighted the crowd was the spectacle of a toff, a regular toff as I must have looked to them, brown-bagging his lunch to the coronation.

By this time I was certain to reach the Abbey before the downpour resumed. That certainty and the pleasure of strutting a great stage exhilarated me. Triumphantly, I raised my lunch over my head and waved it at the crowd, and was washed with a thunder of cheering and applause that the great Astaire himself might have envied.

That was the high point of the day for me. A moment later I passed into the Abbey and a long day's work.

Except for the coronation, I probably would never have got to London. The coronation was what the trade called a color story, and I had made a reputation in Baltimore for being a good color writer. It was a curse in some ways because writing color meant getting stuck with the dreariness of covering parades, the annual arrival of the circus, and the hubbub surrounding events like the Preakness. These stories soaked up a lot of adjectives because they never produced any news that could be told in lean, exciting verbs. It was fun to do them at first because of the garish writing that was permitted. Since they were always the same year after year, however, a long diet of them led to boredom, then softening of the brain.

My reputation as a color writer should have been the end of me, but I was lucky in death and politics. In 1952 King George VI died and General Dwight Eisenhower was elected President of the United States. The timing of the king's death meant Elizabeth's coronation would take place the following June. Eisenhower's election meant the *Sun*'s veteran correspondents, who would normally have covered the coronation, would be tied down in Washington reporting the beginning of a new government. The coronation might be a grand picnic, a magnificent party, but basically it was just another color story.

Well, I had also done some real news reporting in Baltimore that showed I could also write with verbs. There would be news, too, to cover in London. "Hard news," the trade called it. But the big story would be the coronation. A color story. Buck thought about a color writer who could also use verbs. Then he invited me to lunch at the Chesapeake.

Since television has come of age, spectacles like the coronation have shrunk in importance for newspapers. Television's ability to make a faraway audience feel present at these dazzling shows is incomparable. Once newspapers conceded it, they mostly gave up trying to compete. In 1953, however, television was still learning to toddle, the coronation was still an immensely important newspaper story, and newspapers made expensive efforts to beat each other in the competition. The task of a reporter was to bring it to life on a printed page, to make the reader see it with something of the same intensity that television would later produce with cameras, satellite transmission, and a thousand other technological wonders still to come.

So when I entered Westminster Abbey at 7:30 in the morning I realized that my performance this day had better be good. So far my work in London had been a hit with Dorsey. His visit in March had changed things between us in a way that made me think we were even on a friendly footing. Still, back on his home ground in Baltimore, he was more complicated than my pal Buck, international sightseer; back home, he was also Dorsey the gambling man who had a big bet riding on my performance in London. He had put me there because of the coronation.

This was the day for collecting bets or tearing up the tickets.

If I was not terrified by the trials of the day, it was because of the self-confidence gained from Buck's London visit. It had been a triumph from start to finish, and I knew Buck associated me with that triumph. My wisest move had been to introduce him immediately to Gerry and Alice Fay. I guessed Gerry's wit and man-about-London poise would appeal to Buck's love for sophisticated urbanity, and I guessed the two would make good drinking companions. My judgment proved perfect. Before the week was out they had become friends for life, and the Fays had a standing invitation to Baltimore to stay with the Dorseys.

"Dorsey is an extremely easy guest to entertain," I wrote my mother. "He is a great Anglophile and pronounces himself delighted so far by everything he has seen. He's like a kid wandering through a storybook land. He was saying yesterday he doesn't think he will want to leave here for Paris."

With Gerry and Alice, we made London a weeklong party, and when Dorsey's wife, Becky, arrived on the *Queen Elizabeth,* she joined the party enthusiastically. We drank Pernod in exotic Soho joints, sampled beer in pubs from London Bridge to Chelsea, and sipped vintage Bordeaux, Burgundies, and brandy in London's best restaurants. These included one in Mayfair, where, I told my mother, "A fabulous meal for just three of us cost $40, but fortunately I wasn't paying, so that was Dorsey's worry."

I took him underground to show him the marvels of the London subway system, which left him unimpressed. "Let's get out of here," he said. "People on subways all over the world all have the same defeated look."

The stately black London cabs were more his style, especially the older models in which drivers sat exposed to the weather while passengers rode in the enclosed cushioned depths behind. In these we criss-crossed London. Coming up from Knightsbridge toward Piccadilly one day, he began saying the *Sun* should buy a house in London as a permanent residence for its correspondents.

"That's the house we ought to buy," he said as we passed Hyde Park Corner, and pointed to a handsome stone structure with a large portico.

"That's Apsley House," I said. "I don't think it would be for sale."

"Why not?"

"It was the Duke of Wellington's house," I said.

By the time the Dorseys left for Paris, matters among us rested blissfully on a comforting "Russ" and "Becky" and "Buck" foundation. Leaving London reluctantly for what he anticipated would be the horrors of France, Buck urged me to join them in Paris on the weekend. I didn't. No use pushing your luck.

I had a good seat in the Abbey. It was in the north transept looking down from about mezzanine level onto the central ceremonial theater. It provided a clear, unobstructed view of the queen and the throne in left profile. Opposite in the south transept sat the lords and ladies of the realm in scarlet and ermine. The few good seats allotted American correspondents had been distributed by a lottery drawing, and I had got lucky.

After being ushered up the ramp to the chair I was to occupy for the next seven or eight hours, I took a spiral notepad out of my pocket and began taking notes, just as I would have done at a three-alarm fire in Baltimore, or covering a liquor-store shooting or Santa Claus's arrival in the Thanksgiving Day Parade.

This was by design. After worrying for weeks how to cover a coronation, I had decided to cover it pretty much the way I would cover any routine assignment on the local staff. I would show up, keep my eyes open, listen closely, and make notes on what I saw and heard, just as though I were going to phone the story to Banker or Spry on the rewrite desk. With the coronation, of course, I would have to get back to the office and write the story myself.

My hope was to produce a story that seemed fresh, and I thought this might be possible if I treated it as though I'd just strolled into the newsroom one afternoon and Cauley had come dancing at me and shouting: "They're having a coronation up at the Abbey in ten minutes. Get up there as fast as you can."

This was not the safe way to cover the coronation, but it offered the best chance of doing a good story. The safe way was to write the story before the event was held. This was the easiest way, too. It was also the surest way to produce a lifeless story.

I considered writing the story in advance. It could easily be done. The thing was really nothing more than a pageant, an immense pageant, to be sure, but a pageant nevertheless. Every line of the script, every move in the ceremony, everything was available weeks beforehand. The plot line was as predictable as a Chinese opera. I could write the story in advance, so it would be ready to cable to Baltimore if I couldn't produce a fresh story writing on deadline after getting out of the Abbey.

This idea I discarded quickly. For one thing, I was cocky about my ability to produce a fresh story of several thousand words under deadline pressure. I had always worked well on deadlines, maybe even better than when there was time to dawdle. Also, why go through the tedium of writing the entire story ahead of time if I didn't intend to use it?

So I entered the Abbey with no backup story ready to send in case of emergency, took out my spiral pad, and started jotting notes on what I saw. Tier upon tier of dark blue seats edged with gold. The stone walls draped with royal purple and gold. The stained glass of rose windows transforming the gray outer light into streams of red, yellow, green, and blue high up against the Abbey roof.

Many of these notes were to appear almost unchanged in my story.

"A glistening African woman in a dress of glistening gold jangled the dozen dainty gold bracelets adorning her pudgy arms."

"Yellow men and tan men, black men and pink men, men with *cafe au lait* skins and men with the red veined nose of country squiredom."

"Malayans with bands of orange and brown-speckled cloth bound tightly about their hips . . ."

"Men dressed as Nelson might have dressed when he was sporting in London . . . like courtiers who dallied with the Restoration beauties of Charles II's court . . . like officers in Cornwallis's army . . ."

" . . . violins far away eerily unreal . . ."

Writing to my mother later, I disposed of the coronation in a single paragraph:

"I am so sick of the whole business that I can't write about it. Suffice it to say that I was in the Abbey about seven and didn't get out until four P.M. In this time I ate two sandwiches, several chunks of cheese, went to sleep three times, and drank a half pint of brandy to keep my blood flowing. I was seated in the midst of all the African and Oriental potentates and had a fine view of the staircase leading down to the water closets, where I could see Africans in leopard skins and Chinese dressed like French admirals queuing up to wait their turn to make water. I came out of the Abbey, stiff as a board and woozey, and had to run through a cold driving rainstorm to find a taxicab. Then I had to write for six hours, producing that mass of type which ran in the *Sun*. I didn't feel that I laid an egg completely, because next day mine was the only story from any American newspaper which had parts reproduced in any of the London papers. Considering that papers like the *New York Times* and *Tribune* had twenty-five and thirty reporters to do the job, I felt we did fairly well."

The humility in this last sentence was entirely bogus. By the time I wrote my mother the reaction from Baltimore was in, and I felt I had done far better than fairly well. I felt I had scored an absolute triumph. The day following the coronation, I had a cable signed by sixteen members of the city staff, including Janetta, Banker, Caulfield, and Ed Young. It said:

MAGNIFICENT. YOUR COVERAGE WORTHY OF THE CORONATION, AND OF BAKER.

Pete Kumpa, one of the best newsmen on the staff and an old friend whose regular correspondence kept me posted on events in the home office, reported: "Your story received here in the greatest admiration. Magnificent is the word."

The greatest ego bloater of all, however, was a note from Becky Dorsey marked "Very Personal." She reported various compliments about the coronation piece that Buck had received from various high-and-mighty types in the *Sun* hierarchy, then said:

"The nicest of all—Tom O'Neill said, 'Buck, the boy knows how to use the English language. It's a finished piece, beautifully done'—"

Closing, Becky wrote, "I do not know that Buck would approve of my telling you all this, but on thinking of that fine ignorant old face of yours, I couldn't help myself."

I could have discounted praise from my friends on the city staff. They had been writing glowing reviews from my very first days in London. They were my cheering section back in Baltimore, and for good reason. Being picked from the local staff for the *Sun*'s plum assignment abroad, I was a symbol of hope for them. If one man from the local staff could escape into the glorious world of foreign correspondence, there might be hope for all. They had a stake in seeing me succeed and wrote constantly, applauding and cheering me on to keep my morale high.

Becky's report about Tom O'Neill, however, was not so easily explained away. Nothing could have done more to puff me with self-admiration than those few words about Tom O'Neill's remarks to Buck. I was not the type to have wildest dreams, but if I had been, the wildest I could have concocted would have had Buck Dorsey listening with the respect he always accorded his favorite reporter as the great O'Neill heaped me with praise.

Two months after the coronation had crowned me with glory, my triumph was confirmed in a cable from Baltimore:

TEN DOLLAR MERIT RAISE EFFECTIVE NEXT WEEK FOR YOU. HAPPY AUGUST FOURTH AND ALL THAT. LOVE. DORSEY.

That brought my salary up to $120 a week. I was a $6,240-a-year man.

19

Paradise

Cousin Edwin had not crossed my mind for a long time. The old fantasy no longer entertained me. Life had kept me too busy once Mimi and I were married.

There was the money hardship to worry about, and fatherhood, and family problems that came with creating a new generation, and family problems that came with the aging of the old generation. My mother had started falling inexplicably. A tumble down cellar steps broke her shoulder. There were brief instants when she was disoriented and lost. Petit-mal seizures, the doctor said. While I was in London she had a convulsive seizure, a bad fall. The doctor put her on medication.

Herb's larynx had been removed because of cancer just before I went to England. Afterward, unable to speak, he was out of work for months and hopelessly depressed. It was my sister Doris who saved him, laboriously teaching him to speak again ventriloquially, bringing him back into contact with the world, making him smile again. His unemployment benefits ran out, and money was needed at Marydell Road.

Doris, now married and living in the neighborhood, helped provide it. Doris seemed to have shouldered the full burden of Marydell Road. Far away from it, in London, leading the good life, I felt guilty about leaving the headaches for Doris to handle, and sent a little money, and wrote my mother faithfully every week.

Problems like these probably mean you are grownup and, I suppose, come with the territory. So does the forgetting of childhood fantasies. Getting the London job had gratified my fierce yearning for success instilled by my mother. It was far more wonderful than any realistic expectations I had ever had. I couldn't hold it forever; it was for eighteen months, two years at most; Buck had made that clear from the start. I couldn't imagine any job anywhere in journalism, however, that could make me happier. For the moment, I had fulfilled childhood's dream of glory.

As for losing all interest in Cousin Edwin, that had happened even before my luck turned. He had died in December 1951, and the news scarcely touched me despite all those years of having his greatness held up for my envy. Now I would never meet him, and it didn't matter. Not a bit. I had never really expected to meet him. The whole business had been fantasy. The great Cousin Edwin, no smarter than anybody else, had never been real, so the death had no emotional impact on me.

The *Sun*'s story of his death, however, prompted me to pick up the newsroom copy of *The New York Times*. That was something I didn't often do, pick up the *Times*. It was heavy going, full of writing that made you think of people playing pianos with boxing gloves on. Its obituary on Edwin ran for six columns, a length normally reserved for the world's shakers.

The obit was singularly lifeless, giving no suggestion that he had ever had more than two breaths of humanity in him. By then I had written enough obits to recognize the symptoms. Whoever had written poor Edwin's send-off had been too floored by reverence or fear to dare suggest that he had once been human. Buried in this lump of indigestible dullness about "indefatigable energy" and "unusual competence," however, was a startling piece of information. At age nineteen he had graduated from Randolph Macon College and made Phi Beta Kappa. Maybe Edwin James had been smarter than anybody else, after all.

By the time I had been in London a year, thoughts of Edwin never crossed my mind. I was too contented with the way my own life had turned out. In London I was at the top of the ladder and enjoying excessive praise from Baltimore. All ambition seemed to have been satisfied. My mother had taught if I worked hard I could amount to something, could make something of myself. She had been proved right, yet I was vaguely dissatisfied. Now that I seemed to amount to something, how was life different? Once you had made something of yourself, life should change, shouldn't it?

Though I couldn't put this uneasiness in words, I felt that success ought to make life more satisfying, ought to bring a peace of mind, a maturity, a serenity toward life, which I did not feel. Well, I was not yet thirty. With ambition satisfied, I had half a lifetime ahead to do the fine things: to cultivate my mind and sensibilities perhaps, to develop a philosophy that would put me at ease with the world, to do worthy things for those less lucky than I, to do. . .

I didn't know what.

So when 1954 came around and Buck offered to move me to Washington and become White House correspondent, I jumped at the opportunity. White House correspondent: That seemed even more glamorous, more important, than London correspondent. Living the cultivated life of mind and spirit and doing good and worthy things to enrich the soul could wait a bit. Buck was offering me a chance to be even more successful.

I was discovering, though I didn't realize it then, that hunger for success was bred so deeply into so many Depression youngsters that we were powerless to stop chasing it long after we had achieved it. Or had "made it," as the slang of that era had it. The hunger to "make it" was the motor that ran our ambition, and it was almost impossible to turn off.

If we made it, we were not satisfied. We wanted to make it big. If we made it big, we wanted to make it bigger. About this time, self-mocking people who had been Depression children began talking about the "rat race." The self-mockery didn't stop many from running it, though. Ten years later our own children would strike brutally at us by rejecting the successful lives we had prepared for them, but in 1954 nobody, absolutely nobody, could foresee that terrible time.

Neil Swanson was fired and Buck was given the top editorial job the same day. That was in early January. Buck sent a cryptic cable saying Swanson was no longer with us. A flood of letters from newsroom friends said, "Fired." Explanations were muddled. The most titillating had it that Swanson had outraged the paper's owners by ordering news of his latest marriage placed in the society column, a space sacred to Marylanders of bluest blood, hence verboten to Swanson of Minnesota and his bride, who had written the *Evening Sun*'s column for teenagers.

The larger explanation was plain. The death of Paul Patterson, long president of the Sun company and Swanson's patron, had brought new managers to the head of the boardroom table, and they didn't like Swanson. One way or another, they were going to have his head.

"The unanimity of the rejoicing around the office

surprises even me," Ed Young's letter of early January reported. "There wasn't a tear shed anywhere, and the holiday mood hasn't let up even yet."

Like all great news people, Ed had a glandular compulsion to be the first to break big news, and the Swanson story by this time was old news, so before going into it he went right to the big story.

"This is not official, and I want you to be properly impressed when you hear it from authority, but the present plan is . . ."

Buck wanted to transfer me to Washington to cover the White House. The *Sun* hadn't had a White House man since Joseph Short left the job to become President Truman's press secretary.

Buck's letter came five days behind Ed's. He wrote generously about Swanson, except for a reference to taste that was reminiscent of the lecture he had given me years ago about covering a high-school reunion.

"For five or six years he has been extremely indulgent to me, has let me go my way, has scarcely ever breathed down my neck and in many ways, as you know, he is an extremely able newsman. . . . But it is kind of nice not to have to put up with what frequently seemed to be shocking examples of bad taste. . . .

"Away with these trifles and to business. It is my present plan, which has the blessing of the throne, to send you to the Washington Bureau on a permanent basis somewhere around mid-summer. Unless, of course, you have serious objections. The front office has authorized a replacement for Short and you are my idea of that replacement. . . .

"It will surprise me a great deal if you have any objections because, as you know, our Bureau seems to me the ultimate in American newspapering and since you appear to have decided, after some quakings in the stomach, to make a career of this business, Washington ought to be for you."

This letter came two days before the first anniversary of my arrival in London.

Washington bureau. White House correspondent. These were big, heavy, serious words. I wrote back immediately and started planning to depart London in June. The best year of my life was over.

The scared young man who abandoned his trunk in the fog at Waterloo Station last January was now long gone. I did not kid myself, though, by supposing I had become a man of the world. My childhood theory of God as Cosmic Joke Player still shaped my reaction to life's blessings. *Be careful,* I told myself; this could be the start of a heartbreaking practical joke, so play it cautiously, don't get carried away, don't enjoy it too much.

Still, for the first time in my life I felt almost grown-up. I had been to Paris, sat in the Abbey for the coronation, dined in the Bank of England, lunched at the House of Lords, and driven a peer of the realm up a hill backward.

I had been to the Derby, where Gerry Fay taught me how to bet the horses, and had learned that the Derby was pronounced "Darby."

I had been to Dublin, where Gerry taught me the words to "Kevin Barry" and "The Old Orange Flute." There I had walked through St. Stephen's Green at midnight with ten Dubliners, all of us bubbling with Guinness, and heard them joke about the American passion for tracing Leopold Bloom's route through Dublin and argue to a rage about attempts to revive the Celtic tongue.

I had been to Canterbury, destination of Chaucer's pilgrims, stood by the altar where Thomas à Becket was murdered by Henry II's assassins, and sent my mother a postcard picture of the cathedral on which I scrawled, "Very old town."

I had been to the Isle of Man, where I learned that a Manx cat has no tail. I had been to Scotland, where I learned that the people were called "Scots," their culture was called "Scottish," and the only thing Scotch was their whiskey, which they spelled "whisky" to distinguish it from inferior intoxicants like bourbon, rye, and Canadian whiskey.

I had learned a great deal about drinking. Though weak on knowing when to quit, I knew which ales could be as devastating as a third martini and which caused flatulence. I had developed a taste for French wine and learned that some years produced better wines than others. I had seen this dramatically illustrated at a large luncheon given by the Foreign Correspondents Association at the Savoy when Mimi and I were seated at a table with Ruggiero Orlando, the correspondent for Rome Radio.

Ruggiero was short, intense, voluble, charming, and a passionate conversationalist. His uncle Vittorio Emanuele had been prime minister of Italy during World War One and, with Wilson, Clemenceau, and Lloyd George, was one of the Big Four who wrote the Versailles Treaty. An enemy of fascism, Ruggiero had had to flee Mussolini's Italy in fear of his life. His ability to talk more entertainingly than any other foreign correspondent in London lent him an authority that wine stewards were quick to recognize, and at lunch that day it was Ruggiero who was handed the wine list.

I watched intently to learn what wine this wise man of the Old World would order with this particular meal. Scarcely pausing in his nonstop conversation, Ruggiero glanced at the list, said, "Latour 1947," and resumed talking. The wine steward returned with a bottle, uncorked it, poured a little wine into Ruggiero's glass, and waited for approval. Still talking, talking, talking, Ruggiero lifted the glass, fell silent just long enough to sip, then turned mournful eyes to the wine steward.

"This is not a Latour 1947," he said. "It is a 1949 Lafite."

The wine steward looked at the bottle. Ruggiero was correct, absolutely correct. The wine steward begged forgiveness a thousand times until Ruggiero sent him away with orders to fetch the Latour '47. I had heard of wine expertise on that level, but had always thought it a joke. Having learned better, I was struggling to learn the difference between a drinkable wine and one that was going to vinegar.

I had also seen famous men up close and learned to speak to them without blushing and stammering. Tommy D'Alesandro, Baltimore's mayor, came to London at coronation time.

"We had dinner together and had a long chat," I wrote my mother.

"And oh yes, I went to the Correspondents dinner on Wednesday where I met General Marshall and General Bradley. God, I sound like a gossip columnist. Governor Earl Warren was also there. . . ."

There was a steady flow of celebrated people making themselves available for interviews, ranging from movie stars like Gary Cooper to American politicians like Adlai Stevenson to Foreign Secretary Anthony Eden. Eden periodically talked foreign policy, but not for attribution, with the American reporters, but rarely said anything that justified the trip to Downing Street. British government people traditionally treated their own press with contempt and generally made themselves unavailable to the American press, and since trying to see any of them was a waste of time, I soon gave it up.

Winston Churchill was prime minister. He cultivated an aura of grandeur, very much as General de Gaulle did, by, among other things, withholding the

Presence from all but the elect. His abuse of the press, for which he was notorious, rose from the fact that he considered himself a journalist and regarded his thoughts, speeches, and writings as marketable commodities that were not to be given away so long as American publishers were willing to pay large fees for them.

Being prime minister exposed him occasionally to the press, since it required frequent appearances in the House of Commons. There I saw enough of him from the press gallery to justify talking about him with impressive authority.

The most valuable part of my London education, however, took place in the writing department.

I arrived in Fleet Street with the police reporter's weakness for overwrought language and passion for clichés, and indulged both for the first few months. Some of my early stories read like parodies written for a burlesque on journalism.

Reporting a minor political squabble in the Labour party, I started the story by writing:

"In a stormy four-hour session behind closed doors . . ."

When Moscow reported Stalin near death, my story began:

"London is a tense world capital tonight, keeping a death watch on Moscow and nervously speculating about a struggle for power in the Kremlin."

I had flawless instincts for the worn-out expression: for the "stormy session" held—where else?—"behind closed doors." For the "tense world capital," the tired old "death watch," the "nervously speculating" population, and in the Kremlin the shopworn "struggle for power."

My most shameless performance was a story about the sudden departure of Soviet Ambassador Andrei Gromyko from London for New York:

"A cloak-and-dagger attempt to get out of London in complete secrecy shrouds the purpose of Gromyko's trip in darkest mystery."

With "cloak-and-dagger" and "complete secrecy" up to their old trick of putting a "shroud" around "darkest mystery," I had composed a sentence so rich in newspaper cliché that it was a travesty on the trade. There was no mystery about Gromyko's trip. My own story said in the second paragraph that he was on BOAC Flight 509 and would arrive in New York next morning, while the fourth paragraph quoted him as saying he was going to attend a meeting of the United Nations.

The only mystery was why the *Sun* published it instead of dropping the entire story into the wastebasket.

The answer was that the *Sun* believed in learning by doing. As a beginning reporter, you were thrown into the police stations to sink or swim. If you qualified for assignment to Washington or overseas, the *Sun* assumed you were smart enough to know what you were doing. Copyreaders rarely changed anything you wrote, no matter how dreadful it might be. Once promoted to the big time, you were given a lot of rope. A reporter could also learn by making a fool of himself. So went the theory, and the *Sun* dared to live by it until it became obvious the offender would never learn anything, in which case he was tucked away in an inconspicuous niche where he could no longer embarrass the paper.

The tumult and storm in my writing those first few weeks probably stemmed from my lack of confidence in a job that seemed far too advanced for me. To compensate, I was tearing the language to tatters every time I sat down at the typewriter. This was acceptable tradition in American news writing, though the *Sun*'s best writing reporters, like Tom O'Neill and Price Day, were too good to go that route.

What settled me down was daily exposure to the *Manchester Guardian*'s stories. They seemed masterfully written. Many read like polished essays. I read them with delight and growing fascination, because they proved that journalism did not have to be an assault on the mother tongue. It could be quiet, subtle, understated, or just dully matter-of-fact, yet still make the reader's mind tick over.

Coming from a journalistic tradition that licensed hotshots to make the language churn and steam, I was excited to discover that quiet could often pack more punch into a story than turmoil could. I was profoundly taken with the example the *Guardian* provided in covering a foreign-policy speech by Anthony Eden in the House of Commons. This was the sort of speech always breathlessly described by American reporters as "a major foreign policy address," and I was floundering around at the typewriter, struggling to make the story sound like one of the vital events of the decade, when the *Guardian* story was dropped on my desk.

It was by Harry Boardman, a lovely writer who used pen, ink, and longhand script to compose his daily report from the House of Commons. His opening paragraph on the Eden speech that day said:

"When he rose in the House Mister Eden had nothing to say but made the mistake of saying it at great length, omitting hardly a single flatulent Foreign Office cliché."

It was a revelation. It was breathtaking. The simplicity of it! The rightness! How easy it was to express the truth by keeping the language plain.

I had already written several hundred words of excitable prose about the Eden speech and meant to write several hundred more. Boardman's story changed my plans immediately and changed my theory of journalism forever.

I scrapped the long story in my typewriter and wrote a new one of just four paragraphs. With Boardman's courage, my story dismissed Eden's speech as "long-winded" and offered an example to illustrate:

"The objective is to create the conditions for the expansion of world production and trade and for that purpose to secure international action leading to an effective system of multilateral trade and payments over the widest possible area."

Until that night I had held religiously to the American faith in "objective journalism," which forbade a reporter to go beyond what the great man said. No matter how dull, stupid, unfair, vicious, or mendacious they might be, the utterances of the great were to be reported deadpan, with nary a hint that the speaker might be a bore, a dunce, a brute, or a habitual liar.

For a reporter from an important American newspaper to question the value of "objective journalism" was worse than unthinkable. It was subversive. It was revolutionary. Now I was not just questioning it; I was thrusting my own judgment into the story by calling the speech "long-winded" and by publishing one of Eden's sillier statements, which tended to satirize him. Harry Boardman, a conservative elderly gentleman who wrote plain, quiet English and had no use for typewriters, had set me on the path to revolution. After that I began sneaking my judgments into stories where I thought they would broaden a reader's understanding.

The *Guardian* reporters I knew best would have winced at the overheated stories of my early London days. Getting excited offended their principles, whether the provocation was alcohol or deadlines. The low-key style was their way of life. Though Gerry Fay became a dear, lifelong friend, it was only years later, while reading a book of his autobiographical pieces, that I learned he had landed on D Day in Normandy, a major in the British army under notice that he would probably not live through the day, but lucky enough to survive several days in the thick of the fighting before being wounded by a sniper. Telling war stories was bad form, like writing overwrought English.

Gerry's father, Frank Fay, and his uncle Willie had been instrumental in creating the Abbey Theatre in Dublin to produce the works of Yeats and Lady Gregory, but pride in his family theatrical history did not tempt Gerry to do much horn blowing about it.

By contrast, I'd had an American childhood. "Might as well blow your own horn because nobody's going to blow it for you," was my mother's advice. Blowing your own horn was the American way. Maybe that accounted for the bombast of American journalism. The British of the war generation had no horn blowing in them. Their style was quiet, introspective, ironic.

Though many *Guardian* writers probably had heroic stories to tell, the only one I ever heard was Mark Arnold-Forster's. Mark was short, very thin, very blond, very pale, and very quiet. He looked too frail to send out in a high wind, much less on a mission for heroes. Yet Mark had commanded one of five small torpedo boats that attacked the German battle cruisers *Scharnhorst* and *Gneisenau* as they steamed through the English Channel one day when the rest of the British navy was far away on other business.

I heard the story several times from colleagues who marveled at the courage of it, and tried one day to learn from Mark how it felt to attack a battleship with a torpedo boat.

"It felt jolly good to get back," Mark said, and changed the subject.

After learning to relax at the typewriter and winnow a little of the snorting and roar out of my writing, I began looking for good stories that didn't require shouting. Duty required keeping up with the diplomatic comings and goings and periodically filing some British political news, but I quickly realized that such stuff was small chaff even to the few Americans who kept abreast of great affairs. Britain's shrinkage to small-power status had begun. The stuff that once made big news from London no longer seemed very important to the superpower mentality developing back home.

I abandoned the pretense that the empire hadn't folded and started reporting Britain as a big, gaudy feature story. I wanted to shake free from outdated press claptrap about worried Whitehall, fearful Downing Street, and the uneasy Bank of England and concentrate on material that would make readers back in Baltimore feel what it was like to be in England at this moment when an old order was dying.

This kind of coverage fit my need to try a quieter, more intimate style of journalism. What's more, you didn't have to strain to find story material. For a reporter who thought the human comedy was a better story than the balance-of-payments deficit, England was a paradise.

There was always a good story to be had from the sin front. One day it might come from the Church of England's newspaper, denouncing apartment-house living as "licentious, corrupt, and ungodly" and attacking the typical apartment dweller as "a pagan living a life of materialism and concubinage."

On another, the House of Commons might be quaking before the anger of the Lord's Day Observance Society. This was a powerful lobby whose purpose was to prevent repeal of Sunday blue laws enacted between 1625 and 1780. In 1953 these accounted for what was known as "Gloomy Sunday," because they forbade dancing, billiards, sporting contests, and theater performances, and shortened pub hours. When a member of Parliament named Parker proposed repealing them, the fury of the gloom lobby was so intense that the House of Commons voted five-to-one against him. In the debate, Parker disclosed the dangers of threatening a Christian's Sunday calm:

"I have never received so many abusive letters as I have since I put my name to this bill. Some of the sentiments expressed are very surprising. Many people have wished me to drown with a millstone round my neck; others have said they would like to see my eyes put out and be there when it is happening."

This naturally led me to a pub at Sunday noon to report on what beer drinking was like on a day when pubs could open for only two and a half hours.

"Sunday beer drinking is pursued at a murderous pace. Knowing that he has exactly 150 minutes before the taps run dry, the Londoner storms the pub door on the dot of noon. . . . Neither man nor woman loses time by removing coat and scarf. Beer must be absorbed, guzzled, swilled, choked down, poured in, right down to the final precious second of drinking time, and there is no time for waste motion. . . . The clock is every man's enemy. It must be watched like a traitor, or before he realizes it, the careless drinker will find it has struck the fatal hour and sent him out with volume for one last pint unfilled."

The incessant English struggle to make the punishment fit the sin provided enlightening stories about the motherland of America's puritanism. Hangings were frequent affairs. They usually followed within a matter of weeks after the death sentence was imposed. British acquaintances tended to boast about this swift administration of capital punishment. So unlike the dreadful fuss you people make over it in the States, you know. I'd been there less than a year before a story cropped up which left no doubt whatever, except to embarrassed cops and prosecutors, that they had hanged an entirely innocent man.

I was not yet nervy enough in my journalism to point out that at least they had hanged him without prolonged delay, thus sparing him the pain of prolonged contemplation of the ancient rule that the law and justice need not coincide.

Another day, and the House of Commons had a proposal to restore the ancient punishment of flogging for violent crimes not severe enough to justify hanging. Magistrates and judges were enthusiastic, but not for flogging with the cat-o'-nine-tails. The "cat" made heroes of its victims, one judge observed. "Birching" was the judges' preference. This would involve beating miscreants across the buttocks with a long bundle of water-soaked sticks.

"When laid on by a chief warder who knows his business," Lord Chief Justice Goddard argued, the birch "not only gives them a taste of something unpleasant but leads to considerable ridicule."

There was foolishness everywhere, even in Downing Street, where the British aptitude for getting it all wrong about sex was illustrated when a group of female college students staged a demonstration in bathing suits in February. The coldness of London's February must be felt to be believed. Reading's men, it developed, had invited some French girls to a traditional campus bash, declaring English girls "not glamorous enough." The Reading women wanted to refute this libel in front of the prime minister himself. Hence, the bathing suits. Hence the ghastly blue legs, the goose pimples, the palsied shivering of the young woman who knocked at Churchill's door. The door was opened. A man appeared. He was not Churchill. She handed him a written defense of the Englishwoman's sex appeal and ran for woolen blankets.

I thought Americans would like to know if foreigners were as ga-ga about kid music as Americans were, so when the American howler Johnny Ray opened at the Palladium, I chose to cover that instead of reporting the Foreign Office view of what Marshal Tito's visit to London really meant. Ray was the first crooner in the history of his art to cry his way to the top of the sales charts. His triumph, which came from recording songs about weeping, was said to be symptomatic of some lugubrious neurosis in the American psyche, which manifested itself in delighted squeals when frail young men wept to music.

At the Palladium I established that if there was any neurosis, the British had it too:

"Throughout Ray's performance, his own wailing was answered by the shrill, ecstatic yowls and squeals of the girls. . . .

"The moment everyone was waiting for came when he threw his head back, gulped a great lungful of air and expelled the words: 'If you kah-rie-rie-rie . . .' A girl near the front row screamed, 'He's crying!'

"The entire house strained forward to see better and Ray turned his face full into the spotlight. There, sure enough, tears stood out in the corners of his eyes and his face bore an expression of woe seldom seen except over open graves."

And so forth. Only later did I realize how blessed I was to be working for the *Sun* in London. No other paper would have tolerated such a cavalier approach to covering the seat of the empire or put up with a reporter who believed that the work should also be fun for the reader. It was obvious, though, that with Buck in charge in Baltimore and with Washington—

the White House!—ahead of me, I was in the happiest
of all possible situations.

What happened at that moment was right out of my
wildest childhood fantasy about Cousin Edwin. *The
New York Times* came knocking at my door.

20

Fathers

A month before leaving London, the mail brought a letter from James Reston. His name was typed on the envelope under fancy lettering that said "The New York Times Washington Bureau." It was a thrilling envelope to look at, and I spent a lot of time enjoying the pleasure of looking at it before slitting it open. Getting a letter from James Reston was even more exciting than getting a letter from James Cagney would have been. I didn't want to spoil it by opening it too soon and discovering it was only a form letter asking for ten dollars to help support the Old Reporters' Home.

Scotty Reston was the most exciting man in American journalism. I didn't know much about *The New York Times,* but I knew that much. Like everybody in journalism, I knew he was called Scotty because Scotland was where he was born. I knew his parents brought him to America briefly in infancy, then took him back to Scotland until he was eleven years old, knew he'd gone to a Big Ten college somewhere in the Middle West, knew he played golf, knew he had worked for the Cincinnati Reds baseball team.

All this had been in the news magazines recently when the *Times* made him chief of its Washington bureau. He was journalism's shining new star, the man of the future at *The New York Times*, and, so, a celebrity whose career had been reported as fully as an up-and-coming politician's. Even in faraway London, heavily absorbed in myself, I'd been excited to learn the *Times* had given Reston its top Washington job. Maybe a new age had dawned at the *Times*, a paper where dull, plodding earnestness had become such a tradition that *Time* magazine referred to it with a reverential sneer as "the good gray *Times*."

Good grayness was not my idea of what Americans wanted in a newspaper, and maybe Reston's promotion meant the *Times* was tired of it, too. With people like Buck Dorsey taking over at the *Sun* and Scotty Reston moving up at the *Times*, things were looking up for the business. The stories about Reston suggested he had a romantic touch of the old-fashioned, swashbuckling, cutthroat reporter. He wrote a lean, punchy English that was a model of clarity and spiced it with wit and sass. Like Hildy Johnson and Walter Burns of *The Front Page*, he had a zealot's passion for scooping the opposition.

He also had a genius for saying a great deal in a tight space, as I learned when I finally opened his letter:

"This is just a note to tell you how much I have admired some of the dispatches you have sent from London. I was told that you were coming home soon, and I should like very much to have a talk with you. I don't know whether you are wedded to the *Sun*, but, in any event, I should like to meet you when you get back."

Interpreting this didn't take much skill at reading between the lines.

"I assume he may be thinking of offering me a job with the *Times*," I wrote my mother. "If so, I'd probably be a sap to turn it down, as the NY *Times* Washington office is just about the summit of everybody's

James B. Reston as chief of the *Times* Washington Bureau in 1954 (*New York Times*)

journalistic ambition. Anyhow it is flattering to have the *Times* approach me about coming to work for them. Even if it doesn't pan out."

"Flattering" was not quite the word I was looking for. "Eerie" would have been more accurate. After those boyish fantasies of being sought out by the *Times,* then standing revealed before Edwin as my mother's avenger, if not "eerie" it was a hilarious stroke of irony. As always, my mother showed no undue excitement:

"I was happy to get your letter, especially the news that someone else has noted your writing ability. It may be just the break you need. Anyway, we will be knowing before too long."

With which, she changed the subject. At times like this she could be infuriating. ". . . may be just the break you need." As though she thought I still needed a break. She was maddening.

Here I was, sitting on top of the world, headed to the White House, publicly hailed by Buck Dorsey as the greatest thing since Tom O'Neill, a tantalizing letter in my pocket from the magnificent Scotty Reston, and she still thought I needed a break. It was impossible to succeed enough to satisfy this woman.

Well, she had been through the wars, and probably didn't really ever expect any good news, and was afraid I'd be lulled by an early triumph or two and let ambition burn out too soon. Her letter was a way of saying, all right, things are looking up, you may still make something of yourself, but don't count your chickens before they're hatched.

Her next letter showed that the old Depression worry about money still haunted her. It was all very fine, the fancy international travel, gaudy titles like London correspondent and White House correspondent, praise from big shots, all well and good. But what about money? She had obviously been thinking about Reston and the *Times,* but her letter did not mention it. Instead, she had E. P. Kavanaugh in mind. In my days as a union agitator in the *Sun* newsroom, the financial meanness of the *Sun* was embodied in E. P. Kavanaugh, the company's business manager whose genius for making inflammatory comments had been invaluable for building union morale.

"While dusting your books last week," my mother wrote, "I found a communication from Kavanaugh, in which he stated for the benefit of the union paper that, 'A man who could make more money elsewhere was a sucker to stay on the *Sun,*' and it occurred to me that you might do well to remember that statement in case you got a better offer from another source."

In plainer English, I would be a fool to let sentimental feelings of loyalty tie me to the *Sun* if the *Times* offered bigger money. She made no mention of the *Times* as Edwin's paper and the sentimental satisfaction she might gain if I were to follow those colossal footsteps in service to all the news that was fit to print. In fact, she had mentioned Edwin only once in all the dozens and dozens of letters she wrote to London. It was as though she were determined to stop reminding me of the Edwin connection.

The one slip had occurred months ago after I'd written her about meeting Drew Middleton, the *Times* correspondent newly assigned to London.

"Mr. Drew Middleton might be an interesting contact over here in case the *Sun* has nothing interesting when you get back to Baltimore," she wrote back. "Did you ask him if he knew Edwin James? What a silly question, but I wrote it down before I thought."

With three sentences, Reston had created a complication that was both delightful and painful. I wrote back right away. Well, I was not "wedded" to the *Sun,* but I was very happy there, I said, but . . .

I was full of buts, and they disclosed a mind that was already filling with thoughts of treachery to Buck Dorsey. Happy though I was with the *Sun,* I replied to Reston, I would certainly like to meet him, and would get in touch after arriving in Washington.

The voice of the secretive plotter surfaced in the letter reporting all this to my mother:

"Don't mention this around to anybody as I don't want it to get back to the *Sun* or get around generally that I am toying with the idea of going elsewhere. It might be a good bargaining point at the *Sun,* if nothing else, but I want to handle it my own way."

It took many years for me to understand the bad conscience Reston's letter caused me. Rather late in life, when my own children were grown, I became aware that when they were growing up I had not been a very good father. Not a particularly bad father, at least no worse than most, I suppose. Just not a very good father. At this time people were having smaller families, maybe just one precious baby rather late in life, and men were working hard at being good fathers. My own sons had children by now, and were wonderful fathers, or so it seemed. It made me realize how different I had been at fatherhood.

Well, there were a lot of possible explanations for my shortcomings. Children were plentiful in the 1950s, and you took them for granted, loving them dearly to be sure, but not giving them the royal attention children naturally got later, after babies became such rarities.

Then there was the tremendous prosperity of the 1950s, so different from the relatively hard times that overtook the next generation. The country was so rich in the Fifties. So rich. A typical American family could afford three children, a house, two cars, three weeks at the seashore, a television set, and meat seven nights a week, all on a single wage earner's income. As in our case, the wage earner was usually the husband and father. I'd come of age in this astounding prosperity when a husband's role was to go to the office and become a success while the wife's job was to get the children born and smartened up for a really good college. Men from this world obviously wouldn't give fatherhood the priority, the energy, the study, and the seriousness it required.

There were plenty of excuses like this, none of them quite persuasive to me. Then one day I had a letter from a man, a stranger, with whom I'd had a brief conversation. About what, I couldn't even remember, but his letter got off onto father-son relationships and the rifts between fathers and children that keep them from knowing each other. Something in its tone produced a moment of inner light, a recognition that had escaped me until that moment. I wrote back. It was an extremely personal letter to send to a stranger, but of course it was a letter written to myself, telling me something so simple that the wonder was I hadn't always known it:

"My father's dying when I was very young created the obvious problems we all read about when we first learn to spell psychology. I first invented him, using little more than a handful of memories so fragmented they were like strobe-light freeze frames in the theater.

"Later I began casting about for surrogates. As I settled into journalism I took my father figures from the older men along the way—editors, executives, always authority figures, never reporters; reporters are footloose, irresponsible corsairs according to the newspaper myth of my youth. One wanted to be a reporter. They were the romantic devils. But one would not have wanted a reporter for a father. So I tended toward bosses.

"Rather late in the day, I realized that I had been a somewhat inferior father. Looking back on events, I realized that I had never been much interested in being a father. Of course I loved the children, but nowadays I see fathers whose lives are to some extent devoted to careers in fatherhood. They study the role, live it as a role and take pride in doing it well, suffer when they do it inadequately.

"It never occurred to me to take fatherhood so seriously. Though I had children, I remained a son while my children were growing up. Offhand I don't know when I finally quit searching for a father. But I did, and I slowly and quietly realized that I had turned into the father figure I'd spent my life seeking, and that I wasn't cutting a very good one for my children. I am still not very good at it. The role doesn't come naturally to me. I feel like an impostor, and I laugh privately at myself faking it. Being eternal son was better."

I was on my third surrogate father when Reston wrote. The first was Ed Young, whom I had loved immediately. He was father as best man in the business, the grown-up version of the father who could lick any other father on the block. The second was Gerry Fay, the father as dazzler, a man to make a son's eyes sparkle with delight at his erudition, charm, sophistication, wit, and power to command other good men.

The third, of course, was Buck Dorsey, and I felt bound to him more tightly than I ever did to Ed or Gerry, possibly because the relationship had grown so slowly. It had passed through several of the stages common in father-son relationships. When I first came to the *Sun,* he had been fierce, remote Mr. Dorsey, the figure of ultimate power. He had been the teacher explaining how to do things right, lecturing me on good taste and bad. He had been the beneficent bestower of good things, presenting me with the London bureau. And finally he had become an older friend and companion who confided in me and might even be preparing me to inherit his mantle at the *Sun.*

About all this, of course, I was extremely secretive, never letting on by word or gesture that I had laid private claims on these men who, as it turned out, all had sons of their own blood and would doubtless have been irritated and embarrassed to learn that my respect, admiration, and affection for them were expressions of my secret yearning to be the eternal son.

None of the three, surely, would have been more irritated than Buck, who would probably have found it in inexpressibly bad taste. There was plenty of evidence that Buck liked me well enough, and even that he planned a bright future for me at the *Sun.* After "a long ginny conversation" with Buck in Baltimore, Brad Jacobs, who was to succeed me in London, reported:

"I learned nothing worthwhile except that he has a very high opinion of you. He clings to the notion that Tom O'Neill is the best reporter in the world but, with that one possible exception, he figures you for doing the best London job he ever saw."

Yet, despite my feeling toward Buck, and his for me, it had taken only three sentences from Reston to tempt me to betray him. In business affairs like this, I later was told, there can be no such thing as betrayal, and such talk shows a weakness for melodrama and false sentimentality. Still, this father-son business in which I was secretly engaged made it painful to think of disappointing Buck by playing the ingrate and walking out on the wonderful White House assignment he had arranged for me.

There was another complication. As a gloomy Protestant, I knew that an unpleasant price must be exacted for all this success. As the time in London ran out, I began to realize vaguely that I had made a bad choice in so eagerly saying yes to Washington. Turning down Buck's offer of Washington and asking for another year or two in London was impossible for a young man as greedy for success as I was. In the end, I would eventually have to leave London anyhow, and the chance at Washington might be gone. If you were going to make something of yourself, if you wanted to amount to something, you had to jump when opportunity beckoned. Still, I sensed that the best of times was over.

"It's hard to realize that we have only six weeks left here," I wrote my mother. "We've really had a glorious time and it's going to be heartbreaking to face up to the fact that it is ended once and for all."

*   *   *

The night before sailing, Mimi and I had a farewell dinner with Gerry and Alice Fay that lasted two bottles of wine too long. To make the dinner party, we had to suspend packing. When we got home after midnight, we were not interested in packing. When we awoke with throbbing heads, only three hours remained before the boat train left for Southampton, and we discovered we had far more unpacked goods than we had suitcases for. A desperate early-morning tour of secondhand shops around railroad stations turned up an ancient trunk at the last possible minute. We threw in all the unpacked goods it could hold, left the rest scattered on the floor, and at the last possible moment set out for Waterloo Station.

At the last possible moment we flung ourselves, children, and luggage aboard. The train was exactly like the one that had brought me up to London in the fog with the man who hated America. Now it reminded me of a thousand things I was going to miss about England, and as it sped toward Southampton on a beautiful June morning, Mimi and I drank a final pot of tea while feeling melancholy, uneasy about the future, excited about going home, and hung over.

21

Hagerty

The White House was a serious mistake.

Dewey Fleming took me over there on a hot day at the end of July. Dewey was chief of the *Sun* bureau, an old-timer at the top of his form, wise about government and politics, calm, self-assured, and gentle.

"It's a job that's usually given to older men," he said. "It doesn't involve a lot of activity."

What he meant was that it was a rest cure for the weary. It took me a couple of days to understand that.

"But it's a good place to start learning your way around Washington," he said. "If you start with Congress you've got several hundred people to worry about. At the White House, there's only one."

The *Sun* bureau was on the twelfth floor of the National Press Building. The Treasury was one block west, and the White House occupied the block on the other side of the Treasury. It was an exciting walk, and when we rounded the Treasury onto Pennsylvania Avenue and the view opened out to become the White House, I was exhilarated by the glory of it. I had walked past the White House before, but this time I was going to walk through the gates, go inside, and be part of the great events that happened there.

Coming down from New York, I'd stayed in Baltimore with my mother, and, always goading me to stay dissatisfied, she had said, "Well, Russ, if you work hard at this White House job you might be able to make something of yourself." On this lovely July morning, looking through the fence past the great spreading shade trees and seeing that beautiful white façade with the high portico and serene windows, I could imagine no finer goal to strive for than a chance to work in this noble place.

In very short time I was to discover it was a reporter's graveyard.

We went in at the northwest gate after Dewey showed the guards his White House pass and said we were expected. The guards accepted my driver's license as adequate identification. We walked down the path to the West Wing, went into the lobby, and were admitted to the office of the press secretary to the President of the United States. It was a small office for such a magnificent title. There were a couple of comfortable armchairs, a sofa, a fireplace and mantel, elegant drapes on floor-to-ceiling windows overlooking the front lawn, and a big desk with a very big swivel chair, which contained James C. Hagerty.

I had heard of Hagerty. His name was on the front page of most American newspapers almost as often as the president's. Today he was in his shirt-sleeves. So famous, yet such a regular guy, I thought, in his shirt-sleeves with his feet on the desk. He looked like a tough Irish street kid, the kind who used to threaten to bust me in the teeth because he didn't like my looks. Reddish-brown hair, square jaw, thin lips that could set in a hard line or open into a big, boyish grin. Not very tall, but athletic-looking through the shoulders. Eyeglasses with thick lenses.

Later I came to admire Hagerty and even like him a little, though not too much. If you were part of the White House press corps, the place was too much like

a cage and Hagerty too much like your keeper. He
was good at what he did, and you had to admire that.
Maybe he was the best possible White House press
secretary. Though a wonder at what he did, what he
did was aimed at making his boss look good, and the
reporters, of course, weren't there to make his boss
look good, but to tell the public what was going on.

After the smiling, handshaking, and small talk were
over, Dewey introduced me to a couple of reporters
who were lounging out in the lobby, then left me
alone with American journalism's dream assignment.
White House correspondent! I was White House correspondent for the *Baltimore Sun*!

I was considerably deflated when I got back to the
Sun offices at four-thirty that afternoon. Until that
day, I had been too enchanted by the glory of being
called White House correspondent to wonder what the
work was like. It was a shock at day's end to discover
that there hadn't been any work to speak of. Nor was
there very much work in prospect. The main item of
discussion among the White House reporters all day
had been the president's forthcoming vacation. As
soon as Congress started its summer recess, I learned,
the president intended to get out of Washington for a
month or two of golfing and fishing in Colorado.
White House correspondents, of course, had to follow
him. My foolish ambition had trapped me in a backwater with a future full of inactivity.

By the end of the week I felt sad enough to cry.
Surely I had made the worst decision of my life. With
half an ounce of good sense, I would have said no
to Buck's White House offer and pleaded for a long
extension of the London tour. Instead, I had given
up the endless fascinations of London for this bland
pudding of a city with the climate of a swamp and the
soul of a one-horse town. I had swapped the freedom
to roam one of the earth's great cities and report what-

ever struck my fancy. And what had I got in return? A glamorous job title which entitled me to sit in a confined space listening to my colleagues breathe.

The prospect of eternal idleness was depressing enough for somebody who wanted to make something of himself. Even more crushing to the spirit was the sense of claustrophobia that came with the White House territory. You gave up the reporter's freedom to roam once you walked through the gate and accepted a compact under which you were penned into a small area policed as tightly as a prison exercise yard.

Inside the White House, reporters were confined to the lobby, the pressroom, and Hagerty's offices. The only people you were likely to see in these areas were Hagerty, other reporters, and such White House visitors as Hagerty wanted you to see. Want to talk to somebody on the White House staff? Ask Hagerty to make an appointment for you. And remember: This is a tight ship, as tight as they come. Anybody you talk to is expected to report back to Hagerty about the conversation. That's right, it's not likely anybody on the staff will tell you anything you couldn't find out faster by asking Hagerty.

Anyhow, the one really important staff man, Sherman Adams, the one you'd love to talk to, never talks to anybody from the press. Oh, once or twice a year, he may go to a private, off-the-record dinner with the Brahmins of the Washington press corps. Arthur Krock of the *Times,* Roscoe Drummond of the *Herald Trib,* Dick Wilson of the Cowles papers. Everybody talks privately now and then to the Brahmins, those men as august as popes, who move through the city looking so wise, such enviable grandees, so full of secrets that they are, alas, sworn not to disclose.

Yes, Sherman Adams may speak to men like these. This is a small town where the lions recognize the existence only of other lions. If you are not a lion, but merely a glamorous White House correspondent, you may cover the White House every day for a year and never lay eyes on Sherman Adams, or have physical proof that he exists. This is a tight ship.

Some of the correspondents had covered the 1952 election campaign. Everybody gets chummy with the press on the campaign. Get a good-fellow reputation on the campaign and maybe the reporters will give you the edge in the paper someday when it counts. So, having covered the campaign, some of the correspondents had established confidential relationships with people inside this sealed White House cocoon, though none of them seemed to profit much from their campaign friendships. This was a tight ship. After the *Time* man and the *Newsweek* man had their private meeting with old campaign pals on the White House staff, their magazines were enriched with anecdotes illustrating the president's firmness, decisiveness, energy, alertness, glowing good health, zest for living, and a thousand other gee-whiz qualities. It was a tight, tight ship.

Not having been around for the 1952 campaign, I realized almost immediately that we were all prisoners to Hagerty's version of the news. Any greenhorn with swashbuckling ideas about eluding Hagerty's control and wandering around the White House offices knocking on doors was swiftly disillusioned the instant he put a toe out of the prisoner's box and found himself face to face with an extremely serious young man wearing a business suit with a pistol bulge. The Oval Office was situated only a few feet from the reporters' lounging area. Secret Service men were everywhere.

Seeing how things were, I resigned myself temporarily to the rest-home quiet of the lobby. It was a large, windowless, gloomy, rectangular space generously furnished with soft leather sofas and armchairs. Several oil canvases hung on the walls, including a large painting of Lincoln and his Cabinet. At the far end, an open passageway led to the Oval Office. Visitors who didn't want to face reporters could enter from a side door on West Executive Avenue and scurry along this corridor before the press could get to them.

For people who didn't want the press to notice them coming and going, there were many secret routes where constant traffic flowed to the Oval Office unseen by reporters. Cabinet officers, the Joint Chiefs of Staff, the director of the Central Intelligence Agency—these were the people whose White House visits might tip reporters to real news. They came and went constantly, but the White House correspondents were almost always the last to know about it.

As news makers, most of the people who passed through the lobby so the reporters could have a crack at them were, in the words of Jerry Greene of the New York *Daily News,* "not worth a paragraph back in the truss ads."

Usually they were milk-and-graham-cracker celebrities who had never been touched by scandal, nor were likely to be: a successful football coach who made his players pray before every game, an entertainer beloved by the whole darned family, a rich man who had given away money without expecting a dime of profit in return, a publisher who had called for a rebirth of patriotism, a famous evangelist. For variety, Thanksgiving brought the farmer who had grown the biggest turkey or pumpkin in the farm belt, and the opening of money-raising charity pleas brought beautiful children suffering from dreadful afflictions.

On a typical day there might be two or three lobby interviews to give lounging reporters the illusion they were working. The content of these interviews rarely varied: The president looked absolutely wonderful, he was doing a magnificent job, America was lucky to have him there, he was a great man, this was the most wonderful day in the caller's life, and so on.

Reporters who couldn't stand the excitement of the lobby could retreat to the pressroom. This was a light, airy space with big cheerful windows on the northwest corner of the West Wing. Long afterward, in the Nixon years, the press corps was ejected from this choice location to make room for Henry Kissinger and sent down to eternal night in the White House cellar; but in 1954 it was the site of a more or less nonstop game of nickel-a-card fan-tan played on dingy, shopworn desks to the jangle of telephones. Little else of consequence ever went on there.

The lobby may have been a desert for news, but with its comfortable sofas and chairs, it was a wonderful place for reading, dozing, or just sitting around chewing the fat. I passed many comatose hours in those cushions working on crossword puzzles, deploring the baseball incompetence of the Washington Senators, and listening to assorted White House correspondents breathing softly and regularly over paperback mysteries which drooped in nearly lifeless hands.

Besides covering traffic through the lobby, the reporters were briefed twice a day by Hagerty, morning and afternoon. There were rarely more than a dozen of us. We stood around his desk while a secretary passed out mimeographed announcements of routine news: appointments to this and that, tomorrow's scheduled callers, resignations of minor functionaries, presidential statements on the importance of National Rutabaga Week, transcripts of the president's welcoming remarks to the visiting prime minister of Zippity Zap. Sometimes there was even something close to news.

Over Hagerty's desk we traded banter, asked a few cheeky questions to which we didn't expect answers, and a few serious ones, to which Jim said, "No comment," or "I'll check on that and get back to you."

We all called him "Jim." To him we were "Smitty," "Marvin," "Bob," "Larry," "Andy," "Eddie," "Chuck," "Ray," "Russ." Everything was on a first-name basis. It was a small, exclusive club of professionals. The members were not required to like each other especially, but everybody was supposed to behave by the rules. It was civilized.

So was the routine. At lunchtime, Hagerty announced a "lid." This meant no news would be released until after the lunch hour. "Lids" were faithfully respected, though not even Hagerty could stop the world from turning until after lunch, so the wire services kept people around anyhow. For a wire service, being twenty seconds behind the opposition reporting a big story could be a catastrophe.

Normally the White House press consisted of maybe fifteen reporters, three photographers, a newsreel cameraman or two, and a couple of sound technicians for radio and newsreel film. Television technologists, who later turned White House coverage into heavy industry, were still undreamed of in 1954. CBS and NBC, however, kept full-time reporters on hand, covering for both radio and television. The United States Information Agency also assigned a regular reporter. The other outfits with full-time reporters were the *Chicago Tribune, New York Times,* New York *Daily News, New York Herald Tribune, Washington Star, Washington Post, Newsweek, Time,* and *U.S. News and World Report.*

The most important members of the group were the three reporters for the Associated Press, United Press, and International News Service. These three wire services fed into every newspaper and broadcast outlet in the country, including the *Baltimore Sun.* This meant I didn't have to waste time covering routine material because Baltimore could pick it up from the A.P. Theoretically, this freed me to work on the kind of stories you couldn't get from a wire service. Well, theoretical was one thing, actual was something else. The way Hagerty had the White House buttoned up, the kind of stories you couldn't get from a wire service couldn't be got. It was a tight ship.

I was sitting on a lobby sofa with Joe Loftus one day discussing Hagerty. Joe was the *New York Times* man on the White House that summer, though his regular beat was labor. He looked the way the *New York Times* man ought to look, I thought. There was something stolid and dependable in the way he stood, and there wasn't a fancy touch anywhere on him. He was middle-aged, his hair was going gray, and he wore it crew-cut. His eyeglasses were plain, no-nonsense steel rims. His suit was plain, square, off-the-rack, and probably washable. He looked slightly grumpy and seemed to be standing apart from the dullness of White House routine, as though he considered it silly and would prefer people not to know he was part of it. He struck me as an honest man set down in a slightly phoney world.

"Hagerty?" he replied, in answer to my question. "Well, he's the enemy of course."

As we talked, I became aware of someone approaching and glanced up. So did Loftus.

"Hi, Scotty," he said. Then to me:

"You know Scotty Reston?"

There was an old-fashioned, boyish look about him. With black hair, slightly curly, and a wide mouth that smiled readily, and a brow so serene that it seemed never to have scowled, at first glance he looked as if he might have stepped down from an old photograph over the velveteen settee in a 1912 parlor. The eyes told a rather different story. He had the shrewdest, wisest, most disconcerting gaze I had ever seen on an honest man. Old-fashioned or not, he was the most self-confident person I had ever met, and I liked him instantly.

It was love at first sight. Only forty-four years old, he was just a shade too young to be my father. A big brother perhaps. During the talk that followed I was so dazzled that later I could remember nothing that passed between us.

22

Jumper

That fall I took the train over to Baltimore for the last lunch with Buck Dorsey. On the phone I'd told him there was an important matter to talk about, and he said something like, "Why don't you come over here and we'll have lunch?" So I found myself back in Hasslinger's looking at another martini.

I had become a two-fisted drinker. Like heavy smoking, it was one of the things newspapermen were supposed to do in those days, and I drank because it was the thing to do, not because I needed it. This day, however, I needed it and welcomed the martini because it was a drink that did its work fast.

While waiting for the gin to give me courage, I made small talk about the president, telling Buck what Eisenhower was up to and what he was really like. Seven years ago, when he was awesome Mr. Dorsey, I'd sat amazed in his office while he asked somebody in the Washington bureau what Truman was up to. It had seemed the most exciting thing in the world. Now I was telling him what Eisenhower was up to, and it didn't matter, it was just White House lobby wisdom about Eisenhower trying to pretend he wanted the Republican Congress reelected despite the agony it had given him the past two years.

I was careful not to go to a second drink before I told Buck what I'd come to tell him. In the grip of the second martini, solid ground quickly turned treacherous, and I didn't want to say anything false or foolish or maudlin.

What Buck expected to hear, I never guessed. Maybe he thought I was trying to get up the nerve to ask for more money and wondered why I didn't come right out with a demand, the way Tom O'Neill would have done. He obviously knew I needed more money because he had got the company to give me a twenty-dollar raise on moving to Washington. Twenty dollars was a big salary boost for the *Sun,* but even that left me relatively poor compared to the London life with its easy expense accounts, office car, and $250 monthly living allowance.

Whatever he may have been expecting, he showed absolutely no surprise when I said Scotty Reston had offered me a job in the *Times* Washington bureau and I intended to take it. Telling it was painful. When I got it out, I couldn't let it go quietly, but launched into a meandering, apologetic explanation: how dearly I loved the *Sun,* there was no newspaper to match it for excellence, certainly not the *Times,* it was the hardest decision I'd ever had to make, I hoped Buck understood that I wasn't leaving because I thought the *Times* was a better paper than the *Sun,* or even as good. . . .

Buck listened, poker-faced. He was a gambling man, after all. A gambling man didn't let his face betray his mind. I was aware that I was babbling.

"Would a little more money help?" he asked.

Absolutely not! Money had nothing to do with this. I tried to suggest that if it were only a question of money I wouldn't dream of leaving the *Sun* because a man didn't walk out on the most important things in his life for mere money. There was a more compelling reason. . . .

This may even have been true, but it's still hard to know for sure. I felt so guilty about walking out on Buck that I had persuaded myself I was doing it not for shabby money reasons, but in response to a summons from some mystic power. For the first time, I told Buck about Cousin Edwin. Despite the family tie, I told him, I had never approached the *Times* and asked for a job, but now that the *Times* had come to me, I felt duty bound to fulfill a family destiny.

This must have sounded strained and improbable to Buck, because he didn't take up the invitation to argue against the mystic power of destiny, but returned the conversation to a more rational level. He was flattered, he said, that *The New York Times* wanted to hire his people. They knew the best paper to look at when they wanted quality. It showed Reston had good judgment, and though he didn't want to lose me, he felt honored in a way, because the *Times* was a great newspaper.

"Tom O'Neill says it's the only real paper," Buck said, "though I don't agree entirely."

It was the only time I ever knew Buck to be in even partial disagreement with Tom O'Neill.

We were well into the second martini when Buck made the only argument he was ever to make for my staying with the *Sun*. He pointed out that if I made the switch, I would be sacrificing a place near the top of the tree at the *Sun* for a relatively minor spot in a very large outfit. In a way, it would be like starting over again. It might be harder than I imagined.

"At *The New York Times* you're going to be a little fish in a very big pond," he said. "With the *Sun* you're a big fish in a small pond."

Come on now, the *Sun* wasn't exactly a little pond,

I said. It might not be a gigantic organization like the *Times,* but . . .

"The question," he said, "is, do you want to be a big fish in a little pond, or a little fish in a big pond?"

We went to a third martini, and there was more talk about fish and ponds, but it didn't change things, and Buck probably didn't expect it to. He probably realized my mind had been made up when I phoned him. When lunch ended we were surprisingly clear-headed and making sense, though not having the good time we'd had with gin in the past. Finally we talked about when to cut the cord. Buck hoped I could stay on through Election Day to cover Eisenhower's campaigning. I said of course and we parted outside on the street after Buck said, "If you ever want to change your mind, just let me know."

I had known him seven years. He didn't come back into my life until another seven years went by.

It was the tedium of White House vacationing that persuaded me to accept Reston's offer. In our first meeting back in Washington, unable to make up my mind, I'd told Scotty I had emotional ties to the *Sun* and asked for time to think things through; then left Mimi and the children in Washington to get settled in a rental house off Connecticut Avenue, and went off for what turned out to be an eight-week presidential vacation in Denver.

There the White House correspondents were quartered luxuriously at the Brown Palace Hotel. Most of us breakfasted largely and leisurely on fresh trout, huge melons, waffles, elegant egg dishes, and anything else that took a long time to eat. Some golfed in the afternoon, some napped, some caught up on their reading. Bob Donovan of the *Herald Tribune,* a canny veteran of presidential vacations, worked on a scholarly book about presidential assassins. There was a pressroom at Lowry Air Force Base where the president and a small staff had office space. In the morning there were usually a couple of reporters waiting for Dr. Walter Tkach, the deputy White House physician, to give them vitamin B_{12} shots for hangovers. For professional company and the illusion of being close to the action, I spent a lot of time at Lowry playing fantan and Scrabble.

Day after day, week after week, we wrote stories about the president playing golf, signing bills, and reacting. Jim Hagerty made sure the president did plenty of reacting while on vacation. The president might not be doing much, but Hagerty kept him in the news by having him react to people who were.

IKE PRAISES STEVENSON E.D.C. STAND was a story that got me twenty inches of type starting on the front page. Story: Hagerty said Eisenhower was "delighted" with a diplomatic message Adlai Stevenson carried to France. EISENHOWER PLEASED WITH TEXAS RESULT ran for ten inches. Story: Hagerty said "the President is highly pleased" with primary election results in Texas.

There was also a regular trickle of presidential visitors available for interviews. Frank Leahy, a onetime Notre Dame football coach, came out of Eisenhower's office to report, "I think every one of us ought to get down on our knees and thank God we have him." Politicians emerged saying they had talked vital political strategy with the president. Generals came out declaring that the president believed in strong national defense. Vice-President Nixon showed up to give "wholehearted approval" to everything the president was doing in a congressional political campaign in which the president, at this stage, was doing nothing.

I used a lot of the *Sun*'s money wiring such trivia to Baltimore by Western Union. My first instinct was not to bother with it, figuring Baltimore could use the

President Eisenhower talking to the White House press at Denver vacation headquarters

A.P. story if any of it seemed worth printing. All the other reporters, however, were sending at least one story a day, and some were sending two and three. It seemed sensible for a new man on the beat to do as the old-timers did.

The theory was that since the home office was paying expenses for a long vacation, you should at least pretend you were working. So you filed the trivial routine. If you didn't file it, you wouldn't file anything at all because there was nothing but trivial routine to report. When President Eisenhower vacationed, he vacationed with all his might and main. The story of this Homeric vacationing was quickly told:

The president and Mamie had settled into his mother-in-law's modest, gray-brick house on Lafayette Street. There were blue canvas awnings on the front porch. His mother-in-law was Mrs. John S. Doud. The president called her "Min." The neighborhood was not notably flossier than Marydell Road, where canvas porch awnings were also part of the summer decor, and Mrs. Doud's house was not much bigger than my mother's.

Modern presidents have got us used to thinking that men so great must always be housed in sprawling grandeur, but in Eisenhower's time the small, middle-class ordinariness of Lafayette Street did not seem remarkable enough to rate more than a sentence near the end of my first-day arrival story. Remembering how much racket Uncle Gene could make in a house that size and how hard it had been for Herb to get his rest, I often wondered whether Ike, like Herb, didn't sometimes feel like climbing the walls. Information about domestic relations inside Mrs. Doud's house, alas, was impossible to come by.

Daytime the president usually spent on the golf course at Cherry Hills Country Club. Some evenings he stayed at home with Mamie and her mother. Others he played bridge in a penthouse suite at the Brown Palace with some of the country's richest corporate leaders. With his military sense of rank, Eisenhower felt socially comfortable only with men at his own level of importance. These men, who ran giant oil corporations and companies like Coca-Cola, qualified by Eisenhower's measure. Larry Burd, the *Chicago Tribune*'s correspondent, christened them "Ike's millionaires" in new lyrics he wrote for the old Depression song "I've Got a Pocket Full of Dreams":

> We're Ike's millionaires,
> We're Wall Street's bulls and bears,
> And we've got our pockets full of dough . . .
> We're Triple-A in Dun and Bradstreet,
> We've got fleets of Cadillacs,

And we calculate
We're overweight
In income tax . . .

A White House reporter's isolation from the president was as complete in these lazy vacation weeks as it had been in the no-nonsense atmosphere of the White House. We were permitted to watch him tee off at Cherry Hills only once while the photographers took his picture. If you kept close watch on his office at Lowry Air Force Base, you might see him coming and going, but it wasn't very rewarding. His manner was polite and correct, but there was always a cool distance between him and us. There was no striving to be a regular guy. He was always the five-star general; we were always enlisted men, and not very heroic ones either. The only regular White House correspondent I ever heard him call by his first name was Merriman Smith of United Press, and his pronunciation suggested he thought Smitty's first name was "Mariam."

I had come on the White House beat thinking I would enjoy some personal contact with the great man himself. Why not? Everybody had seen dozen of pictures of White House reporters gathered around Franklin Roosevelt's desk and chatting with Harry Truman as he took his morning walks around Washington. It was gall to discover that under Eisenhower a reporter was little more than a courtier swelling the presidential scene. In a way, I suppose, Jim Hagerty was trying to help us all save face by providing a never-ending stream of junk news with which to justify our existence.

After we had been in Colorado a while we were ready to accept anything that could pass for news. When the president retreated from Denver for a week's fishing at Fraser, up on the far slope of the Continental Divide, I admitted our desperation in a piece for the *Sun*. Herbert Hoover, then in his eightieth year, had joined Eisenhower up there, and a squad of reporters with nothing to do and nothing to write were leaning on Hagerty for help.

"What did the president eat? How did he cook? How many fish did he catch? Did he play bridge with Hoover? How does he relax when he's not in the trout stream? What do the two call each other—Herb and Ike, Dwight and Herbert, or are there two 'Mr. Presidents'?

"Hagerty, wearing a New York Yankees' baseball cap, a wool shirt, blue jeans and looking in desperate need of some relaxation for himself, was testy about such queries. First, he clamped a news blackout on the chow picture. There would be no reports on what was eaten for lunch, he decreed. The president was up here to relax and he was entitled to privacy.

" 'How's it going to stop him from relaxing if we print what he eats?' asked one man, but Hagerty was adamant. No chow releases. This put the press on his back, and a flurry of warm-tempered, mocking questions ensued. Did Hoover wear a 'Herbert Hoover' collar when he fished? Was it true that the President was feasting on smoked dove for breakfast?

"Hagerty relaxed and gave ground. President Eisenhower, he revealed, was doing a twenty-four-hour cooking job on a vegetable soup of his own recipe. . . ."

It was no secret that neither Hoover nor Eisenhower had much affection for the press, but somehow Hagerty, that wonderfully resourceful scoundrel who knew how to win the hearts of the reporters he exploited, got us into the ranch for a few minutes to see the two presidents together while the photographers took pictures.

Eisenhower, wearing natty sports attire, bore the invasion patiently, turning sirloins on a charcoal grill while the photographers worked. During the hubbub,

Hoover came out of the cabin wearing a gray, double-breasted suit, a wrinkled gray shirt with a necktie, and a tan straw hat. To most of us, Herbert Hoover was only a sad legend whose name evoked memories of sad, sad times, so it was worth the trip into the Rockies for the chance to hear him speak. And speak he did, about presidential privacy.

"Thirty years ago we used to believe there were only two occasions on which the American people would protect the privacy of the President. That was at prayer and fishing. I now detect"—and he turned to Eisenhower—"that you have lost that last one. The press no longer regards the privacy of the President when he's fishing. That is one of the degenerations of the last thirty years."

I thought Hoover was displaying a dry, ironic sense of humor appropriate for a basically silly situation. Most of the reporters couldn't see it, though. That business about our work being "one of the degenerations" was too close to the truth for comfort.

Late that summer Scotty Reston turned up at the Brown Palace and sat in on one of Hagerty's briefings. Afterward we went down to the coffee shop. He asked if I'd made up my mind.

I didn't say yes, and I didn't say no. I talked more than necessary, and what it meant was "Well . . ."

"If you're going to jump, jump," Reston said.

I thought, *Oh, oh! Sounds like his patience is running out. With all my delicate hesitating, maybe I'm throwing away a golden opportunity.*

I jumped.

Afterward he explained I would have to spend three months working in New York. Turner Catledge, the managing editor, insisted on that. Turner wanted all new correspondents to know their way around the home office. Reston said I would also have to be interviewed by Catledge, but needn't fear Catledge would veto me, the interview was just a formality. Funny, I hadn't thought about the managing editor having any say-so in all this. Mindlessly, I'd assumed Reston was supreme.

"Mimi, darling, I know there's no valid reason for sending you letters, but, as expected, I have nothing but time on my hands."

I was writing from a desk in *The New York Times* city room on West Forty-third Street. It was Sunday night, November 7, my first day in the newsroom Cousin Edwin had once ruled. The place was vast and bleak. Desks, aligned as neatly as stones in a military graveyard, stretched from Forty-third Street on my right to Forty-fourth Street on my left.

About halfway down the block several men in shirtsleeves were playing bridge. Here and there others were working crossword puzzles or browsing in newspapers. All newsrooms were quiet on Sundays, but the vastness of this one made its silence funereal. Distances were so great that the city desk had a microphone tied into loudspeakers for summoning reporters from remote corners. Now and then the quiet was broken by an amplified voice calling for Mr. Perlmutter, or Mr. Phillips, or Mr. Robinson to come to the city desk.

In my experience, reporters who sat around doing nothing didn't keep their jobs long, so I was writing to Mimi partly to look busy:

"Having read the *Times* word for word, through the ads, obituaries and classifieds, and having neglected to bring 'The Decline and Fall of the Roman Empire' with me, I'm at a complete loss for something to do, so will give you a blow-by-blow account of my first day with the NYT. Exceedingly bleak. I mean by that, having to sit in a city room all day with nothing to do."

Under the routine, I would spend five days in New York, then get two days off to be with Mimi and the children in Washington where we were renting a house, then go back to New York for another five days. I'd come up from Washington this first morning on the Pennsy.

"The train ride was sleepy. I bought the Sunday *Times,* but it kept putting me to sleep. I ate breakfast as soon as I got on in Washington and was finished by time we arrived in Baltimore, which was a mistake—eating too fast, I mean—since it put only forty miles of the trip behind me. . . ."

This was a letter from a man with a thousand hours to kill.

"In New York I checked bags at Penn Station and having ninety minutes to kill, strolled leisurely up to Times Square. It was a sunny, cold day and the streets, as usual on Sundays, were all but deserted, and you know how drab New York looks under strong light when there is no one about. I felt very unhappy, and went to Child's for lunch, which did nothing to raise my spirits. Then to the office, up to the third floor and to the city desk. I wouldn't have been altogether shocked if Caulfield had spun around in his chair and said, 'You've got the west side.' He didn't. Instead—what an efficient organization the *Times* is— one of multitudinous assistant city editors handed me my police card, keys to a locker, and a memo reminding me to meet the personnel director at one P.M. tomorrow for a two-hour interview."

Personnel director. This turned out to be a cheerful little man named Dick Burritt who was Turner Catledge's idea. Catledge had succeeded Cousin Edwin as managing editor, but, as I later discovered, his admiration for Edwin's management skills was very low. He judged Edwin had made a mess of the personnel situation, principally because he wouldn't lay a firm managerial hand on his correspondents, shake them vigorously, and remind them they had a boss in New York.

Catledge meant to change all that. He was already shaking correspondents vigorously and would have liked to shake Scotty Reston especially vigorously, but was apparently forbidden to do so. Apparently he couldn't even stop Reston from hiring his own people for the Washington bureau. He could, however, make Reston's new troops sit in the home office long enough to realize that there was a home office and that Catledge was its master.

"A kind man by the name of Murray Shumach gave me a guided tour of some of the building. National desk. Picture desk. Foreign desk. Wire room. Radio room. Composing room. Library. Morgue. Editorial writers' department. Etcetera. Hung around the city desk for a while. Nobody seemed to know what to do about me. Finally sat down at my desk and started reading the paper. Wrote two three-paragraph stories. Then a third-assistant editor from the foreign desk asked me to write three paragraphs from the handout of a North African lobbyist.

"That done, an assistant city editor invited me up to dinner. Nice cafeteria; mediocre food. I asked the editor I ate with how many people he had on the city staff. He seemed shocked at the question and didn't really seem to know himself, though he estimated about 175, 'if you include all the side departments that are nominally under the city desk.' Looking over the city room here, I can count about 175 desks."

The Catledge interview was pleasant enough. It was conducted in the big managing editor's office that had once been Edwin's. So here I was at last, just as I'd imagined in my childish revenge fantasy, except that I got there too late to catch Edwin.

Tall, florid, and beautifully custom-tailored, Catledge

didn't look like a managing editor. Buck Dorsey looked like a managing editor. Catledge looked like one of those southern senators who ran all the important committees on Capitol Hill and were always described as "powerful." He had bright button eyes set in a round face that was born to grin from ear to ear with the self-satisfaction of a cat that has just finished off the canary. He was from Mississippi, had one of the fast-talking southern accents, and was always described, quite correctly, as polished, courtly, and charming.

He had also been a top-drawer Washington political reporter during the New Deal and war years and knew what it was to be at ease with men who ran the Congress, men who ran for president, as well as with President Roosevelt himself.

Trying to look like a suave man of the world while facing him across Edwin's big desk, I was a child in the hands of a master but too young to realize it. He was so easy to talk to. I decided to impress him, so told him my mother was first cousin to the man who had occupied this very office.

"Mister James," Catledge said. Yes, he had worked with Mr. James for several years. Mr. James was a wonderful man. Then, Catledge was suddenly being confidential with me, talking to me like an old friend, like another man of the world with whom he could exchange gossip about the mighty.

Mr. James was a wonderful man, but he had made a serious mistake.

Really?

Yes, Mr. James had made a serious mistake when he let his own son, Michael, go to the Paris bureau.

Paris for Michael was a mistake, was it?

A serious mistake. It gave the Paris correspondent, C. L. Sulzberger, a hostage he could use to resist New

York's efforts to take control of the paper's foreign correspondents.

Catledge might just as well have been speaking in ancient Babylonian dialect because I hadn't the least notion what he was talking about. I didn't even know Edwin had a son, and the reference to what was obviously some antique and obscure piece of office politics was completely beyond me. I tried not to look baffled, though. I was flattered that the managing editor, the man who held Edwin's old job, this impressive man, so powerful, so polished, should confide deep company secrets to me. Secrets about the weakness of Cousin Edwin, for heaven's sake!

I tried to put on a face that looked wise, noncommittal, but gravely reflective, and Catledge gave me the ear-to-ear grin, stood up, pumped my hand again while maneuvering me out the door, and committed me to my three-month term in the newsroom.

The close of my first night's letter to Mimi said:

"Critique on the day: Depressing.

"I'll probably write you every night if this job maintains its searing pace."

It was Mimi who got me sprung before I'd served my full sentence in New York. Just before Christmas she got exasperated and phoned Reston. With two small children and a third due any day now, she was left alone in Washington to cope with the horrors of an American Christmas while I sat in the New York newsroom week after week reading Dostoyevsky. Reston must have heard desperation in her voice. A day or two later Frank Adams, the *Times* city editor, interrupted my reading with the news that I would be freed for good at two A.M. on Christmas morning.

At the last minute I had the nastiest experience of my newspaper life.

Christmas Eve fell on Friday that year. Around

eleven o'clock that night the wire services started moving bulletins about a bad airplane crash in Prestwick, Scotland. It was a big Boeing Stratocruiser. London to New York. It looked as if everyone on board had been killed.

About one o'clock in the morning we had a list of passengers. Four had New York addresses. Some ghoul on the city desk decided we could print the list if we could make sure the names and addresses of the New York passengers were correct. He handed me the list with orders to get busy on the phone.

All I had to do was find if there was a phone number for each address, dial it, tell whoever answered that the *Times* wanted to know if a person who spelled his name this particular way happened to live at this particular address. If the answer was yes, you asked if this particular person was expected home for Christmas aboard BOAC's night flight from London.

The first number I rang produced a sleepy feminine voice. She said yes, and yes, and yes, before her mind shook off sleep's cobwebs and she realized a phone call from the *Times* before dawn on Christmas morning could only be bad news.

"What's wrong? What's this about? Has something happened?"

"No, no. Just a routine check," I said, disconnecting before she could demand to know more.

It was cowardly and terrible, but all the other possibilities were worse.

Fortunately, the desk man behind this enterprise had already enlisted another reporter to check two of the four names. This left me only one to go. I spent a lot of time talking to the telephone company and finally came up with a phone number for the address, but not the name on the passenger list. A dedicated reporter would have phoned the number anyhow, but I never kidded myself that I was one of the great ones.

I told the city desk there wasn't any number, got a "Good night" and a "Merry Christmas" from the desk at two in the morning, and took a taxi down to Penn Station, where I drank coffee and nodded over the morning papers until the dawn train pulled out for Washington.

The seven weeks in New York hadn't been a complete waste of time. I had read a lot of Dostoyevsky after realizing that you weren't expected to work much at the *Times*. With so many to cover so little, a reporter improving his mind in the classics was a greater blessing to editors than the ambitious pest hanging around the desk asking for something to do.

The paper seemed comically overstaffed. Remembering nights at the *Sun* when we had half a dozen reporters to cover the whole city, I marveled at the swarms in the *Times* newsroom with nothing to do for days at a time. At the *Sun*, I had written two thousand words a night without feeling overworked. At the *Times*, writing a six-hundred-word story seemed to be considered a whole week's work. Some reporters never seemed to write anything.

Sander Vanocur, who worked there briefly before I came, was dismayed by the excess of manpower. As an American in London, he had done a little freelance work for the *Manchester Guardian* and had come to New York in hopes of getting back to Europe as a foreign correspondent. Catledge hired him, and he was given a desk so far back in the newsroom that he was practically in Sardi's restaurant. Catledge immediately forgot him.

Sitting there one night, feeling blue and forgotten and wondering how he had managed to get himself buried, Vanocur found his glum expression had attracted the sympathetic attention of sweet-tempered Meyer Berger. Berger was a superb reporter and the brightest ornament of the New York city staff, as well

as a gentleman and a historian. He had written a loving history of *The New York Times* and learned a
great deal about Adolph S. Ochs, the Tennesseean
who had bought the *Times* for a trifle and built it into
a colossus of journalism.

"Mister Vanocur," said Berger, "I know it looks
strange here with all these people sitting around playing bridge and doing crossword puzzles, but it's always
been this way since Mister Ochs's time. Mister Ochs
always liked to have enough people around to cover
the story when the *Titanic* sinks."

When I first sat down in that great sea of tedium,
I thought somebody at the *Times* was trying to make
me feel humble about working for the paper that
printed all the news that was fit to print. Everything
seemed aimed at making me feel like the smallest fish
in the biggest pond on earth.

For housing, I'd been put into the Dixie Hotel,
directly across Forty-third Street from the *Times* building. The Dixie had not yet achieved fleabag status,
but was working on it. In my first few days there, the
chambermaids finished off a fifth of whiskey I'd
brought from Washington. The lobby was heavily traf-
ficked by the kind of men who wore sunglasses at
midnight escorting dramatic women they had just met.
A far cry from my days of Savoy grandeur in London,
it made me suspect I was dispensable to the *Times*.

At the office, somebody occasionally remembered I
was there and asked me to do an obituary on a businessman dead in New Jersey, hold it to three paragraphs, please. Once I was sent to help cover a fire
on the East Side. It was out before I got there, but I
was reprimanded for taking a taxi instead of the subway. The craziness of it! A newspaper that kept a
hundred reporters on the payroll to do nothing bridled
at spending cab fare to cover a fire. Another night I

was allowed to do legwork for a reporter covering a political rally at Madison Square Garden.

These were jobs for kid reporters, but I quickly realized I'd be flattering myself if I supposed the *Times* was trying to haze me as the new boy on the block. This place was so big that I didn't even exist. With so many reporters on the staff, there just wasn't much for anybody to do. Things moved much more slowly here than at the *Sun.* Much more slowly. Much . . . more . . . slowly.

In seven years at the *Sun,* I had gone from beginner police reporter to White House correspondent, had learned to do rewrite, write features, edit copy, do makeup, crop pictures, write captions, and compose headlines that fit. For a new man to get that much experience at the *Times* would take seven hundred years.

The vastness of the place produced comical situations. Visiting one day in the newsroom, Peter Lisagor of *The Chicago Daily News* was talking to two *Times* reporters he knew when he realized they didn't know each other, and introduced them. There were editors who didn't know the names of reporters they passed in the corridors. Looking out over the newsroom one night, Tad Szulc told me, "This room is filled with people waiting for Catledge to think of them, and he doesn't even remember their names."

Once I understood how things were there, I started reading Dostoyevsky and got through *Crime and Punishment* and *The Possessed* and was started on *The Idiot* when Christmas came.

At the *Sun,* people who had been around five years were old hands, and ten years on the staff was forever. At the *Times,* everybody was contentedly planning to stay until life's sunset. This made for pronounced dullness in the newsroom.

"Drink is the curse of the *Herald Tribune,* and sex

is the curse of the *Times*." This ancient pronounce-
ment on New York journalism was several times
recited to me by *Times* men, who always seemed
pleased to think of themselves as potential slaves to
sex. During my New York term the curse seemed very
feeble. There was a famous telephone romance going
on between a woman reporter and an underworked
editor, both of them of advancing years. Whenever
the two were on their phones at the same time, somebody was apt to nudge you and point, first down to
her section of the city room, then up to his at the far
end, and wink.

There was also a youthful Don Juan, whose exploits
were certified later in a book, thinly disguised as a
novel, by his angry wife. After the turmoil of the *Sun*'s
newsroom, however, the *Times*'s seemed a sedate
place of contented, middle-aged folks in business suits
going home happily to their families. For one whose
idea of a newsroom had been formed at the *Sun,* the
Times's felt like an insurance office.

Inactivity, the Christmas blues, the midnight train
rides every week to Washington, the Dixie Hotel, and
Dostoyevsky combined to put me in low spirits as
November gave way to December. How had I got
myself into this dreary pickle? The year had started
so brightly in London when I seemed to be on top of
the world and was ending in grimness. I had made
two terrible decisions. One had ended the joys of London and replaced them with the boredom of the White
House. The other had brought me from the comfortable security of the *Sun* to the chill of this immense,
inhumane bureaucracy.

What's more, I'd picked up enough gossip about
office politics in New York to realize that there was
some kind of rivalry going on between Catledge and
Reston. I realized, too, that I was not Catledge's man,
but Reston's man, and that I had come to work for

an outfit where your entire future might depend less on how well you did the job than on whose man you were.

Buck had cautioned that I might not like being a little fish in a big pond, but my silly, mother-driven ambition to amount to something, my nonsensical fool's fantasy about being bigger than Cousin Edwin had brought me from the felicities of London to the Dixie Hotel and that huge murky pond right across the street that I didn't like at all. It had been a year of letdown.

The train got me to Washington on Christmas morning in time to have a late breakfast with Mimi, Kathy, and Allen amid Santa Claus's ruined wrappings. It was Saturday. On Monday I reported for work at the *Times*'s Washington office at 1701 K Street. Nine days later our third child was born at George Washington University Hospital. We named him Michael Lee, not after anybody in the family, but just because we thought it sounded like a good name. He was born around dawn. By noon I was at the Capitol to do a feature story on the Joint Session of Congress meeting to hear the president's State of the Union speech. The *Times* ran it for a full column under a jazzy headline. It was my third big by-lined story that week.

Washington suddenly looked quite wonderful. So did Scotty Reston, who had brought me to this place where so much glory suddenly seemed possible in the world's greatest newspaper.

23

Johnson

On a spring morning in 1958, Mimi answered the phone and said it was Senator Johnson's office asking for me. It was Saturday. We were eating a late breakfast, and Senator Johnson didn't know me from Herb, Uncle Gene, or the Jolly Green Giant.

Saturday was a lazy day in Washington. The president golfed at Burning Tree, Congress shut down for the weekend, and children nagged fathers to take them to Glen Echo and ride the Ferris wheel. There was an unwritten agreement that government and press would not annoy each other unless there was a genuine crisis.

"Lyndon Johnson?"

Probably a joke. At the office last night, Wally Carroll had told me I'd be the *Times* Senate correspondent starting next week. Wally ran the Washington desk and was Scotty's right-hand man. He had a pixie sense of humor. In honor of my new job, he might have got somebody with a cornpone accent to call up and pose as the Senate majority leader.

A woman with a lovely, soft southern accent said good morning, Mr. Baker, Senator Johnson wants to speak to you, please, and gave way to a big male voice that said, "Russ, this is Lyndon Johnson."

It was, indeed. Lyndon Johnson, the genuine article, Democratic leader of the Senate, nobody could
doubt that. He had one of the most distinctive voices
in town.

"Russ, I hear you're going to be working up here
on the Hill, covering the Senate . . ."

I was saying something, but didn't know what. By
now I had covered a lot of famous people and was
used to talking easily with them, but this strange
Saturday-morning call from Lyndon Johnson had me
too flustered to keep command of the conversation.

Maybe it was the unabashed heartiness with which
Johnson kept calling me "Russ," as though we had
been pals ever since boyhood down on the "Purd'nallis"
River, and never mind that he wouldn't recognize
me if I tapped him on the shoulder at this very
moment.

He said they'd been telling him I was taking over
Bill White's job covering the Senate for the *Times*.
Bill White was a wonderful man as well as a wonderful
reporter and he'd done a wonderful job for the *Times*,
and he'd been able to do it so well because he understood the Senate, knew how it worked . . .

In fact, Johnson really had known Bill White almost
forever. Their friendship went back a quarter century,
to early New Deal days when both were new boys in
Washington. Bill, however, had now arrived at Reporter's Nirvana, a syndicated column of his own, for
which he was quitting as the *Times*'s main man on the
Senate.

So the politics of this Saturday-morning call was
amply clear. I'd been around Washington long enough
now to understand that politics was fundamental to
the human condition everywhere, only more so in
Washington.

Johnson was saying, Russ, the two of us are going
to get along just fine.

I sure hope so, Senator, I was saying, while thinking this man is really a piece of work. Just last night I hear I'm going to be the new Bill White, he probably knows it before I get to bed, probably has to be restrained from telephoning me in the middle of the night to say, "Russ, we're going to get along just fine, you and me . . ."

It was no secret around town that Lyndon Johnson wanted to be president. Big-time television was still in the wings waiting for the 1960s, so it was no secret among men who wanted to be president that being written about with awe and wonder in *The New York Times* was one of the most wonderful things that could happen to you.

"When there's something in the Senate you want to know about, I want you to feel you can come ask me, and I'll be glad . . ."

This kind of talk made me edgy. You didn't have to be terribly Washington-wise to know that Lyndon Johnson, if not actually offering a deal, was probing to find out if I was willing to trade favors. He was saying he could make me look good at the *Times*. He didn't have to tell me what my end of the deal would be: to make Lyndon Johnson look good in the *Times*.

The offer put me off for several reasons. For one, Johnson was too big a story, so it was dangerous to give him most-favored-senator treatment. Everybody watched him constantly, and everybody read the *Times;* a sweetheart contract would be recognized at once. That couldn't do me anything but harm.

Another reason: I had never been much interested in getting "inside" information and scoops. Such stuff was important to a newspaper, but it wasn't what I did well. On the Senate beat I hoped to give the reader accurate and absorbing pictures of the fascinations that occurred there daily. I wanted to let readers know that senators billed as titans of statesmanship were also human. That the Foreign Relations Committee's stately Walter George of Georgia was also the senator from Coca-Cola, that Senator Fulbright also worried about keeping the board of Arkansas Power and Light pacified, that the oil industry often called tunes for senators like, well . . . Lyndon Johnson.

If I had to cut, doctor, fake, and censor constantly to promote Johnson's ambition, my theory of coverage just couldn't work.

During this eerie Saturday morning phone conversation, I didn't think things out so carefully as I now suggest, but I was instinctively trying to keep distance between us. This was never an easy thing to do with Lyndon Johnson, even on the telephone. One of his favorite postures for conversation was leaning down over you and pressing his nose down toward yours until your spine was bent so far back that you couldn't think of anything but your aching vertebrae.

So while he went on calling me "Russ," I kept saying "Senator," determined not to get palsy by saying "Lyndon." Toward the end, I suddenly became aware that this was not a phone conversation. It was a broadcast.

The phone company sold a device that sat on your desk and worked as both mouthpiece and earpiece. You could lean back and talk from a distance and still be clearly heard, and the reply from the person you were talking to came through it so loud and clear it was heard all over the room. The defect was that it sometimes transmitted an echo. Johnson, who loved all gadgets, had one, of course, but I didn't suspect it until I heard my own voice echoing in my earpiece a millisecond after I'd spoken.

This prompted me to listen more closely, and—what do you know!—I could hear the shuffling of bodies moving around in chairs, and even a faint laugh from somebody not Lyndon Johnson. Johnson's phone call was a performance being given for an audience. I was not having a phone conversation; I was playing to a crowd.

This left me feeling clammy. That faint laugh had been especially unnerving. Was Johnson making a fool of me to amuse his audience? Who was in that audience? Any reporters who covered the Senate for other papers?

Johnson returned to his major theme: his eagerness to do me immense kindnesses, to dole out the most secret information. All I had to do was come to him, tell him what I needed, it would be mine for the asking, that was how kindly disposed he felt toward me. Then he concluded with a line I hear clearly in my head to this day because it made me laugh so many times in the years that followed:

"For you, Russ, I'd leak like a sieve."

In my four years covering the Senate, he never "leaked" me a single piece of information that had the slightest news value.

Maybe he wrote me off as useless after that first phone talk. More likely, I suspect, he never "leaked" anything to any journalist unless it was something self-serving. The most useful information for a Senate reporter in those years was what Lyndon Johnson was up to, and I soon learned that Johnson was the last person to ask.

The best person to ask was Styles Bridges, the Senate Republicans' slippery gray eminence, whose mind, like Johnson's, had a Florentine subtlety when it came to politics. Bridges instinctively understood Johnson. Though of opposing parties, they had a fellowship of mind. This enabled Bridges to make an accurate guess about what Johnson was up to, even when he didn't know for sure. Often, of course, Bridges did know. Among Senate Republicans, he was the power behind the power, and since Democrats rarely had more than a one-vote majority in the Senate, Johnson had to deal with Bridges.

If I could find Bridges I could get an authoritative reading on Johnson's latest maneuver. The problem was to find him. Bridges had more hideouts than a movie gangster. Since he rarely appeared on the Senate floor I spent many a futile afternoon wandering half-secret corridors of the Capitol maze, knocking on unmarked doors, asking strangers, "You know where I can find Styles?"

On rare occasions they did, and he was worth the search. In Senate press gallery lore, he was said to be the slickest of scoundrels, but like so many politicians famous as rogues, his word could be trusted—at least when he talked about his colleagues. When he said, "I don't know," it meant he either didn't know or was bound to silence on the subject. When he said, "I don't know, but maybe . . . ," he meant he didn't know for sure but had this pretty good guess. When he answered a question with a piece of information, you could safely assume it was not a lie. Bridges was a classic illustration of why reporters so often give their hearts to rascals.

It was Johnson who fascinated me, though, because he was a writer's delight, a human puzzle so complicated nobody could ever understand it, but what a glorious time a writer could have making the effort. The Senate of the 1950s swarmed with men who had run for president, intended to run for president, or were destined to run for president though they didn't yet know it.

Most were remarkable men. John and Robert Kennedy were both there, John as a junior senator in the back row, Robert as chief counsel of an important committee. Richard Nixon and Barry Goldwater were there; so were Hubert Humphrey, Stuart Symington, Estes Kefauver, and Richard Russell. Down the corridor in the House of Representatives were Gerald Ford and Eugene McCarthy, soon to move over to the Senate. Almost everybody who was to afflict the country for the next generation was there. Remarkable men, all of them, but from a writer's point of view, they were long magazine pieces who might at best, with plenty of coffee and cigarettes, be stretched into thin campaign biographies.

Johnson was the exception. Johnson was a flesh-and-blood, three-volume biography, and if you ever got it written you'd discover after publication that you'd missed the key point or got the interpretation completely wrong and needed a fourth volume to set things right. He was a character out of a Russian novel, one of those human complications that filled the imagination of Dostoyevsky, a storm of warring human instincts: sinner and saint, buffoon and statesman, cynic and sentimentalist, a man torn between hungers for immortality and self-destruction.

Fascinated by him, I passed endless hours leaning over the press gallery watching him on the floor below and wasted too many hours sitting in offices listening to him talk, talk, talk. To a writer, he was irresistible, and monstrous, and delightful, and, if you were trying to convey a sense of him for a mass-circulation journal, terrifying.

A year before I took up the Senate beat, Bill White wrote a long portrait of him for the *Times Sunday Magazine*. To call it flattering would have been understatement. Bill believed Johnson could be one of the nation's great presidents, though at that time, the mid-1950s, there seemed little chance that an oil Texan with a southern accent could ever get to the White House. Bill's *Magazine* piece emphasized Johnson's statesmanlike qualities so fully that it never got around to suggesting Johnson might have a defect or two of the most trivial sort.

Normally Bill talked to Johnson at least once a day, but for three days after publication of the famously flattering *Magazine* piece, Johnson refused to see him. On the fourth day, Johnson relented, Bill went to his office, they discussed business, and, since Johnson obviously didn't intend to raise the subject, Bill asked if he had seen the *Times* magazine article.

Yes, Johnson had seen it. He spoke now in his tragic voice, a tone he often fell into when reflecting on the persecutions to which he was subjected. He had seen the piece, all right. To his sorrow, he had seen the piece.

Was something wrong with it?

Johnson's reply was so outrageous that Bill, one of Johnson's oldest friends, couldn't resist telling us about it back in the office. Johnson said:

"If I thought I was the kind of man you wrote about in that piece, I wouldn't like myself very much."

Old friendship got Bill off easy compared to the punishment visited on Sam Shaffer, who did the reporting on an unabashedly flattering *Newsweek* cover story on Johnson. Johnson did not leave Sam dangling, but called him into his office the day the magazine appeared, abused him extensively, and declared, "Anybody who'd write something like that about me would rape my wife."

Sam sat in Coventry for three weeks before Johnson would speak to him again. Then they resumed relations as though nothing had happened.

Knowing Johnson was capable of these tantrums, I was always uneasy writing about him, yet covering the Senate meant writing about him almost constantly. People who keep a tiger for a pet must feel the same uneasiness; it's a fascinating creature to be associated with, but you have to be careful about taking liberties. As a result, sometimes when he did things that made him look bad, I leaned backward to give him the best of it in the paper. There are a hundred ways a reporter can handle an unpleasant story about a politician without putting the boot into him very hard, and I sometimes took it easier on Johnson than an upright, conscientious reporter should have. I rationalized my shame by telling myself I had to keep up good relations with Johnson to do a good job covering the Senate for the *Times*.

I was lying to myself, of course. Johnson provided me with little of news value except colorful copy, which anybody could get without keeping on his good side. Truth was, I let him keep me mentally a little bullied because I enjoyed the personal contact with him which the job made possible.

He had a gift for finessing the awkward question with a comic vulgarity.

"Don't you think the Senate ought to be discussing this situation in Laos?" I asked him one day when that mysterious little Southeast Asian country was in the news.

This was in the 1950s when most senators, including Lyndon Johnson, I suspect, couldn't have found Laos on a map. Instead of admitting he didn't have a single idea about Laos in his head, Johnson went on the attack, came out of his chair, leaned into my face, and whacking his hands on his buttocks in rhythm with his words, shouted:

"Low Ass! Low Ass! Low Ass! All the things I've got on my mind and you come in here wanting to talk about Low Ass!"

His sense of humor sometimes extended even to himself. In a mellow chatty mood in his office one day, he told me a story about Little Juan, a Mexican-American boy in Duval County, Texas. Duval County was a sensitive subject with Johnson because of the 1948 Democratic primary that sent him to the Senate for the first time. In that election, 988,296 votes were cast, and Johnson won by the amazing majority of 87 votes. Naturally, everybody said his people had stolen those votes, and Duval County was supposed to be where the critical stealing was done.

Because of his eighty-seven-vote majority, Johnson acquired the nickname "Landslide Lyndon." If you wanted to stay on his good side, you didn't call him "Landslide Lyndon" or otherwise joke about that election. This day, however, he had to tell me this joke, "one they tell about me in Texas," he said.

About Little Juan sitting on the curb crying. Along came a friend. "Juan, Juan, why are you crying so?" asks the friend.

"Because my father is dead," says Little Juan.

"But Juan," says the friend, "your father died three years ago."

"But yesterday," says Little Juan, "he came back to vote for Lyndon Johnson and he did not come to see me."

Though I dealt with Lyndon Johnson off and on for seven years, sometimes in close personal contact, sitting around his office chewing the fat, joking, telling stories, he never knew who I was. He knew I was *The New York Times,* of course, but I don't think he ever for more than a second or two thought of me as anything but an important newspaper that he didn't want to antagonize.

This was dramatized in unflattering fashion on a day in 1962 after I spent nearly an hour alone with him in his Capitol office listening to one of his marathon monologues. I had known him seven years by then. He had become vice-president, knew he was the butt of cruel humor among many of President Kennedy's people, and was trying to pretend it wasn't so, that he still counted as he had counted back in the Fifties when he was Johnson the Genius Who Ran the Senate.

He spotted me outside the Senate this day, clapped my back, mauled my hand, massaged my ribs, just as he'd always done in the glory days of old, all the time hailing me as though I were a long lost friend and simultaneously hauling me into a big office he kept across the corridor from the Senate chamber. He sat me down and launched his monologue. The part he obviously wanted me to note, in case I published some of this in the *Times,* dealt with a private dinner for three at the White House at which he had supped alone with the president and Mrs. Kennedy.

He had been profoundly moved when Mrs. Kennedy had reached across the table, touched his hand, and said, "We need you, Lyndon."

I strongly suspected this story was about eighty percent fiction, but his eyes glittered so happily that he seemed to have persuaded himself every word was God's truth, and I wasn't disposed to ask skeptical questions. For one thing, he'd told me I couldn't quote him directly on anything he said, and I had no intention of reporting this touching story of Jackie Kennedy's dinner-table endorsement on my own say-so.

For another thing, I felt sorry for him. If you had once been the great Lyndon Johnson, master of the Senate, it was hard being the nonentity called vice-president, it was painful to be laughed at and called "Cornpone" by people you thought of as arrogant, smart-ass Ivy League pipsqueaks.

Looking for something that could be printed, I shifted ground slightly toward the famous frustrations other powerful men had experienced in the vice-presidency. His fellow Texan, "Cactus Jack" Garner, Franklin Roosevelt's vice-president, had said, "The vice-presidency isn't worth a jar of warm piss." It was the only memorable line Garner had ever uttered.

No such thing, said Johnson. John Garner had

never said any such thing. He had known John Garner very well, had often talked to the old gentleman back in the early New Deal days. Garner had always known the job was vitally important. Nothing as silly as that statement about a jar of warm piss could ever have been spoken by John Garner.

And so it went, on and on. During our chat Johnson scrawled a few words on a piece of memo paper and sent it to his outer office. A few minutes later his secretary brought him back a message on a small piece of paper. Johnson looked at it, crumpled it, and threw it in a wastebasket. A reporter who knew me happened to be idling in Johnson's outer office during this exchange of messages, so knew what it was about and told me as we walked away from the office together.

"Do you know what was in that message Johnson sent out while you were in there?"

"No. What did it say?"

"It said, 'Who is this I'm talking to?' "

My vanity needed that blow. Like so many Washington newspaper people, I had begun to kid myself that these terribly important people talked so readily to me because of my charm. I needed to be reminded that they were not talking to me at all; they were talking to *The New York Times*.

I first met Johnson in 1955. It was at a dinner party in the garden at Bill White's house on one of those early-summer Washington nights still soft enough to dine out of doors. I had been with the *Times* only a few months, and Bill had taken an interest in me. This was flattering because he was one of the bright stars of American journalism.

Before the *Times* he had worked his way in the A.P. from small-bore stuff in the Houston office, to Washington in 1933 covering Texas regional news, to war correspondent, then to top-drawer writer during World War Two. He had been in the armada that landed in Normandy on D Day. He was a professional, a generation older than I was, and with his rugged profile and graying black hair combed straight back, he looked more like a senator than most senators. In fact, Bill was probably more powerful in some ways than many senators. Part of the Texas old-boy network that pretty much ran Washington in the 1950s, he knew most of the people who counted.

After I switched to the *Times*, Bill noticed me hanging around on the fringes of the Senate looking for feature stories and took me to lunch at the Mayflower one day. There he tried to instruct me in a thousand subtle things about power in the Senate and how it worked. This was the highest flattery. I felt like a rookie baseball player at spring training camp who had attracted the attention of Ted Williams.

Arriving at his place for dinner that night, Mimi and I were dismayed to find we were the only people there that nobody had ever heard of. We knew it was going to be a heavy evening when we stepped through the gate and saw Dean Acheson, former secretary of state and architect of the Western world's cold-war policy. It was that kind of crowd: famous congressmen, a famous judge, a famous newspaperwoman. Except for Mimi and me, the least famous guests were a couple of lawyers named Abe Fortas and Edward Bennett Williams, and I knew they were big-time, too, because I'd seen their names in newspaper stories about big-timers.

Lyndon Johnson was only moderately famous. He must have felt almost as out of place as I did. Why else could he be chain-smoking one cigarette on top of another and pouring down Scotch whisky like a man who had a date with a firing squad? During the drinking hour before dinner, I watched him taking in rivers of smoke and whisky and waving his hands and weaving his long, skinny torso this way and that, all the while talking nonstop to a group of four or five who seemed enthralled by the performance. It was just Lyndon Johnson being himself, of course. He always operated like a runaway motor, but I didn't know that at the time.

There were four or five tables for dinner, and when we finally sat down to eat I discovered Bill White had done me another favor by seating me next to Johnson. Bill's wife, June, introduced us and told him I'd been working in London. As food arrived, he stubbed out a cigarette, lit another, finished his Scotch, called for another, and asked how the House of Commons compared with what little I had seen of the Senate.

I'd been surprised at the lack of debate in the Senate, and said so. In the House of Commons, debate seemed to be far more important than in the Senate, where, I said, most talk seemed commonplace, inaudible, and inconsequential, as though it didn't really matter.

Johnson had taken only two or three mouthfuls of food, and now he shoved his plate aside, stubbed out his cigarette in the food, lit another smoke, drained his whisky, and called for another.

Speechmaking didn't count for anything when it came to passing bills, he said. What mattered was who had the votes.

He was being the forthright schoolteacher, trying to instruct an innocent pupil about life's realities.

But what about the history books with their stories of the great debaters? What about Webster and Clay? What about . . . ?

Johnson had a child on his hands.

"You want to hear a speech? I can get somebody to make any kind of speech you want to hear. What kind of speech do you want?"

Another cigarette was being stubbed out in the

food, another cigarette was being lit, the Scotch was getting low in his glass again.

"You want to hear a great speech about suffering humanity? I've got Hubert Humphrey back in the cloakroom. I've got Herbert Lehman. I've got Paul Douglas . . ."

This man obviously absolutely hated oratory. As he talked on, another butt fizzled out in the green beans, another match flared, the empty glass was replaced with a filled glass. . . .

"You want to hear about government waste? I can give you Harry Byrd. States' rights? I've got Jim Eastland, I've got Olin Johnston, I've got . . ."

Another cigarette was squashed, another lit.

Dessert was brought. He waved it away and called for a drink. I had seen people smoke and drink dinner before, I had done it myself once or twice. In those days when health was not yet an obsessive social passion, drinking and smoking too much were not the revolting things they later became. Still, until now, I had never seen it done by anybody really famous. Famous people didn't have to carry on like that, did they? This Johnson did, though. He did it like a man trying to kill himself.

A few weeks later, at a Sunday afternoon party with a similar group in Middleburg, Virginia, he had a severe heart attack. In the ambulance, he later told me, he reached for a cigarette, and Senator Clinton Anderson, himself a heart patient, took the pack out of his hand, saying, "You won't need those anymore."

Even before I inherited Bill White's job, I had seen enough of Johnson to marvel at the theater he provided. Often it could not be reported in a family paper. Phil Potter, the *Sun*'s Senate man, and I went to his office to tease him the day he joined a big political crowd to welcome Vice-President Nixon home from a disastrous trip to South America. Nixon had been mobbed on the trip, and might have been killed, so the airport welcome-home was a patriotic display of affection for a brave, death-defying vice-president.

The irony was that the Democrats almost universally despised Nixon. If you were a Democrat in the 1950s, you were expected to despise Nixon, whether you despised him or not, so press cynics like Potter and me were amused to learn that the great Senate Democratic leader had led the handshaking as Nixon descended from his plane.

Late that afternoon we found Johnson in a small office off the Senate floor and, straight-faced, asked him if he now intended to concede that Nixon might indeed be a great American. Aware that we were tormenting him, Johnson replied with a comment calculated to keep him out of the paper:

"I can tell chicken shit from chicken salad."

By the time he telephoned, calling me "Russ" and promising to leak like a sieve, his great concern with the New York papers was his stand on civil rights. He wanted to be president, and Democrats who wanted to be president needed all the help they could get from the New York papers. In New York they liked civil rights. In New York they didn't understand the hellishness of the trial facing a man from Texas who championed civil rights. In New York they looked down on Texans, and needed to be shown that a man from Texas could be just as liberal as a man from New York, though it was ten times harder for a man from Texas.

So periodically, wandering into his office, I would be brow-beaten by Johnson reading an endless list of liberal legislation he had got through the Senate or intended to get through the Senate. After a while I began to know the list by heart. One of my favorite items was the vote by which he had got the Senate to defeat something called "the Bricker amendment," a right-wing attempt to cripple the Supreme Court.

At this point on the list, Johnson usually recalled that Anthony Lewis, our Supreme Court reporter, had been especially concerned about the Bricker amendment. Defeating the thing was a great deed done for liberalism, Johnson always said. Or, as he once put it while running down the list:

"Bricker amendment defeated—I saved Tony Lewis's little Supreme Court for him."

To get right on the civil rights issue, he finally cut free of his old ties to the southern race baiters, brought a bill to the Senate floor, and endured a filibuster to get it passed. After I hadn't called on him for a couple of days, he must have feared that the *Times* was losing interest in the filibuster, because his secretary got me out of bed early one morning—Saturday again—with a request to hurry immediately to the Capitol because Senator Johnson wanted to see me.

I got to Johnson's office, still sleepy-eyed, to find Don Irwin waiting outside. Don was the *New York Herald Tribune*'s Senate man. Whatever this was, it must be very big because Johnson wasn't risking the charge that he had favored one New York paper over another.

Don and I were admitted to the sanctum together. There we found the great man clad in silk pajamas lying partially covered on an army cot. We were to take it that, like all the other senators tied to the Capitol by the filibuster, Johnson had spent the night on this Spartan rack. He gave us his most worried, most thoughtful, most solemn expression.

"I've called you all down here this morning," he said, "because I need your help."

Don looked as uneasy as I felt. With Johnson, who could tell? Maybe he really was going to ask us for help.

He rose from the cot and stood in full pajama magnificence in the center of the office. He was no longer the skinny beanpole I'd first seen at Bill White's dinner party. He looked big, heavy, almost ponderous.

"Tell me how to end this filibuster," he said, speaking directly to Don.

That was why he'd got us out of bed and brought us down here without breakfast? To play games, asking reporters what he ought to do next so he could impress them with how dumb and incompetent they were?

That was the reason, all right.

Don was so flabbergasted he could hardly do more than stammer. Johnson turned the question on me.

"I need advice," he said. "I'm asking you to help me. How do I end this filibuster?"

It was the only time I ever came close to sassing him. I said something like, "For God's sake, Lyndon, I'm an irresponsible young newspaper reporter with no constituency to worry about. How can you expect somebody like that to tell you how to deal with ninety old men who are responsible to hundreds of different pressures?"

With that, the conference petered out quickly. Johnson's older daughter, Linda Bird, burst in with coffee and after a little socializing, Don and I were dismissed. Johnson, I always assumed, felt reassured that he had done what he had to do to keep New York from forgetting that Lyndon Johnson was fighting it out for civil rights on the cot front.

He did for an instant know me by name one afternoon several years later. It was during the 1964 presidential campaign. He knew he was going to win big, big, big, and he was euphoric about it. One of the few things troubling him was a scandal involving Bobby Baker, a young man, said some, whom he had once loved like a son. Bobby was now out of his life, except as a political embarrassment, and Johnson was enjoying probably the supreme moment of his life. He was running for president, and everybody, absolutely everybody, was going to vote for him.

Flying across the country on Air Force One, he often sat up far into the night drinking Scotch and savoring the miracle of it all. You didn't sleep through a time of glory and happiness as wonderful as this. You stayed up, enjoying it, talking about it. He talked about it one night with the handful of pool reporters assigned to his plane, telling them that all the great leaders of the world were dead now, replaced by minor figures. He, Lyndon Johnson, was the last of the big men left on the international scene. One reporter said what about President de Gaulle of France, who had just completed an unexciting visit to several South American capitals.

"Aren't you forgetting General de Gaulle?" he asked Johnson.

Johnson snorted in contempt.

"De Gaulle! He's just an old man who went to South America and fell on his ass."

Flying the country in this extraordinary state of elation, he landed at Los Angeles a few minutes behind the chartered jetliner the rest of the press was flying. As Air Force One rolled to a stop, I stood back from the photographers to get a long view of the scene and saw him come down the ramp laughing and talking and waving for the cameras.

As his feet touched the tarmac, he glanced into the distance and saw my face. Some extraordinary chemistry, produced no doubt by the joy of the season, helped him match my name to my face at that instant. Waving happily at me, he shouted, "Baker for president! Baker for president!"

Then, an instant of dreadful recognition! This film, shown on television, could be a disaster. Everybody would think he was shouting about the scandalous Bobby Baker. So he waved again, and again shouted, in an even louder voice:

"RUSSELL Baker for president! RUSSELL Baker for president!"

A year and a half later, mired fatally in Vietnam, his presidency was already headed for ruin, though he didn't know it. Except for that brief campaign moment, I hadn't covered him as president. I had been writing a newspaper column, which was often critical of his Vietnam policy. On a May day, eleven years after I had first met him, he recognized my name on a list of guests invited to a large, not very special White House reception.

The document is in his presidential library in Austin. It is a memorandum from the office of Eric Goldman, who was Johnson's house intellectual:

"Jim Jones phoned to say that the President has okayed everyone on the guest list for the Presidential Scholars ceremony except in category 17, newspapermen.

"On that list the President wants removed the following:

"Russell Baker, Art Buchwald, Robert Donovan, Walter Lippman, Peter Lisagor, James Reston."

It was a pretty distinguished company to find myself in. The chief qualification for membership, I suspected, was having got under Johnson's skin by criticizing his Vietnam policy. I didn't learn about it, however, until some fifteen years later when a friend doing research in the Johnson library found it in the files.

Funny thing, though: I remembered going to that reception. It was the only time I'd gone to the White House socially since Eisenhower had left. Somebody had slipped up, and I had got an invitation in spite of Johnson's veto. It must often be like that, even after you are president.

Unaware that we were supposed to be scratched, Mimi and I went. I followed Mimi through the reception line, coming up toward Mrs. Johnson and Lyndon in the Blue Room, wondering if, when my name was announced, he might stop me for a word of reminiscence about the old days.

He didn't. He just looked at me with his official, brief reception-line expression as we shook hands. It was the look you get from people who look you right in the eye and haven't the faintest idea who you are. After all those years, he still didn't know me from Herb, Uncle Gene, or the Jolly Green Giant.

24

Lawrence

Bill Lawrence covered politics for the *Times*. He was the only reporter I ever knew who looked as if he might beat you up if you didn't tell him what he wanted to know. He was stocky, could look as merciless as a mob enforcer when he wanted to, and had a gravel voice that got instant respect from politicians.

With Scotty and Bill White, he was one of the bureau's Big Three star reporters, and knew it, and acted accordingly, which meant doing pretty much what he wanted to do. When there was something he wanted to do, there was nobody better. Because there was a lot he didn't want to do, the bureau needed somebody to play second fiddle to the maestro, and the job fell to me.

That's why I was sent back to Denver in 1955 to cover another Eisenhower vacation. In years without an election to cover, Lawrence liked covering the White House. For him, it was pleasant work in a dull year. White House stories meant automatic front-page by-lines, and it was a short walk to the National Press Club, where he enjoyed being a big wheel in club politics. Disappearing into Colorado on another endless Eisenhower vacation did not appeal to him.

Scotty seemed shy asking me to take over for Lawrence on this one. When he'd hired me I told him he had to promise I would never have to cover the White House again. It was only a joke, of course, but he seemed to have it in mind when he said, "You know the go-around out there, why don't you rent a place and take Mimi and the children and make it a long vacation."

So we went, all of us, taking the B&O's Royal Blue sleeper to Chicago, and transferring to the Union Pacific next day for Denver. Mimi had found a two-story apartment on Josephine Street, and I settled into the old routine.

August 14, my thirtieth birthday: PRESIDENT BEGINS DENVER VACATION; PLANS WORK, TOO.

August 15: "Newsmen were permitted to follow him to the first hole. Par for the hole is four. The President took five strokes."

August 17: "President Eisenhower paused this morning between his palette and the trout stream to sign the new Executive Order. . . ."

August 19: "This is a story about a President and a seven-year-old scene stealer. . . . His name was David Eisenhower. His age, seven. His grandfather never had a chance. . . ."

August 27: PRESIDENT FISHES, THEN COOKS CATCH.

September 6: NIXON TO HEAD STUDY OF NATION'S PHYSIQUE.

September 23: "President Eisenhower returned to Denver and the golf course today after four days of fishing in the Rocky Mountains."

If Bill Lawrence was counting his blessings back in Washington, he stopped counting next day.

September 24 was a Saturday. The United Airlines public relations department had offered to fly the White House correspondents to Colorado Springs to see a football game that afternoon. I was planning to stay around Denver for a lazy afternoon with Mimi and the children. Things were so slow for the White House staff that Hagerty had left Denver and put his assistant, Murray Snyder, in charge.

Reporters checking in early at the Lowry Field presidential offices that morning noticed the president wasn't in and asked Snyder why not. Snyder said the president had suffered "a digestive upset during the night."

When I got there about nine o'clock, everybody was quietly nervous. "Digestive upset" didn't sound like much of a story to people who lived, ate, and drank as White House reporters did. Should they cancel the football junket for a story that might evaporate in a little bicarbonate of soda? They began pressing Murray Snyder for guidance.

A former *Herald Tribune* reporter, Murray was the antithesis of the hard-driving, hard-drinking, hard-hitting Hagerty. Tall, handsome, and dressed like a fashion plate, he was a cool, soft-spoken gentleman, always ready to give you a pleasant little smile, but always unhelpful. His problem was Hagerty. He seemed scared to say or do anything that might make Hagerty explode. He was a number two man who acted like a number seventeen man.

By noon we were all leaning on him. He had said nothing since 8:10 that morning when he issued the "digestive upset" report. At ten minutes past noon, he called us to the briefing room for reassurances. He had talked to Eisenhower's doctor. The doctor had told him that "this indigestion is not very serious, that it's the same kind of indigestion that many people have had."

He was telling us there was no story. Most reporters without Saturday deadlines went back to the Brown Palace. Still, this indigestion story was just troubling enough, and suddenly nobody wanted to fly to Colorado Springs for a football game, so the excursion was canceled.

Saturday deadlines fell especially early in Denver. There was a three-hour time difference between Mountain Standard and Eastern Daylight Saving Time, so noon in Denver was already three in the afternoon in New York where the first edition deadline was six o'clock. That close to deadline, I stayed in the press room, wrote a few paragraphs too many about the presidential indigestion, and kept an eye on Murray Snyder's office for any unusual bustle.

Sure enough, at two o'clock, commotion. Word ran through the press room that Snyder's staff was phoning all the absent correspondents to return immediately to Lowry Field.

This was that rare moment that justifies the White House reporter's existence. The beat, among other things, is a death watch, and the White House man's inescapable responsibility is to be there at the terrible moment. When the president's plane crashes, when the assassin fires, when a blocked artery brings the president to his knees in terminal agony, the White House man is supposed to be there. That's why his bosses spend so lavishly on his job, that's why he is allowed all that glorious travel and vacationing: So his paper, network, magazine, wire service can say their correspondent was there at the historic moment. In the White House reporter's worst nightmare, he is somewhere else, goofing off at a movie, or in a saloon, or at a football game, when the dreadful thing happens to the president. This is the ultimate disgrace for which there can be no atonement. The White House reporter knows that if it happens to him, he will become a joke notorious among generations of White House reporters yet unborn.

Sensible of his obligation to the reporters Hagerty had entrusted him to care for, Murray wanted to get them all back to Lowry so none would be humiliated. Hearing what he was doing, everybody knew this was going to be a big, big story.

By two-thirty everybody was present. Murray ordered the door to the briefing room closed, then said he had a statement to read. It said:

"The President has had a mild anterior—scratch that—a mild coronary thrombosis. He has just been driven to Fitzsimons Hospital."

White House reporters in 1955 were not steeped in medical lore as they later became, so, just to make sure everybody knew what we were talking about, Marvin Arrowsmith, the A.P. man, asked, "Is it a heart attack?"

"Yes," said Murray, and the stampede for telephones and typewriters left him standing alone in the room.

A president with a heart attack was an extraordinary piece of news in 1955. There had never been one before. How serious Eisenhower's might be was anyone's guess, but a reporter would be foolish to believe the White House statement that it was "mild," for the simple reason that the White House would be foolish to say it was "grave," even if it was. All we knew with reasonable certainty was that people often died of heart attacks, that the president had suffered one, but was still alive.

I wrote the story quickly in the pressroom at Lowry. At this primitive stage, it was an easy story to write, basically just another piece of police rewrite, and Western Union got it into New York fast enough to make a decent showing in the first edition. As afternoon faded into night, a stream of reporters who were strangers on the White House beat began appearing in the pressroom. Watching the press crowd expand, it slowly dawned on me that this was not just a big,

big story, but the biggest story in the world, and likely to remain so for several days to come.

The biggest story in the world, and it was all mine! Reporters thrive on the world's misfortune. For this reason they often take an indecent pleasure in events that dismay the rest of humanity. At the age of thirty, ambitious to get ahead and amount to something in the business, I immediately saw Eisenhower's heart attack as a blessing to my career. Here was the great chance to show the *Times* how good I was. I had been on the paper less than nine months without getting a crack at the big eye-catcher stories. Now I had one, and it came like a gift from the gods. I had been packed off on this dim vacation story to fill in for Bill Lawrence because nothing was supposed to happen, and the biggest story in the world had just fallen into my lap.

My exultation did not last long. In the dark confusion of that hectic night, I had a wire from the national news desk in New York announcing that Bill Lawrence was flying to Denver and would arrive in the morning.

I probably deserved this comeuppance for my arrogance in thinking I could handle such a big story alone for the *Times*. Most of the other big metropolitan dailies represented in Denver were handling it with one man, but the *Times*'s strengths included that vast pool of talent and a management willing to spend money to bring large teams of players into action. Sending another reporter, or even two or three, was to be expected of the *Times*. But why did it have to be Bill Lawrence? It meant the *Times* didn't consider me up to a story this important. They were sending the big fellow to take charge.

As things developed, Lawrence was only half able to make the story his, and I clung to the other half. The central question always was: Will the president die? This meant round-the-clock coverage at the Lowry Field pressroom, a narrow corridor connecting the base headquarters building and the officers' living quarters. Army cots, set up in the B.O.Q. hallway, were usually filled with exhausted and snoring reporters in the quiet hours before dawn. Eddie Folliard of *The Washington Post* came off his cot at three o'clock one morning and stamped into the pressroom complaining that the night sounds of his colleagues sounded "like hogs eating slops by a waterfall."

Before Lawrence had been two days in Denver, I was glad to have him there, and the obvious hardship of taking over all of a round-the-clock story made Bill grateful for having me to share it. The upshot was that we took turns writing the daily lead story and stayed reasonably rested. We got along well, too, but I never knew whether this was because Lawrence liked me or because he had sized me up as a lightweight who couldn't threaten him.

The story ended badly for Bill. In his second week at Denver, he collapsed and underwent a complicated appendectomy that knocked him out for several weeks. This left me alone with the story seven days a week. New York sent out W. Granger Blair to help, but cautioned that he wasn't to write any leads, which left him with little to do and probably made him think me a worse story hog than Bill Lawrence.

When Bill was fit to go home, Hagerty arranged his flight back to Washington in a plane with a bed. Naturally it was the president's plane, the *Columbine,* the propeller-driven forerunner of Air Force One.

Covering Eisenhower's heart attack, I scored the one journalistic feat likely to earn me a place in the history of journalism. Dr. Paul Dudley White, the heart specialist in charge of the president's case, gave an extensive press briefing two days after General Eisenhower was stricken. As a reassuring medical sign, he cited the fact that the president had had "a good bowel movement" that day. I quoted Doctor White's report exactly in deference to the *Times*'s policy of providing the fullest possible coverage, but buried it in the story's fifty-third paragraph in deference to the *Times*'s distaste for offending the social conventions. Thus I became the first reporter in history to report a presidential bowel movement in *The New York Times*.

Being the poor man's Bill Lawrence paid off the following year. It was a presidential election year, which left plenty to do even after Bill took the big stories, and gave me my first submersion in politicians. In April I went to Florida to watch Estes Kefauver and Adlai Stevenson run against each other in the Democratic primary for the right to be crushed in November by General Eisenhower.

That spring, of course, not everybody knew the general was unbeatable. I didn't realize it myself until after the November election. In late October when campaign reporters were asked how they thought the election would go, I said, "Don't be surprised if Stevenson pulls an upset." Well, I never claimed to be as good a political reporter as Lawrence.

My amateur's incompetence at it showed in a suggestion I made that year to Robert Kennedy. I had covered him a little because he was chief counsel on what had once been Joe McCarthy's Red-hunting Senate committee. I knew he had the position because his father was rich and had used his influence with Joe McCarthy to get his son the job.

Fatherless me, with nobody to use influence and get me flashy jobs, I despised nepotism and came to those hearings predisposed to dislike young Kennedy. Young? He was the same age I was. In those days, age thirty, I felt like the youngest reporter in Washington, hated being young, and feared I would never be old enough for great men to talk to me seriously, the way they talked to Bill Lawrence, Bill White, and Scotty.

At first it was easy to dislike this rich, favored, young Kennedy. As a committee counsel, he was clearly incompetent. He stammered, got confused in his questions, blushed, got angry, lost his poise, seemed childish, a boy trying to do a man's job. Except for the famously rich father, I thought, he would be lucky to find work as a file clerk.

I moved to covering other things and didn't come back to his committee for several months, and was surprised to discover he had grown up, and had done it very quickly. Now his questioning was calm, shrewd, and to the point. He had picked up the self-confidence needed to keep him in control of touchy situations in the hearing room. Surprising in a daddy's rich boy, he had a sense of irony, a sharp wit, and the gift of humor. I began to forgive him, then to admire him. He was a credit to the country's thirty-year-olds. I began thinking he was wasting his life as counsel on a rather shabby Senate committee. I thought he had a bright political future, and wondered why he didn't start working on it.

I raised the question one day while we stood out front of the Senate Office Building. We had been chatting about some crook who had been before the committee that morning, and with that out of the way, feeling kindly disposed to him, I told him I thought he should be running for some important public office and asked why he wasn't.

Well, he said, his brother already had one of the Senate seats for Massachusetts, and there didn't seem to be a lot of other opportunities available to him.

"Why don't you go back to Massachusetts and run for mayor of Boston?" I suggested.

From that instant, he probably never again thought

of me as anything but an idiot about politics. I may have been the only journalist in Washington who didn't know that getting involved in Boston politics was sure death to dreams of national political glory. Worse, I may have been the only one without sense enough to know the Kennedys had their sights on fancier goals than anything Boston had to offer.

So I needed to learn a little politics when I went down to Florida that spring and plodded around in the heat watching Estes Kefauver try to shake hands with the whole world. It was hard afterward to explain America's fascination with Kefauver in the 1950s, because all that showed in the old films was the comical about him: the coonskin cap topping off the austere business suit, the big jack-o'-lantern grin, the big hand extended limply out in front of him inviting other hands to drop in and be shaken.

He was a big, long, thick log of man who moved in a dreamy, stiff jointed walk as though he had no knee joints. His public manner was gentle, folksy, downhome. Getting out of his chartered Greyhound at a central Florida prayer meeting, he stood at the front step, rigid as a cigar-store Indian, and let the people come to him to shake that famous hand, and murmured a little something to each.

"Ah'm Estes Kefauver and Ah'm runnin' for president. Will you he'p me?"

"You'll he'p me, won't you?"

"You gonna he'p me?"

"Estes Kefauver, ma'am. I need your he'p."

To test my theory that he was punch-drunk with fatigue and so groggy he was running on pure reflex, I got in the handshaking line one day to test his reactions. I had been on the Greyhound with him for three or four days. Earlier that day I had been one of four people who chatted with him over lunch at a Cuban restaurant in Tampa. I thought he might smile and crack wise when he found me waiting for my hand-shake, but there wasn't a flicker of recognition in those eyes when I laid my hand in his paw and said, "An honor to shake your hand, Senator."

Looking through me at something five thousand miles away, he said, "I hope you're going to he'p me," then dropped my hand and reached for the next one.

Central Florida was back country in those days. Evenings he stood on small-town bandstands under the naked light bulbs and red-white-and-blue bunting limp in the sultry air and gave them his small-town speech. It usually included the name of some relative of his, generally a female cousin, who lived right there in that very town, he said. Cousin Mary, Cousin Susie, Cousin Carrie Lee. He had thousands of cousins, to hear him tell it up there on the bandstands.

"Will you he'p me? I grew up in a little, small town, and I have the same ambitions, the same aspirations that most of you have. You'll he'p me, won't you?"

And, "If you can't give me your votes, remember me at least in your prayers."

My own ambition seemed trifling compared to ambition on the Kefauver scale. Even my mother might have thought Kefauver had a little more gumption than was good for a man, no matter how much he wanted to amount to something. Kefauver hadn't a prayer of becoming president, but never admitted it to himself.

The professional politicians, the "bosses" he constantly attacked, still had the last word in the Democratic party in 1956, and they were not merely opposed to Kefauver, they hated Kefauver. There were many reasons, all complicated, but the nub of it was that they thought he was a dangerous maverick, an egomaniac, and a populist demagogue. Southern Democrats despised him because he favored granting black people their civil rights. Northern machine

Democrats wanted vengeance on him for his televised hearings on organized crime, which had publicized the links between the mob and big-city Democrats.

With the professionals dead set against him, campaign money was scarce and his chances of winning in a convention nil. Professionals ran conventions in those days. So Kefauver set out to prove that nobody loved him but the people. There were enough states with primary elections that year to give him a chance to prove he was a hero to the masses, and if he could do that, the mean old "bosses" would have to think twice before burying him at the convention. Kefauver's strategy was to go into primary states and shake hands with each and every one of the millions who constituted the people and ask for their he'p. It was a way of letting ambition kill you.

Earl Mazo, who was covering in Florida for the *Herald Tribune,* wrote some fresh lyrics to "Sweet Betsy from Pike," which explained everything:

I'm Estes Kefauver from old Tennessee,
And all that I want is the Presidency.
The bosses despise me all over the land,
That's how they made me a handshakin' man.

I was fascinated by Kefauver, I suppose, because he was the first politician I'd ever seen close up when the terrible, destructive heat of ambition was on him so intensely that he seemed to be killing himself. Often he seemed to be running on pure alcohol. I knew he was drinking, of course. Everybody knew he was drinking, though he never seemed out of control. A believer in the power of Sen-Sen to cover up a telltale breath, he chewed the stuff day and night. Earl Mazo told me about getting a glimpse of the drinking Kefauver one day in Miami.

Dick Wallace, Kefauver's press man, had told Earl

he could see Kefauver alone for a few minutes after his lunchtime nap at the hotel. Wallace met Earl at the door. Though the room was darkened, Earl recognized Kefauver lying on his back, flat out on top of the bedspread, completely naked, and sleeping the sleep of the dead. Dick Wallace filled a water glass almost to the top with straight Scotch whisky, carried it to the bed, and touched Kefauver's shoulder, saying, "Senator, it's time to get up."

Kefauver began to rise stiffly. As he came toward the full sitting position, one arm rose as though grasping for something to pull himself up with. Wallace put the glass of whisky in the outstretched hand, and Kefauver brought it to his lips and drained it.

Like most high-powered politicians I got to know, Kefauver seemed haunted by the same sort of childhood devils that had driven me through life with taunts to quit sitting around like a bump on a log, to quit acting like a good-for-nothing, to show a little gumption, to get out and make something of myself, to amount to something.

Like Jack Kennedy, the man he was destined to fight and beat for the worthless vice-presidential nomination that summer, Kefauver had been second son in a family that expected great things of the first. As in Jack Kennedy's family, the brilliant first son had died before he had his chance at glory, and Estes, the second son, had felt compelled to undertake the awful job of being his own big brother. Life is probably difficult for most second sons; a second son who feels obliged to compensate for a parent's loss of the golden boy must have to contend with demons.

Whatever the explanation, there was no joy in Kefauver in Florida that spring. Maybe there had never been. With the coonskin cap, the handshaking, the thick Tennessee accent, the Cousin Marys, the Cousin Susies, and the Cousin Carrie Lees, he had created a false public portrait of himself as a simple rustic from the frontier with the memory of mud between his toes and the spirit of Lincoln in his soul. The fact was not so romantic. He was a Yale-educated lawyer with a mordant sense of humor and a subtle mind that had been a match for the shrewdest Wall Street lawyers when his committee investigated behind-the-scene actions of investment bankers in Tennessee Valley power projects.

Kefauver, not Stevenson, was the true egghead of the party, but he was cunning enough to construct a public image of himself that had just enough buffoon in it to throw egghead-hunters off his trail.

Stevenson was in Florida, too, but he was not so intriguing as Kefauver. Everything was up front with Stevenson: the playful subtlety of the mind, the erudition, his liking for people, and the charm, above all, the charm. It was impossible not to like Stevenson. The smile was absolutely genuine; so was the twinkle in the eyes. Reporters loved him. He was thoughtful and articulate. Campaign fakery and flapdoodle bored him. He was genuinely interested in public affairs and thought out loud about them in graceful speeches, which he wrote himself.

Yet he was not very interesting. You met him, were charmed by him, and went away liking him, but there were no unplumbed darknesses of the soul in him. He seemed to be a happy man and, probably, a good man. One of the hardest things in all writing is to write a good novel about a good man, and I was covering politics much as a novelist might do it, rather than in the Bill Lawrence style.

What fascinated me was the cast of characters, not their ideological principles. The ideological differences between them were too slight to interest anyone but a newspaper columnist. They were all huddled in the political center, and though political journalists wrote

melodramatically about leftists, rightists, conserva-
tives, liberals, moderates, and centrists, the real difference between any two of them was the difference
between a tittle and a jot. Everything was really about
character, personality, and appearance. The best political reporter, I thought, would be a literary critic who
loved fiction.

After a pleasant week traveling with Stevenson, it
was still Kefauver who stuck in my mind. What I
remembered of Stevenson were the trivialities. Stevenson shaking hands with department-store crowds, feeling a hand nudging his back, whirling to grab it,
finding he was shaking hands with a mannequin. Stevenson on a college campus, eyes popping in amazement when student Democrats, unable to find a
donkey, presented him with a huge jackass. Stevenson, without missing a beat, saying, "I have been presented with sundry donkeys in my time, but this is the
first I have ever received that's big enough to kick an
elephant to death."

Returning to Washington, I was sent back to the
White House one more time so Bill Lawrence could
be free to roam the way a political reporter must in a
presidential election year. I made the most of it by
boasting that I was covering President Eisenhower's
reelection campaign. That sounded like an awesome
job to people who didn't know much about the business. Actually, it wouldn't have been much of a challenge to an alert copy boy, because the Eisenhower
people, figuring the general was a cinch to win, had
decided to do just enough campaigning to avoid looking smug.

Still, being thought of as the poor man's Bill Lawrence paid off again when Scotty included me in the
battalion of *Times* people covering the Democratic
convention at Chicago. There I worked side-by-side
with Bill on the platform, writing a running feature

story while he pounded out the daily convention leads. There I goggled in wonder as governors, mayors, senators, and notorious political bosses bellied up to the platform barrier to be the first to tell Lawrence the news of the moment. There I came to admire him as the best political reporter in the trade, and to find in him a generosity I hadn't suspected, and to like him.

With Bill Lawrence at 1956 Democratic national convention in Chicago

We worked closely together trying to get it all right during the pandemonium when Kefauver and the upstart Kennedy fought it out for the vice-presidential nomination on the convention floor. We didn't realize that we were covering the last great convention floor fight for a nomination, of course, nor that while Kefauver had won the battle, Kennedy would win the war. Still, when the stories were wrapped up, there was a wonderful sense of warmth and comradeship between us, as between two buddies who had come triumphant out of a brawl against superior forces.

When the day ended, Ernest Von Hartz, the *Times* editor handling copy on the platform, lifted the big pile of copy Lawrence had written and said, "It's all there. It may not be literature, but it's all there." It was, too, and it was right. Those were Lawrence's strengths. He got it all, and he got it right.

Bill's great weaknesses were insecurity and love. He needed constant assurances that he was a man of consequence. He once confided to a colleague that as a young reporter for United Press in Nebraska his dream was someday to own a camel's hair coat. By the time I knew him, he needed gaudier buttresses to support his self-confidence.

He was proud, for instance, of his membership at Burning Tree, the most exclusive golf club in Washington. The president golfed at Burning Tree. All the great men golfed there. Reporters were unwelcome. Bill's membership was a tribute great men had paid him. He liked to drop tiny references to Burning Tree into the conversation, maybe to comfort himself as much as to impress the listener. He was a good golfer. Later he was to golf with Jack Kennedy a good bit, to the advantage of both.

He had also worked himself into position to become president of the National Press Club, a job that struck me as just two notches above total dreariness. Bill, however, looked forward to the job like a child anticipating Christmas. It entitled the holder to introduce the luncheon speakers, who were usually famous, or at least notorious.

His need for the love of good women had become a need for the love of good, famous women by the summer of 1956. He was dating both Virginia Warren, daughter of the Chief Justice of the United States, and June Lockhart, the actress who played the mother role in the *Lassie* television series. The Republicans met in San Francisco that year to renominate Eisenhower, and both women turned up. It was a dull convention. Reporters had a lot of idle time to study matters nonpolitical, and soon Bill Lawrence's squiring of two beauties was a big gossip item.

Traveling with the White House party, I got to town too late to study how Bill managed to keep them apart, if he did, but not too late to play an unusual variation on the poor man's Bill Lawrence. Bill was obviously enjoying the envy he'd stirred by having not one but two glamorous beauties in his company, for the second day I was in town he took me aside and confided, quite happily, that he had a problem, and would I help him out?

Would I help Bill Lawrence? What else had I been born to do? Just tell me what to do, Bill, and watch me leap to the task.

Well, he had promised to meet June Lockhart at the Fairmont bar for a drink before dinner, but he had also promised to meet Virginia Warren someplace else at the same time, and he was in a bind. Could I go up to the Fairmont, have a drink with June, tell her he was tied up with a vital news story, and would be rather late getting there?

It was another of the many blessings I enjoyed from playing second fiddle to Bill. I had the rube's awe for picture stars, and the chance to meet one in the round sent me scurrying eagerly up Nob Hill. Miss Lockhart proved to be such bright company that she raised my opinion of Lawrence. At least he chose stars with a touch of class.

After this experience, I was only mildly startled late in the campaign season to find June climbing aboard the Eisenhower press bus when the president arrived in Seattle to start a campaign tour down the Pacific coast. A presidential campaign trip was one of the great American shows. It was natural that June, who seemed interested in almost everything, might want to see one from the inside. I guessed Lawrence had arranged with Hagerty to let her come along for the ride.

We greeted each other as old acquaintances, but I was more than mildly startled when, with a mischievous grin, she showed me her press credentials. She was accredited as a reporter for *The New York Times*. I suspected important people at the *Times* would feel obliged to be shocked if they knew that, so I never mentioned it in my phone conversations with New York as we toured down the coast to Los Angeles.

The trip was otherwise uneventful. First day back in Washington, Scotty called me into his office and wasted little time on the formalities.

"Was June Lockhart on that trip?"

"Yes."

"Accredited to the *Times*?"

"Yes."

Scotty was angry enough to curse. That was serious anger, because Scotty was a real Presbyterian, the genuine article, a product of the wee kirk in his Scottish boyhood. He believed in the old values and did not casually take the Lord's name in vain, so when he now did so I knew he was seriously angry.

"That Lawrence," he said, in a voice combining anger with sorrow. "He's in second childhood."

That, I thought, was said in disgust.

Scotty and Bill had always been close pals in the bureau, or so I thought, so the anger in Scotty was startling to me. Long afterward, when I found myself caught in the events that ended Bill's career on the *Times,* I wondered if Scotty's anger that day in 1956 was the beginning of it.

It wasn't until the Kennedy-Nixon campaign of 1960 that I realized somebody important at the *Times* had a suspicious eye on Bill Lawrence and that it might be Turner Catledge. Whoever it was, Bill was in trouble by the middle of the campaign, and gone the following spring.

25

Player

After Eisenhower's reelection, I spent a year covering the State Department, so lost sight of the politicians for a long time. Then I inherited the Senate beat from Bill White and became too busy learning the tricks of lawmaking to spend much time watching the political sharks cruise.

Obviously Lyndon Johnson wanted to be president. I could tell that by the vigorous way he denied it, but he could never make it: too deep in Texas oil and too thick with the southern segregationists who ran the Senate committees.

I knew Hubert Humphrey wanted to be president, too. Humphrey had been born wanting to be president.

All humanity knew that Richard Nixon wanted to be president, but as 1958 faded into 1959 I was surprised to pick up rumors that Stuart Symington also wanted to be president. In Symington's favor, he was a Hollywood casting director's dream of what a president ought to look like.

I was especially surprised to learn that Jack Kennedy wanted to be president because he looked less like a president than anybody else in the pack. In fact, he looked like a kid, which was how I thought of him. He wasn't much older than I was. In the Senate he had a desk in the very back row, which was reserved for greenhorns, and I rarely thought of him because he was there so little. He was such a small figure in heavy Senate business that I almost never had occasion to deal with him.

In our first encounter, he ran an errand for me. Covering Senate action on a bill one day, I needed to see a document on the presiding officer's desk, but couldn't get at it because reporters were barred from the floor while the Senate was in session. Phil Potter of the *Sun,* an old hand on the beat, was sitting beside me in the gallery.

Was there any way to get the text of that document off the floor?

Looking down over the Senate, Phil said, "There's Jack. He'll get it for you."

Jack?

Jack Kennedy, said Phil. Didn't I know Jack?

Well, sure, I knew who he was. I'd been there that crazy day in Chicago when he almost beat Kefauver out of the vice-presidential nomination. But I'd never met him.

Come on, said Phil, heading for the elevator that went down to the Senate floor level.

"Jack's a nice guy, and he likes reporters. He'll get it for you."

Phil sent in a message that the *Sun* and the *Times* would like to see Senator Kennedy if he was free for a moment, and he came out. Potter introduced us and said I had a problem and maybe he, Jack, could help out.

Kennedy said he'd be glad to help any way he could.

I said there was this document on the desk. Could he bring it out long enough for me to copy some of the more salient lines?

He'd be delighted to do that, he said, and did, and

waited while I copied what I needed, and smiled so
warmly when I thanked him that I was never again
able to think of him seriously as the genuine senatorial
article.

When I began hearing that he wanted to be president, it seemed comical because he had once served
as my copy boy.

I was really surprised to discover that Gene McCarthy also wanted to be president. A canny veteran of
the House of Representatives, McCarthy was elected
to the Senate in 1958. I took to him right away. A
Catholic intellectual and that rarest of creatures in
American politics, a genuine wit, he was a delight to
consult on the problem of the day. Talking presidential politics one day in the Senate dining room, he
said, "If the Democrats are going to run a Catholic
liberal, they ought to nominate me; I'm twice as liberal as Humphrey and twice as Catholic as Kennedy."

I thought, *Hey, he's not kidding.*

Like Adlai Stevenson, Kennedy was blessed with a
personality beguiling to reporters. On the other hand,
Nixon, poor Nixon, was cursed with a personality
reporters loved to loathe. Even Nixon partisans on the
press bus conceded that liking him took a lot of exer-
tion. There were darknesses in his soul that seemed
to leave his life bereft of joy. He was a private, lonely
man who never seemed comfortable with anyone,
including himself, a man of monumental insecurities,
for whom public life, I thought, must be a constant
ordeal.

The stock presidential candidate is expected to be
an exuberant, self-confident extrovert whose face
lights up with joy when he is out among the people
because he is the friend of all mankind. Nixon fitted
none of the personality specifications, so had to fake
it. All right, a lot of good people in politics had to
fake it; Nixon's problem was that you could see him

faking it. "Tricky Dick," the nickname that afflicted him, was false and misleading. He had no talent whatever for fakery. His attempts at it were so transparent, so wooden, so reminiscent of the lead in the eighth-grade class play, that they invited laughter and contempt.

My first close experience with Nixon came in 1958 on a ten-day campaign trip from West Virginia to California, and I was fascinated. Not with the campaign. That was small-bore political stuff. Nixon was campaigning for Republican congressional candidates. What struck me was how different he was from the man I expected.

Familiar with his reputation for championship Red-

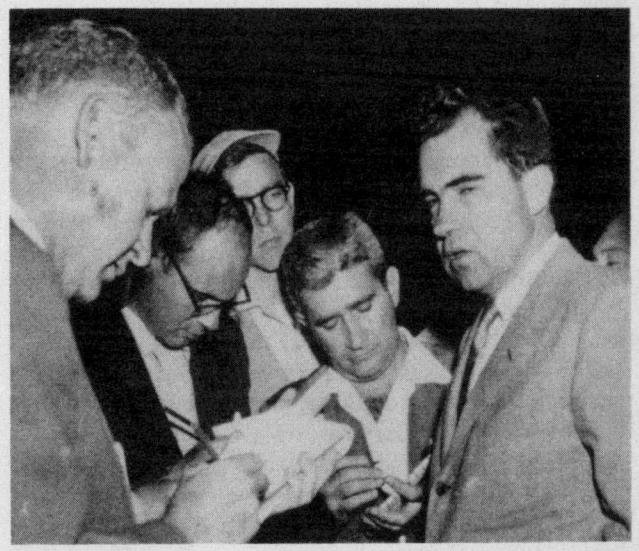

Vice-President Nixon, arriving at vacation White House, chats with reporters (l. to r.) Warren Duffee, Jack Sutherland, Russell Baker, and Earl Mazo

baiting and bare-knuckles campaigning, I expected to see a first-class demagogue exulting in his power to raise the rabble. What I saw instead was a painfully lonesome man undergoing an ordeal. As a campaigner, he had no natural talent for the stirring stump performance, for mingling joyfully with the people, or for strutting triumphantly when the crowd roared. He seemed to do everything by the numbers, without feeling the rhythm, the pleasure, the sensual delight it could provide when you felt it in the bones and really loved it.

You could watch him telling himself, now it's time to put on the big smile, now jab the air for rhetorical effect, now throw the arms high in the air, now turn to wife Pat and smile the faithful, loving husband smile. I was moved by the awfulness of his performances. I felt sympathy for his discomfort with the obligatory routines of his chosen profession and felt bemused admiration for the mechanical determination with which he forced himself to go through with them anyhow. It touched something a little painful in myself.

Growing up, I had missed learning to dance, and felt shamefully defective about it, so got a book and tried to teach myself by marking arrows on the floor and counting as I walked through the patterns.

"One, two, feet together, sidestep three, feet together four. One back, two, feet together . . ."

The trouble was, I never made any connection between the steps and the music, so the idea that dancing was supposed to be a graceful, sensuous response to lovely sounds never registered with me. On the dance floor I moved woodenly through patterns memorized from books while silently counting, "One, two, sidestep three, feet together four. One back . . ."

It was so graceless, so awkward, so terrible that I became painfully self-conscious of doing it poorly, which made my movements even more comically mechanical. I finally gave it up, avoided situations where I might be challenged to dance, and in the end even learned the courage, if dancing was suggested, to say, "Sorry, I don't dance."

Nixon's public political performances were like my dancing. He was doing everything by the numbers. I could give up on dancing because my mother never decreed that dancing was vital for boys who wanted to amount to something. Nixon was not so lucky. In the line of work he'd chosen, public performing was essential. He could never give it up. No matter how artificial he looked at it, he had to keep it up, had to keep counting. One, two, sidestep three, feet together four . . .

No wonder he couldn't stand the reporters. They were an audience that would never stop watching him do something he didn't do well. They were witnesses to the profound joylessness with which he pursued his terrible ambition. I never liked being watched while doing things I didn't do well, so I guessed Nixon didn't either. It must have deepened the natural melancholy of his spirit to have that awful audience always there, watching, so many of them with the supercilious smiles of critics who would sneer at his performance.

Some of the price he paid is told in an incident Pete Lisagor of *The Chicago Daily News* noticed on a campaign trip when we were sharing the same chartered plane with Nixon. It was all propeller flying, very slow by modern standards, and we were droning away somewhere over the great desert, most of us dozing in exhaustion. Nixon and his wife had the front seats, and Lisagor could see Nixon, chin sunk on his chest, apparently sleeping soundly.

As Lisagor watched, Alfred Eisenstaedt, a photographer for *Life* magazine, glided up the aisle, then dropped to his knees, and, camera at the ready, edged

toward the sleeping Nixon. Lisagor watched Eisenstaedt raise the camera, pause a long moment, then
lower his camera without shooting, turn, rise, and
head back toward his seat. As Eisenstaedt went past,
Lisagor stopped him and asked what went wrong.

"This man is amazing," said Eisenstaedt. "Even
when he's asleep he knows he is being photographed."

My assignment on the 1958 campaign swing was to
get an accurate record of what Nixon was saying in
his campaign speeches. There were horror stories
about well-poisoning speeches he supposedly made in
1956, accusing several Democratic candidates of trea-
sonous tendencies. There was no record that he had
ever said anything of the sort, but the suspicion
thrived, partly because many people judged him capable of saying it if he thought nobody could prove he'd
said it.

To get a reliable record of the 1958 tour, the *Times*
equipped me with a small German-made wire recorder.
There was no such thing yet as a lightweight, portable
tape recorder. Even my wire recorder was a curiosity
on the press plane.

Its main defect, aside from the wire's maddening
habit of getting itself tangled in knots, was its limited
range. Unless you got it within six or eight feet of the
speaker, it was useless. This meant I had to be constantly pressing close to Nixon while holding this small
green machine toward his face.

He had probably never before had to worry that
absolutely everything he said was being recorded and
might come back to haunt him. The low state of
recording technology up to then had given politicians
great freedom to deny their most outrageous statements after they had registered their effect. I noticed
Nixon looking at the green machine with annoyance
now and then, and by the time we got to Wyoming
he was set to explode. I lit the fuse at the end of a

grueling day by asking a tough political question during a small news conference for the local papers, then
thrusting the green box up toward his face.

"That's the kind of question I'd expect from *The
New York Times*," he began, his face black with rage
at me or the *Times* or, more likely, the wire recorder
with its constant hint that he was not a man who could
be trusted without mechanical devices to keep him
honest.

This was the first time I had ever been the target
of intense fury from a grown man more important
than a high-school teacher. Under the shock of it, my
reporting reflexes failed so completely that I flipped
the wrong button on the wire recorder and lost every
word of the great eruption. All I knew was that he
was so outraged with me that for a few seconds he
lost control of himself. He must have realized almost
immediately, though, that he couldn't afford a public
temper tantrum because he calmed down in time to
frame a reasonable answer to my question before
moving to the next one.

An hour later he was already in his front seat of
the chartered plane when the rest of us boarded to
leave Cheyenne for Denver. As I came past, he
touched my arm to stop me and said he was sorry
about the way he'd behaved in the news conference.
He was getting the flu and felt terrible, he said; I
probably knew from experience how flu affects you
sometimes.

I didn't know what the etiquette was for handling
personal apologies from men who want to be president, but forgiveness and absolution were what I
granted him.

It was nothing, don't worry about it, I knew exactly
how he felt, I felt as if I might be getting the flu
myself, this had been a brutal trip, take good care of
yourself, you've had a hard week. All this I mumbled,

too stricken with embarrassment to say something witty and memorable, something that might have prevented him from telling himself all the way to Denver, "Now there's another one who hates Nixon."

Bill Lawrence took a year off from the *Times* to enjoy being president of the Press Club and came back in 1960 to cover the presidential campaign. He sized up the huge field of candidates, then started spending a lot of time with Kennedy. Like too many reporters that year, he fell harder for Kennedy than he should have.

In his memoir, *Six Presidents, Too Many Wars*, he wrote proudly about the "really close" relationship he formed with Kennedy early that year and described how it thickened until, after the convention, he and Kennedy became regular golfing companions at Hyannisport.

Lawrence was playing a dangerous game, but one that a lot of other political reporters played routinely. After a while you knew which reporters were betting on Nixon, which on Johnson, or Humphrey, or Kennedy, or Stevenson. Publishers and editors knew it could lead to journalistic malpractice, but seldom objected when it paid off in big scoops for their papers or invitations to state dinners at the White House.

To politicians, newspapers still mattered more than television in 1960. Friendly coverage in one of the big papers was something winning candidates remembered. It inclined them to dispense favors. For a reporter who lived or died by the big exclusive story, having a president who owed you a favor was heaven on earth.

There were other seductive reasons for playing the game, especially if you had the kind of ego that rejoiced in glory by association. If your man won, you could fancy yourself a king-maker who had helped put your choice in the White House. You might be invited to join the social circle of the powerful, bask in the invitations that were the envy of all Washington, be asked to join the president in his leisure hours, welcomed into the private family quarters upstairs in the White House. Such stuff was powerful juice in Washington, even for the most grizzled reporter. Imagine having a president who returned your phone calls!

So political reporters often broke the chastity vow and played the game, and the playing itself could be exhilarating if you had a touch of big-time gambler in your soul, because it was dangerous and the stakes were so high. Even if gambling was not your weakness, there was the wonderful satisfaction of being a player. A reporter spent his life sitting in the best seat in the house to watch the rest of the world playing its fascinating games, but the price of that wonderful seat was tremendous: The reporter could only sit there; he could never play.

This was an especially brutal price in Washington where the games could be of deadly importance. After long careers there, many reporters succumbed to the urge to break free of the confining bystander role and become players. In forming that "really close" relationship with Kennedy, Lawrence became a player in 1960.

In the early months, with few reporters on the story, he began covering Kennedy's national quest for delegates. Among his other contributions to the campaign, Joseph Kennedy, the senator's father, had given his son a twin-engine Convair airplane. Kennedy named it *Caroline* after his baby daughter. Bill spent a lot of time traveling aboard the *Caroline*. It was the ideal size for a candidate moving around the country to beat the bushes for delegates: big enough to let Kennedy relax in comfort but cozy enough to allow for easy contacts with people you invited on board.

Lawrence found it delightful traveling with Kennedy. He enjoyed the in-flight conversations. Kennedy seemed interested in Bill's personal life. They talked about women. Somewhere along the way, Bill fell in love with one of the women working in the Kennedy entourage. He was forty-four years old and had been divorced twice.

Bill's campaign friendship with Kennedy paid off handsomely for the *Times* in important stories. In the end, though, Bill became a heavy loser when the *Times* got edgy. Adolph Ochs, founder of the modern *Times,* had pledged it "to give the news impartially, without fear or favor." Kennedy's political opponents began complaining that Lawrence was violating the "favor" part of the credo by the way he was covering Kennedy.

In his memoir twelve years later, Bill was still fuming that Lyndon Johnson made "a personal attack" on him before the editors of the *Times*. As for the Republicans after Nixon lost the election:

"The Nixon people never forgave me, and in the bitterness of defeat, Nixon often would mention Bill Lawrence as one of the reporters responsible for his defeat."

Back in Washington covering the Senate routine, I was pretty much oblivious to the political maneuvering. Political reporting was not my strong suit, anyhow. Nor did I work at the exalted level where Lawrence operated. When presidents were being made, the *Times* sent Bill Lawrence. If there was space for a color story, I tagged along. So I never expected to become an important player in the Bill Lawrence drama, and when I did, I was so out of things that I was surprised to know it was even going on.

Only afterward did I learn the burden of the case against Bill. It went something like this:

Part of Kennedy's strategy for winning the nomination was to create a steamroller psychology that would make various bosses with big convention delegations line up behind Kennedy before the train pulled out of the station. Lawrence's critics accused him of aiding Kennedy's strategy by his coverage of the West Virginia primary election and by his stories just before the convention that said Kennedy seemed likely to win on the first ballot.

In Protestant, Anglo-Saxon, low-income West Virginia, conventional political wisdom said Catholic, Celtic, rich Kennedy would have a hard time beating Protestant, Anglo-Saxon, poor-boy Hubert Humphrey. Kennedy encouraged this view. Why not? If he lost, nobody would be surprised. If he won, everybody would be astonished at the breadth of his appeal. The game was to maintain lowered expectations.

Bill's reporting did nothing to challenge the conventional picture. When Kennedy easily beat Humphrey, people back in Washington first said they were amazed and then asked how come the reporting from West Virginia never gave a hint of Kennedy's real strength, or mentioned that Kennedy's father had papered the state with greenbacks, or talked about the impact of Franklin Roosevelt Junior suggesting to West Virginians that Hubert Humphrey had been a draft dodger in the war?

Lawrence had got into a fast game. The Lyndon Johnson, Adlai Stevenson, and Stuart Symington people were furious about West Virginia. If they could stop Kennedy from being nominated on the first ballot, they believed one of them could win as Kennedy's strength faded on later ballots. The West Virginia surprise, however, had doubled the steam in Kennedy's campaign and brought him a rush of delegates eager to get on the team early.

So the Johnson, Stevenson, and Symington people

were hurt and furious, and, when the stakes are presidential, it's dangerous to annoy people who are in such a mood. As the man told his wife about the Mafia hit squad, "These are serious men." The game got very nasty indeed for Bill. Washington seethed with poisonous stories impossible to verify. One story had it that Kennedy had deceived the press by leaking fake polls showing Humphrey far ahead in West Virginia and that Lawrence had bought the fake though he must have known better.

This was a backhanded tribute to Bill's political reporting. He was the premier political reporter of the day. Everybody knew Bill Lawrence was too good to be fooled by politicians. When there was a big political story in the back room, Bill got it when everyone else missed it. He was the best, the absolute best. When he missed something as big as West Virginia's move to Kennedy, it was easy for the Washington crowd to believe he could have found it out if he'd wanted to.

In the Sicilian intrigue of the presidential campaign, everybody was ready to believe the worst of everybody else. Around Washington I began hearing suggestions, just the faintest suggestions, not the sort of thing anybody could call character assassination, or even accusations, but I knew Washington well enough now to decode the message. It was that Jack Kennedy had Bill Lawrence in his pocket.

At the Democratic convention in Los Angeles I fell into the familiar role of second fiddle to Lawrence, and once again worked side by side with him on the platform. This time I thought he wasn't enjoying the work as he had four years ago when I'd seen him revel in it at Chicago. That was a little odd because this convention was closely fought, highly exciting, and full of dazzling moments so dramatic they might have been scripted in Hollywood down the freeway.

Lawrence's problem was that he was suffering the agony of the player. He knew he was being criticized and was in a sullen rage about it. His fury was particularly intense toward Johnson, who had denounced him before the *Times*'s editors. Johnson had insisted the *Times* publish a statement in which he criticized Lawrence by name and said Bill's "sloppy work was the product of reportorial fatigue." The *Times* ran the statement inside the paper.

Unfazed by rumors that he was playing the Kennedy game by helping to create a steamroller psychology, Bill was writing long before Los Angeles that Kennedy seemed sure to win the nomination, probably on the first ballot. This, of course, was waving the red flag at the bull. I never doubted it reflected his professional judgment, which everybody said was the best, but it put him in a bad spot at the convention.

After forecasting a first-ballot win for Kennedy, whose opponents were fighting to stop Kennedy on the first ballot, Bill was now going to be the most humiliated political reporter in Los Angeles if Kennedy didn't win, preferably on the first ballot. Having his professional reputation dependent on a Kennedy victory was a terrible situation. Kennedy's cause had now become his cause. No wonder he wasn't having the time of his life in Los Angeles.

I had got there a few days before the opening and found no reason to disagree with Bill's reporting. Assigned to cover Symington, who was everybody's second choice if Kennedy were stopped, I was astonished by the deathly silence in Symington's headquarters suite. There was nobody there. Absolutely nobody.

Doors were open. I could walk around freely. All the fittings of a headquarters operation were there. There were desks, typewriters, mimeograph machines, telephones, a Coca-Cola machine. Everything was untouched. No work had ever been done in those rooms. It was spooky. I loafed around for a while, thinking eventually somebody would show up and say something printable, but nobody did, so, discovering that the machine was geared to issue Cokes free, I drank one and went back to report that the Symington campaign didn't exist.

I was not a political reporter of the Lawrence class, but I wasn't a complete dolt either. If everybody's second choice had folded, it seemed possible that his backers realized Kennedy was a cinch to win.

By Saturday I had seen enough and talked to enough people and studied the A.P. reports on the state delegations closely enough to surmise that the convention was ready to be stampeded for Kennedy. I wrote as much for the Sunday paper, since Lawrence was taking the day off. "On the verge of a stampede," I said. The one group I avoided before writing the story was the Kennedy crowd.

The day of the balloting produced the most memorable political speech I ever heard. It was delivered by Eugene McCarthy nominating Adlai Stevenson. There was fire in McCarthy that day, and he spread it through the galleries and across the floor until the place was howling with passion at each of McCarthy's oratorical strokes.

On the platform, battered by waves of shrieking that made the arena vibrate, I was thrilled by the melodrama of the moment. Was it still possible for a single, great speech to shatter the meticulously laid plans of political technicians, to move people so deeply that it might bewitch and capture the convention as William Jennings Bryan's "Cross of Gold" speech had done at the turn of the century?

It was an exciting moment to be on that platform, and I was pounding away at the typewriter, trying to convey some sense of the pandemonium, when Bill Lawrence leaned into me and said, "It's all coming from the galleries. Stevenson's people have packed the galleries."

Bill looked worried, though. Glancing over the floor, I saw plenty of delegates whooping just as gloriously as the gallery crowd. Was Bill also wondering whether this speech could change things in a way that would be devastating for him?

"Stevenson's people have packed the galleries." Was he giving me information, or was he trying to reassure himself that the uproar was meaningless noise that could not spoil the first-ballot Kennedy nomination he now needed?

And it did not. Kennedy got his majority from Wyoming almost at the end of the rollcall.

In the uproar, Bill leaned toward me and smiled a smile of pure delight and said, "First ballot. Just like I said it would be."

Surely there has never been a campaign in which so many reporters were dying to be players. In the tradition I'd learned at the *Sun,* reporters were supposed to hate the candidates. Well, not really hate them, of course, but keep them at arm's length, stay alert for monkey business, and, in general, play the adversary.

This was easy to do on the Nixon campaign, but on the Kennedy campaign a depressing number of really fine reporters lost their skepticism and went ga-ga over the candidate.

It was alarming to hear so many calling him "Jack," as though he were an old high-school pal. Reporters calling famous men by first names always seemed bush league to me, though most of us did it now and then after long service on a backslapping beat like the Congress had bred familiarity. To veterans covering the Senate, Humphrey might be "Hubert," Johnson might be "Lyndon," Kennedy might be "Jack." It was harmless in the intimacy of the Senate, but such familiari-

ties were bad business, I thought, once their subject
was involved in something as heated as a presidential
campaign. It created an unhealthy, hothouse atmosphere of fraternity between press and candidate, and
even if it didn't corrupt the reporting, it looked bad
to the outside world.

Lawrence and I alternated covering Kennedy and
Nixon. I started by traveling two weeks with Nixon
while Bill traveled with Kennedy. Then we switched.
When I joined the Kennedy people after two weeks
with Nixon, I was astonished at the change of atmosphere. I had come in on a love feast.

The most startling case was Phil Potter of the *Sun,*
one of the few reporters for whom my respect
approached worship. He was that good. And tough.
Nobody could be tougher, meaner, more disrespectful
when dealing with the great muckety-mucks than Phil
Potter.

Long, lean as dried beef, graying hair clipped close
to his skull, complexion dark, eyes angry, face like
the Indian on the buffalo nickel, Potter was God's
angry man in the press corps. People as diverse as
Chou En-lai and Joe McCarthy had learned not to
take him lightly. Old Asian hands remembered Potter
in China, being angered by a press conference remark
made by Wellington Koo, one of Chiang Kai-shek's
main men, standing up in the crowd, starting his question by saying, "Koo, you're a goddamn liar."

Yet here was Potter on the Kennedy campaign,
addressing the candidate by his first name and pro-
nouncing him an absolute prince.

"You're going to love Jack," was his greeting to
me. "He's got class."

To myself I said something like, *Good Lord!
They've brain-washed Potter!*

Phil had covered Nixon for years, but would have

gone gaily to the firing squad rather than call Nixon "Dick" in the presence of another reporter.

I was not going to call him "Jack," and I was not going to melt under his fatal charm. I felt no temptation to become a player, be in with the winning crowd at the White House, have gaudy names to drop, play touch on the lawn at Hyannisport. I was temperamentally disinclined to such pleasures. More and more, my interest in politicians was confined to study of the species, and my pleasure came from trying to learn what made them run. These were the pleasures of the zoologist, not the player with his fatal urge to shape events.

What's more, I had just had a sobering talk with Turner Catledge in New York. From this I realized for the first time that becoming a player had harmed Bill Lawrence worse than most people suspected. Turner had called me in to tell me that I was to cover all the forthcoming network television debates between Nixon and Kennedy.

This was a lightning bolt. Everybody assumed the four debates would probably be the biggest stories of the campaign. Covering the biggest stories of the campaign was Bill Lawrence's job. I hadn't the nerve to ask Turner, "Why me? Why not Bill?"

To make sure I heard him right, though, I said, "You mean I'll alternate with Bill covering the debates?"

"No, you'll cover *all* the debates," he said.

At last, Lawrence was to play second fiddle, though I didn't think of it that way. What I thought was, "Turner doesn't trust Bill to treat Kennedy objectively anymore."

Arriving on the Kennedy campaign, I was on notice that becoming a player was now dangerous business.

To cover the first debate in Chicago, I worked by a TV monitor in an unused studio across the corridor from the debate studio. Since I was on deadline and had to get the story to New York by filing separate paragraphs as the debate progressed, I kept my head down, listening, taking notes, and typing throughout.

It was surprisingly dull, hardly a debate at all, and I thought Nixon had a slight edge in what little argument there had been. With no real blows struck, the event seemed a dud, and my story's lead said the two had "argued genteelly."

With the story finished, I went out into the hall to find the Kennedy people ebullient. Pierre Salinger, the press man, greeted me with an ear-to-ear grin and said something about scoring a great triumph. I figured this was Pierre trying to influence my coverage, but as I talked to more and more people it was clear they thought Kennedy had indeed won a great victory.

And of course, he had. I missed it completely because I had been too busy taking notes and writing to get more than fleeting glimpses of what the country was seeing on the screen. Most of the country had been looking, not listening, and what they saw was a frail and exhausted-looking Nixon perspiring nervously under pressure. It was a Nixon catastrophe.

That night television replaced newspapers as the most important communications medium in American politics. After that, the Bill Lawrences of the press would gradually yield the stage to technicians of the electronic arts until we came to a time when it no longer mattered how newspapers treated you as long as you could handle yourself well on camera.

The irony of it was funny. After all those years playing second fiddle for Bill Lawrence, I had finally got the big job at the exact moment it ceased being a big job. I doubt that two dozen people bothered reading my front-page story on the first debate. Everybody else had probably seen it and had a better grasp of what had happened than I did.

Afterward, I covered the other debates, but it seemed like just another chore that had to be done because the *Times* was the "paper of record." Writing the stories, I thought, was like talking to myself.

In early spring of 1961, Wallace Carroll, who managed the Washington bureau for Scotty, offered me an unusual assignment. I could go to Norway to cover a meeting of the NATO foreign ministers in Oslo, then go down to Geneva for a big diplomatic conference on Southeast Asian problems.

President Kennedy was scheduled to be in Paris in June, then meet Nikita Khrushchev in Vienna. Since I would be in Europe anyhow, I might be sent to Paris and Vienna to help in the coverage.

Bored stiff covering a Senate that suddenly seemed lifeless, I jumped at the offering. I'd never been in Geneva or Oslo. Spring in Paris was an enchanting idea.

Still, it was a curious assignment. Most of it would be diplomatic coverage. Though I had covered the State Department in 1957, I hadn't been very good at it, and I had nothing to recommend me for a NATO story. The Geneva conference would be a big show because the Russians were coming and the mysterious Chinese Communists were also going to be there. I had no Russian or Chinese expertise and didn't even know the new Kennedy people at State who would be on the American delegation.

So it was curious, but, slow as always to smell the smoke, I went off happily. It was an adventure, and what was journalism for if not a little adventure?

Meanwhile, back in Washington, Bill Lawrence was covering the Kennedy White House with considerable distinction, having become "very close friends" with the president. Bill was looking forward to the president's European trip. Aside from the glamour of it, he anticipated a reunion with the woman with whom he had fallen in love during the campaign. She was now working in the Paris embassy.

So he was stunned a few days before the departure to learn that he would not be making the trip. New York's plans for coverage called for sending correspondents from some of the foreign bureaus as well as Washington. Scotty Reston would represent the Washington bureau. And since the *Times* already had another Washington man in Europe who was experienced at White House coverage, Bill was told, he would not be needed.

I was the other man already in Europe, placed there six weeks earlier to work in Oslo and Geneva.

Bill's shock quickly turned to rage. He could see no logical explanation for what was being done to him. Leaving the regular White House man off a presidential trip this important was highly unusual, if not an insult. Bill sensed a plot. With his closeness to Kennedy, he thought, he could be expected to break big exclusive stories for the *Times* in Europe. It made no sense to deny him the trip.

After fuming for several days and talking it over with Kennedy, who sympathized with him, he decided to quit the *Times*. His pride and his dignity were hurt. He was from the world of rough-and-ready where a man did something about it when he was offended.

He talked to James Hagerty, who had become chief of the news division at the ABC network. Hagerty offered him a television job and sweetened it with an offer to put him on the ABC team covering Kennedy's European trip.

Lawrence told Wally Carroll he was offering his resignation and needed immediate approval so he could work on the Paris trip for ABC. What he hoped for at this point is uncertain. Later, writing about it, he said he told Carroll his resignation was not a negotiable decision, yet he was angry at Clifton Daniel, the assistant managing editor, for accepting it brusquely, as Lawrence thought.

Maybe he hoped his resignation would be sent for review to someone higher, Turner Catledge perhaps, or even the publisher, and that he might be asked to reconsider, maybe even asked to go to Paris for the *Times*, after all. He was angry at Daniel for undertaking to accept it so quickly.

His quitting the paper was a sensation in Washington, where the *Times* without Lawrence was as unthinkable as Rome without the pope. Hearing the story in Paris, I was astounded, first of all by the grandeur of the gesture. I'd always known Bill was generously endowed with ego, but never suspected it was so heroic. I was also a little embarrassed by the suspicion that I had been used as cat's-paw in somebody's game to cut him down.

In Paris I saw Bill from a distance working for Hagerty, but not to talk to, and I was glad about that. We couldn't have had much to say to each other. He probably thought me part of his calamity, and though I thought he'd made too many bad decisions since he first stepped aboard the *Caroline*, I admired him too much not to feel bad about the mess he had made of his career.

We had never been friends really, though we had worked well together sometimes. We hadn't much in common. He was of the old school that cherished the scoop, and was willing to deal to get it. I thought most scoops were overrated and not worth the cost. He was only nine years older than I was, but we were from different generations.

It bothered me that he was willing to be a player because I admired him as a reporter, and reporters who become players are usually in danger of demeaning themselves and their papers and betraying their readers by becoming propagandists. It is hard to become a player and stay in the business without ending up contemptible. Or a columnist.

The odd thing was his blaming Clifton Daniel as the author of his tragedy at the *Times*. It wasn't Daniel who told me, back in the 1960 campaign, that Lawrence would not be covering those debates. It was Turner Catledge.

26

Zeus

For years I expected to die at the age of thirty-three. This was a heritage from my father. He had died at thirty-three. Therefore, I might too.

It was silly, of course, and I pushed the idea as far to the back of my mind as possible and tried to bury it there. A young man trying to make something of himself could never get to the top if he sat around brooding about dying young.

I suppressed it the way people suppress a childish superstition they are ashamed of but cannot help believing in. It surfaced now and then when I needed an excuse for drinking too much or was straining to impress desirable women who might have a tender streak for a doomed youth. Most of the time, though, I must have suppressed it very well because I had never turned down a single chance to get ahead in the world by saying, "It's no use, I'll be dead at thirty-three."

Suppressed or not, it existed, and when I reached my thirty-fourth birthday in robust health the sense of relief was wonderful. I had escaped my father's bleak destiny. I was going to live, after all. I would know what it was to have gray hair and see my children grow up and make something of themselves.

Mimi was as happy as I was. Now, she said, she would no longer have to listen to me talk about dying at thirty-three when I got into the gin.

That birthday on which I became older than my father had ever been was the beginning of the end of my days as a reporter. Before that, I had been just a little unsure there would be a future. Now I was presented with a gift that had been denied my father. A gift of time. It would be terrible not to use it well.

I became haunted by a fear that I was using it badly. At home the children seemed to be growing up without me. I seemed to be constantly packing to take to the road. The good times seemed to have vanished. The youthful pleasures of living in airplanes, hotels, and campaign buses had worn thin. I no longer rejoiced in hopping from Washington to Indianapolis to Salt Lake City to San Francisco in a day and cramming India into a three-day presidential visit. Was this all there was?

I felt life's possibilities slipping away as I trudged through roaring crowds with a suitcase clutched in one hand, a portable typewriter in the other, and a dirty raincoat slung over my shoulder.

Sometimes, arriving home in the middle of the night, bowed under the weight of these tools of the trade, I thought a reporter was not so different from the pathetic Willy Loman in Arthur Miller's *Death of a Salesman*, wasting life in pursuit of a fool's dream of glory.

I was starting to worry about fatherhood. I couldn't be a very good father, could I? Always away from home, or sleeping till noon because I'd worked the night before, or coming home in the middle of the night smelling of booze served on the press plane from Denver or Chicago or Miami.

Sometimes I seemed so consumed by the job that I had no time for fatherhood. It was Mimi who walked

Kathy and Allen to school every morning, usually pushing Michael along with her in a stroller. One morning she left Michael in my care. Returning home, she was astonished to see a police car going down Connecticut Avenue and one of the policemen holding a baby on his lap. What astonished her was the baby's startling resemblance to Michael.

Rushing home, she found me sound asleep and Michael gone. Having worked late the night before, I had been too groggy with sleep that morning to hear her say, "Watch Michael until I get back." Thinking himself alone in the house, Michael walked out wearing nothing but a diaper and was three blocks away strolling Connecticut Avenue when the police picked him up.

Very late in my reporting days, there was another Michael incident that made me feel like the father who wasn't there. I was due home in the middle of the night after a long trip, and Mimi came downstairs at midnight to find Michael, now seven years old, standing in the hall by the front door. What was he doing out of bed at that hour of the night? asked Mimi.

"I'm going to stay right here until a certain thirty-seven-year-old man walks through that door," he said.

I was beginning to feel guilty. Maybe I was so absorbed in newspaper work that I was cheating my children out of a father. There were Freudian possibilities to be explored here, I suppose. I had always felt cheated of a father by death. Still, the easier explanation, I thought, was that, not having had a father to study under, I didn't know how to do it.

Whatever the case, I was finally having grave thoughts about something other than newspapers. I was finally discovering there were other aspects of life that needed just as much care as the pursuit of success. I was finally becoming a family man. I guess I was finally growing up. Or maybe just getting old.

Either possibility could account for a growing sense that the good times were behind me, and the serious times ahead.

My fatigue with the reporter's life became apparent slowly through an accumulation of small incidents.

Scotty Reston and I were headed across Farragut Square to lunch one day when two cars ran together a half block behind us on K Street. Police reporting had made me a connoisseur of auto accidents. Some people could tell a fake Rembrandt from the real thing; I could tell a run-of-the-mill fender bender from a real accident.

On hearing the crash, I glanced back briefly without seeing much. I didn't have to. Heavy traffic was moving at such a crawl that the crash couldn't have done much human damage.

"Just a fender bender," I told Reston without breaking stride toward lunch.

"Let's see what happened," Reston said, turning and hurrying back toward the source of the bang.

I started to say nothing could possibly have happened, let's go get lunch, but Reston had already put distance between us, so I tagged along, amused by his boyishness.

Here was the most influential newspaperman in Washington running to a minor accident. Even if there were blood, Reston was wasting time. Newspapers didn't devote much space anymore to death by car. It was too commonplace. *The New York Times* was certainly not going to report Washington's traffic fatalities. Why didn't we just go to lunch?

After on-site inspection assured Reston the accident was indeed routine, we did go to lunch, but as we crossed Farragut Square, I realized this trivial incident

contained a message I ought to heed. It dramatized
the difference between a great reporter and a reporter
who would never be special.

The great reporter was never too big to investigate
the faintest hint of news. He went through life fueled
by a bottomless supply of curiosity. When fenders
banged, his very soul needed to know what happened,
and he was powerless to go blithely off to lunch until
he was sure he wasn't walking away from a story.

The great reporters took nothing for granted. That
was true not just of Reston, but of Tom O'Neill, Phil
Potter, Bill Lawrence, Harrison Salisbury, Homer
Bigart, and a half dozen other veterans who were
superstars of the trade. They had reporting in their
genes. Most reporters lost the passion for it by middle
age, but the precious few seemed just as fervid about
it at sixty as they'd been the first day they walked into
a newsroom.

The more I thought about that car accident, the
gloomier it made me. My amusement at Reston dash-
ing to the scene told me very plainly that my passion
for reporting had faded with age.

Hearing two cars collide, Reston instinctively heard
the possibility of news. Sure, it might be just a fender
bender, but if you walked away without checking, how
could you be sure one of the passengers wasn't the
secretary of state with a bump on the head so bad
he'd forgotten who he was? My instinct, by contrast,
was to make an unwarranted assumption—"just a
fender bender"—that wouldn't spoil the prospect of a
pleasant lunch.

When a reporter avoids a possible story because
he'd rather eat lunch, it is time to think about doing
something else.

After the political excitements of 1960 and the
European adventure that brought Lawrence's resignation the following spring, I returned to the Capitol to

discover that I had had enough of the Senate. I knew how it worked now. I knew pretty much what it would do in most situations. I even knew what most of the senators would say when they rose to speak. I now looked on most Senate doings as little more than high-level fender benders.

I had loved covering the Senate when everything was new and strange. It was like attending the best graduate school of political science in the world. When you had a question, you called the appropriate senator off the floor, and he came out and talked to you. You got one-on-one lessons from masters like Lyndon Johnson, Styles Bridges, Everett Dirksen, Richard Russell.

When you stop learning, though, even the best school may feel like the end of the line. In 1961 I was thirty-six, had been fourteen years in the business, and was restless. I had begun to think of myself as grown-up. I had decided that while reporting was a delightful way to spend a youth, it was not a worthy way for a grown man to spend his life. At least not for this grown man. The indignities of the reporter's life no longer seemed like fun, but just indignities.

I was sitting on a marble floor in a corridor of the Senate Office Building one day when I experienced a moment of vivid inner clarity and realized that I was sick of it.

With a half dozen other reporters, I was covering a meeting of the Armed Services Committee. The committee usually met in private, doors locked against the public. Doing public business in private was common practice at the Capitol, so reporters spent a lot of time idling outside closed doors. Afterward, a couple of senators usually came out to posture for television and issue hollow, misleading, or deceptive accounts of what had happened.

Sitting there, looking down the long marble tunnel

toward the elevator, I thought of my father. Maybe it was the marble that did it. He had been a stone mason. I thought:

"Here I am, thirty-six years old. When my father was thirty-six he had been dead three years. Still he managed to build something, to leave something behind that can still be seen, touched, used. Given three years more than my father had, how have I used the time? I have built nothing worth leaving and don't even know how. Instead, I spend my life sitting on marble floors, waiting for somebody to come out and lie to me."

From that moment on, I was emotionally ready to end my reporting days. What else could I do, though? I seemed caught in a job toward which I would become progressively more contemptuous as it became a familiar, then boring, series of annual routine events. This was the fate of too many aging reporters. When I was full of youth's sassy zest, I had often facetiously declared that most reporters by the age of forty should be hanged if they refused to step aside and let youth replace them. Now I confronted the tiring reporter's destiny myself.

As he had before at other moments crucial to my life, Buck Dorsey descended to save me. I say "descended" because his timing was so close to perfect that it reminded me of those climactic interventions in my high-school *Aeneid* when Juno or Minerva or Venus, this god or that, sent down agents or came down themselves from Olympus to save one of their favorites from destruction. What Buck did now was so timely that afterward I was half tempted to think of him as great Zeus the Father looking after me from the Olympian heights.

Seven years had passed since our good-bye lunch in Baltimore. He had cautioned me that day about the potential problem at the *Times*. Was I going to be content being a little fish in a big pond? Maybe he had understood all along how deeply ambition had infected me with restlessness. I hadn't seen him since, but had not forgotten his farewell words: "If you ever want to change your mind, just let me know."

Now, seven years later, like great Zeus who knew all, he stepped back onto the scene, not appearing in person this time, but sending an agent. This was Price Day, whom Buck had elevated to the office of editor in chief of the *Sun* editorial pages. That spring Price Day phoned from Baltimore with an invitation to lunch.

Price was a Texan who had gone to Princeton, been a cartoonist, written fiction in the Thirties for the slick magazines, been a city editor somewhere in Florida, covered the Italian campaign for the *Sun* in World War Two, and gotten the Pulitzer Prize for his reporting on the partition of India. He wrote with an essayist's touch and spoke so softly you could hardly hear him sometimes, but with the humor and irony of a man who had been everyplace and seen everything.

We met at the Mayflower. It was a very dry lunch by Buck Dorsey standards. Price came to the point after the first martini. Buck wanted to know if I would be interested in returning to the *Sun* to take the best job at his disposal.

What might that be?

Would I be interested in writing a column for the editorial page?

What kind of column?

Travel where you want to travel, write what you want to write, said Price. Washington. New York, California. Move around the country as much you like. Write from abroad when you want.

He was offering every newspaperman's dream.

I would be very, very interested if the *Sun* were to make such an offer, and said so.

A column meant the end of routine reporting and freedom from the obligation to keep judgments out of the paper. Columnists were paid to make judgments. A columnist was a player. Some of them were big-time players. Reston, Walter Lippmann, Joseph and Stuart Alsop—these were columnists in whom presidents confided.

Price was offering the stuff that dreams are made of, but I wasn't so deeply mesmerized that I forgot the *Sun*'s lean way with a paycheck.

Yes, such an offer would be tantalizing, I told Price. If Buck were to make it. But—well, I was paid very well by the *Times*. As he knew, the *Times* paid top dollar.

How much were they paying me?

I told him and did not lie by inflating the figure because I was sure it was already enough to make a *Sun* man gasp, and, after all, I didn't want the column offer withdrawn.

Price thought the *Sun* could match that, but he had to talk to Buck. If I was interested, of course.

I said I was very interested.

Price promised to get back to me quickly, and did. Miracle of miracles! The *Sun* offered more than the *Times* was paying.

But don't forget, said Mimi, at the *Sun* that will probably be the last raise you ever get. Still, she was as enthusiastic about it as I was.

On the phone I told Price I would be delighted to take the job and would immediately give notice to the *Times*. Through all this, Buck and I neither met nor talked.

My discontent with the *Times* was more complicated than a case of boredom with the work. Buck had put his finger on it when he warned about the difficulty of being a little fish in that big *Times* pond. Besides being bored with the job, I had gone as far as I could go on the *Times,* and it wasn't far enough.

For too many years I had been under mother's orders to amount to something and borne the obligation to pursue success with plenty of gumption so I might be worth more than the powder and shot it would take to blow me up with.

In life as my mother taught it, no matter how successful you were, you never rested. You started working at something bigger, higher, grander. That was the only way to amount to something. This was her tradition, and I went through life with it like a fever in my bones. In the end you had to be a fish so big that no pond was big enough.

The better the assignments the *Times* gave me, the unhappier I became about the certainty that the *Times* would always consider me just another second-rate-hotel man. Second-rate-hotel man: That was a classification of *Times* reporters I invented in 1960 after being reprimanded for billing the paper for the price of a first-class hotel during a trip to New York.

Bob Garst, an assistant managing editor, wrote a detailed letter deploring my expense account, scolding me for "spending at too free a rate," and explaining how things stood.

"One item is connected with your recent visit to New York during which you and your wife stayed at the Dorset Hotel at a cost of $28 a day. You followed the proper practise of deducting one-third for your wife, but even so the cost to the *Times* ran around $20, which is much too high for hotel accommodations. It should run nearer $10 or $12 normally. . . .

"Please understand that in such matters as your staying at the Dorset, the *Times* is not trying to tell you where to stop when you are in town. But we are saying that there is a limit to the amount the *Times* will contribute."

I took this as official notice that the *Times* considered me small beans, fit for second-rate hotels. It was doubly galling because the assignments I'd been getting had given me an inflated sense of grandeur.

My by-line had been constantly on the front page for six years. I had covered the White House, the State Department, the Senate, the political conventions, and the presidential candidates on campaign. I had covered Eisenhower felled by coronary thrombosis and triumphally on tour to India, Pakistan, Afghanistan, Iran, Turkey, Greece, Tunisia, Morocco, France, and Spain. I had been there when Kennedy went to the ballet with de Gaulle at Versailles and was bullied by Nikita Khrushchev in Vienna.

The *Times* had supplied material for a lifetime of name-dropping and droning on about places from the Hindu Kush to the Sistine Chapel. The *Times* had broadcast my name and encouraged me to strut when I thought of my excellences, only to strike me low with this crushing notice. No, not a great star of Bill Lawrence magnitude at all, I was only a second-rate-hotel man.

A second-rate-hotel man. That was a terrible thing to have to admit to Mother.

After telling Price I would accept the *Sun* job, I went to Scotty's office next afternoon to tell him I was leaving the *Times* and why. I expected some friendly expressions of regret: It would be a pity to lose me, too bad things hadn't worked out, that sort of thing, but nothing like the vehemence of the reply Scotty made when I finished:

"That's a kick in the balls to me."

This was a stunner. I'd never seen him upset before. Was I letting him down? Impossible. He had been a

good friend to me, pushing me ahead, making the
breaks for me, but the *Times* surely didn't need me.
In that huge pool of talent, I was one among many.

Still, Scotty's tone made me defensive. I tried to
explain about the fatigue with reporting, the sense of
not learning anything new, the need to do something
challenging.

This isn't final yet, is it? he asked.

Well, I had told the *Sun* people yes, I would take
their job.

Hold off and don't do anything more until I get
back to you, he said as I left the office.

I'd been home only a few minutes when the telephone rang.

I said hello and the man on the other end said,
"This is Orvil Dryfoos."

Orvil Dryfoos was the publisher of the *Times*.

"Scotty tells me you're going to quit the *Times*,"
Dryfoos said.

Flabbergasted though I was to find the publisher on
the telephone, I was sure enough about my decision
to tell him, quite calmly, yes, it had been wonderful
working for the *Times*, but I had this offer, an offer
nobody could refuse.

"We're not going to let you quit," Dryfoos said.

Next day I went to New York at Dryfoos's insistence. He and Scotty were close friends, and the
friendship gave Scotty great power in the company. In
New York I saw how great his power could be when
he wanted something very much. The baffling question was why he wanted to keep me from quitting.
That I never understood.

What happened in New York was crazy and wonderful. I talked with Orvil and he took me to talk with
Clifton Daniel, who was presiding in Cousin Edwin's
old office since Turner Catledge was out of the coun-

try. The *Times* needed a new chief of bureau in Rome. I could have the job.

Rome was nice, but it was still reporting, I said. The *Sun* column was what I needed.

Orvil asked about London. Plans called for a new bureau chief in London. Would that interest me?

It almost did. I'd been in London, I said, and loved it. Still, it was another reporting job, so I couldn't be sure. . . .

Clifton intervened. London had already been promised to Sydney Gruson, he said. India was available, though.

Now that I didn't want anything from the *Times* but permission to quit, they were offering me the world. It was childhood's dream of glory come true at last. Not of course with Cousin Edwin saluting my excellence, as I had fantasized long ago, but nothing was ever perfect. And Orvil Dryfoos was a greater figure than Cousin Edwin. Edwin had been a mere managing editor. As publisher, Orvil had power to hire and retire managing editors.

Flying back to Washington, I got home in time for dinner and titillated Mimi with an account of the Arabian Nights quality of the day:

Rome? No thank you.

Unfortunately, London has been promised.

But India is available.

I never kidded myself that either Orvil or Clifton, given their druthers, wouldn't have said, "So long and good luck at the *Sun*." It was Reston who was directing events.

And, as I told Mimi over dinner, Orvil had finally offered a prize beyond anything we could have expected: a column on the editorial page of the *Times*.

This was one of the gaudiest prizes in American journalism. The page had only three regular columnists: Reston and Arthur Krock from Washington and

C. L. Sulzberger from Paris. Reston had devised a way of wedging me in as the fourth, and suggested it to Orvil, who wanted to know if I was interested.

There was an ancient and tired editorial-page column headed "Topics," which was filled by contributions from staff people and copy boys writing casual pieces that read like journalism for going to sleep by. "Topics" ran right down the middle of the editorial page just like Reston, Krock, and Sulzberger.

If I wanted, I could have the space three times a week with my name in modest-size type at the bottom.

Of course I wanted it. It was a column in *The New York Times*. Not so important-looking as the other three, to be sure, but that could be made an asset, and if the thing worked they'd have to put my name at the top eventually.

I had one last condition. It had to have a new name. I didn't care what it was. Anything but "Topics." Nobody, I judged, had read anything under the title "Topics" for a generation. Unless the column had a new title, it would be like shouting down a rain barrel.

John Oakes, who ran the editorial page and hated columns for, among other things, using up his valuable space, graciously agreed to a new title and suggested "Observer."

I telephoned Price Day and told him about the furor Buck's offer had created, admitted I'd been too weak to resist the chance to have a column in the *Times*, and asked him to convey my sorrow and my love to Buck.

I hadn't the courage to phone Buck, and justified cowardice by assuring myself he wanted the entire matter handled by Price. A few days later Price wrote:

"I must say that under the same circumstances I would have done the same.

"I hope to see you soon.

"With every best wish,"

I took this as absolution, though I never heard from Zeus about the matter, nor saw him again. He had been my constant protector and author of my good fortune and someone very like a father, I suppose, though I would never have dared tell him so.

27

Morrisonville

When my mother died in 1984 we went back to the Virginia churchyard where my father and Herb were buried. It was a bitterly cold January day, and the wind off the Short Hill Mountain scattered the preacher's words down the valley and made us cling tight to each other against the icy blasts of winter and death.

"They'll never get me back up there in those sticks," she used to say in the bad old Depression days after she had taken Doris and me out of Virginia and made us city people in New Jersey.

"Back up there in those sticks." She made it sound so forlorn, such a Godforsaken backwater out beyond Nowhere. She said it so often—"back up there in those sticks"—that it became my memory of the place. For years I never wanted to go back. Sometimes I even told people, "They'll never get me back up there in those sticks."

She was talking of Morrisonville, the village where I was born. It lay in the Loudoun Valley of northern Virginia, a long sweep of fat, rich Piedmont farmland cradled between mountains that parallel the Blue Ridge into the Potomac River. Four miles to the north was the New Jerusalem Lutheran Church where Morrisonville worshiped and buried its dead. I remembered going there in a long procession of black cars for my father's funeral on a golden November day in 1930.

"This is the biggest funeral there's ever been in the Lutheran church," an old gentleman told my mother that day, trying to make her feel honored, I guess.

A few weeks later my mother, Doris, and I were gone from Morrisonville. Gone for good, to hear her tell it. "Never get me back up there in those sticks."

She had been brave then. Maybe the bravest of all the brave things she did was giving Audrey, her baby, only ten months old, for adoption by my uncle Tom and aunt Goldie. Uncle Tom, one of my father's brothers, had a good job with the B&O Railroad and could give Audrey a comfortable life, not the kind of adventure my mother was in for as she headed off to New Jersey with Doris and me, off to patching those worn-out smocks in the A&P laundry.

"Never get me back up there in those sticks."

Maybe it was only bravado, which was lost on a boy, but I was in middle age and had seen half the world before I came back to Morrisonville one day and gazed at it in wonder, thinking, *My God, this is one of the most beautiful places I have ever seen.*

Until then, I had never thought of it longingly with love, though it was my birthplace and my father's, too, and had been home to my father's family for two hundred and fifty years. For me it had always been a shabby, mean place "back up there in those sticks" which I had been lucky to escape.

So bringing her back at the end was not a vengeful attempt to have the last word in the lifelong argument between us. It was done out of a sense that a family is many generations closely woven; that though generations die, they endure as part of the fabric of the family; and that a burying ground is a good place to remind the living that they have debts to the past.

This churchyard was where she belonged. It was full of her life.

The grave was beside Herb's. He had died in 1962. My father was a short stroll southward down the slope, beside his mother, Ida Rebecca. Ida Rebecca and my mother had once been bitter competitors in the passionate matter of which one would rule my father. A short stroll westward was Uncle Tom, a good and gentle man who had been a loving father to Audrey.

Down the hillside a few yards from Ida Rebecca and my father were Uncle Irvey and his wife, Aunt Orra. Uncle Irvey was Ida Rebecca's oldest boy, the solemn one, the responsible one. My mother never liked Uncle Irvey, although he and Orra had taken her and my father to live with them at Morrisonville when they were first married and too poor to afford their own place, and though I had been born in Uncle Irvey's house. Maybe she could never forgive Uncle Irvey for having once needed his charity; still, she had dearly loved Aunt Orra.

There was far more of Morrisonville in the graveyard than there was in Morrisonville. Here was my uncle Edgar, one of Ida Rebecca's twin boys, who used to manage the Morrisonville baseball team. Here was my father's youngest brother, Uncle Lewis, who used to put me on a board on his barber chair and cut my hair with artistic scissor flourishes, then douse it with Jeris or Lucky Tiger when my father took me to his barbershop.

Nearby were the husband and wife with whom my mother boarded when she first came to Loudoun County as a young schoolteacher in the 1920s. And the preacher whose Sunday sermons she had attended. The teacher who taught the upper grades in the two-room schoolhouse they shared. Students she had taught in second grade.

That day's ceremony was not among the biggest funerals ever held there. She was in her eighty-seventh year. Except for children, grandchildren, and great-grandchildren, most of her world had passed by. Doris, Audrey, Mary Leslie, and I huddled together under a canvas canopy crackling in the wind. The people we had married stood close behind with some of our children and three or four of our cousins from nearby Lovettsville who remembered her from long ago.

Our sorrow that day was tempered by relief. After six years of the nursing home, of watching her change into somebody else, and then into nobody at all, death seemed not unwelcome. It had been heartbreaking to see her mind run down, fading slowly at first, then swiftly emptying out almost everything but a few old memories that had got wedged in the crevices and the primordial instinct not to give up, not to quit, not to let life beat you, not to die.

"Don't be a quitter, Russell," she used to tell me. "If there's one thing I hate, it's a quitter."

Toward the end, sitting by the bed, holding her hand, I had silently told her, "It's not worth fighting for anymore. Give it up. Let go. It's all right to quit now."

For three days we argued the point in absolute silence. I don't think I won that argument. I don't think she finally quit there at the end. She was just overwhelmed by superior power.

Afterward, I felt bad about having broken the faith. Maybe I had let her down at the end. This was romantic nonsense, of course, because for all practical purposes she had been gone for years, and, in any case, that silent argument over the final three days had not been an argument at all, but only my own mind privately doubting the values she had hammered into me in childhood. Still, even in death, she retained the power to make me dissatisfied with myself by dwelling on the failures.

There was my failure to become the next Edwin James, for instance. Hadn't I disappointed her there? Never mind that I lacked the temperament, the desire, and the talent to run a big bureaucracy like the *Times*'s news operation. Maybe I could have overcome those drawbacks if I hadn't given in to Old Devil Laziness. Or so I told myself when the memory of her battle cries rattled my peace of mind.

"If at first you don't succeed . . ."

"For God's sake, Russell, show a little gumption for once in your life. . . ."

To be sure, the column had been successful enough. I had been writing it nearly twenty-two years by the time she died. It was not a column meant to convey news, but a writer's column commenting on the news by using different literary forms: essay devices, satire, burlesque, sometimes even fiction. It was proof that she had been absolutely right when she sized me up early in life, guessed I'd been born with the word gene, and steered me toward literature, believing that writing might be the way I could make something of myself, could amount to something.

The column had got its share of the medals American newspaper people give themselves, including a Pulitzer Prize in 1979. My mother never knew about that. The circuitry of her brain had collapsed the year before, and she was in the nursing home, out of touch with life forevermore, with the world of ambition, success, prizes, and vanity.

I could only guess how the woman she used to be might have responded to the news of the Pulitzer, but the guessing wasn't hard. I'm pretty sure she would have said, "That's nice, Buddy. It shows if you buckle down and work hard you'll be able to make something of yourself one of these days."

In training me to pass hard judgments on myself, she finally led me to pass hard judgments on the values by which she lived. Long before she died, even before her mind collapsed, I had begun to have a bad conscience about the constant hunger for success that had consumed those good, early years in the business.

Things had come my way too easily. Hadn't I repaid Buck Dorsey shabbily, considering how much he seemed a father to me? I hadn't even been involved in the great stories of my era, as the earlier generation of World War Two reporters had been. Reston, Phil Potter, Bill Lawrence, Price Day, Bill White, Gerry Fay, Eric Sevareid, Harrison Salisbury—tempered by their experience of the war, they all seemed to have a depth of character, a passion for their calling, and a sense that there were things even more important than success, another raise, a promotion, a gaudy title, and a prize citation to hang on the wall.

Well, of course, in my time as a reporter, which was from 1947 to 1962, there were not many great stories to broaden a newsman and deepen the character. Those were the good times, from the summer I started at the *Sun* in 1947 to Dallas in 1963, at least compared to what had gone before and what came afterward. They were especially good times if you were young, ambitious, energetic, and American. Being young makes all times better; being American in that brief moment that was America's golden age of empire made it the best of any time that ever was or will be. Provided you were white.

Good times, though, are not the best times for a reporter. When the country began to pull apart in the 1960s and 1970s, I felt melancholy about being left out as a new bunch of reporters went off to cover the demonstrations, riots, wars, and assassinations; to challenge the integrity of the government my generation had believed in; and, eventually, to change the entire character of American journalism, and change it for the better, too.

Part of the upheaval of that time was an attack on the values my mother had preached and I had lived by. The attack on ambition and striving for success was especially heavy. People who admitted to wanting to amount to something were put down as materialists idiotically wasting their lives in the "rat race." The word "gumption" vanished from the language.

Our children were adolescents now. They brought the fever for change into the house. Not wanting to be the dead hand of the corrupt past, I tried to roll with the new age. I decided not to drive my children as my mother had driven me with those corrupt old demands that they amount to something.

Materialism, ambition, and success were out the window. The new age exalted love, self-gratification, mystical religious experience, and passive Asian philosophies that aimed to help people resign themselves peaceably to the status quo. Much of this seemed preposterous to me, but I conceded that my mother might have turned me into a coarse materialist, so kept my heretical suspicions to myself while trying to go along with the prevalent theory, enunciated best by The Beatles, that "love is all you need."

And then I broke. The trouble was that too many people were not playing the love game. Too many people were still playing my mother's gumption game, and playing it very hard. Gradually I saw that these people were quietly preparing themselves to take over the country. Slowly, I began to fear that our three children—Kathleen, Allen, Michael—were not going to be members of the take-over class. I started preaching the ambition gospel to them.

It was silly, of course. Adolescence is too late to start hearing about gumption. Still, something had to be done. The schools were sending home alarming report cards. Reading that progression of grim report cards, I reached a shameful conclusion: I had failed to fire my children with ambition.

This was a time when, despite the new age, parents talked about getting their children into Harvard the way old folks once talked about getting into Heaven. It was the old rat race. Still going on. And plenty of children not too love-besotted to run the course. Everywhere I saw adults transforming their children into barracuda, pressuring tots for grades that would get them into elite colleges, which would get them elite jobs, where they would eat life's losers.

My children's report cards read like early warning signals. I panicked. Were my lovely children destined to feed the barracuda because I had failed them?

One evening at dinner, when the report cards had been as bad as usual, I heard myself shouting, "Don't you want to amount to something?"

The children looked blank. Amount to something? What a strange expression. The antique idea of life as a challenge to "make something of yourself" meant nothing to them because I had never taught it to them.

I had been at the martinis before dinner.

"Don't you want to make something of your-selves?" I roared.

The children studied their plates with eloquent faces. I could see their thoughts.

That isn't Dad yelling, they were thinking. *That's those martinis*.

They were only partly right. It wasn't the gin that was shouting loudest. It was my mother. The martinis had freed me to preach her old-time religion. The gin only gave me the courage to announce that yes, by God, I had always believed in people trying to make something of themselves, had always believed in success, had always believed that without hard work and self-discipline you could never amount to anything, and didn't deserve to.

In gin's awful grip, I was renouncing the faith of the new age in the power of gentleness, love, and understanding. I was reverting to the primitive faith of my mother. She had embedded it in my marrow, bone, and blood. There, anchored beyond reason's power to crush, it would keep me always restless, discontented, always slightly guilty for not amounting to something a little bit more.

In those days it led me into misunderstanding the children. The bleak report cards did not forebode failure, but a refusal to march to the drumbeat of the ordinary, which should have made me proud. Now they were grown people with children of their own, and we liked each other and had good times when we were together.

One defect of my mother's code was the value it placed on money and position. The children never cared a lot for that. To care, I suppose, you had to have been there with her during the Depression.

The ceremony in the churchyard was briefer than it might have been, because of the icy wind off the mountain, and afterward we went to a house in Morrisonville for food and the warmth of oak logs burning in a stone fireplace.

A house of primitive log construction, it was maybe a hundred and seventy years old, maybe more. Nobody could tell for sure. Some long-dead forebears of mine, names lost to the twentieth century, had probably helped dig the foundation, raise the logs, or mix the chinking. The family had been in those parts since 1730, but they had not been a people who wrote things down, except for an occasional ancient tombstone inscription here and there around the county.

The house was filled with a sense of timelessness

that afternoon. Doris, Audrey, Mary Leslie, and I were children of the twentieth century. Up the road a short distance, I had been babied and spoiled by my grandmother, Ida Rebecca, who was born in the time of the Civil War.

My mother, whose death had brought us there, back up there in those sticks, had spent childhood in the age of the horse, buggy, and Teddy Roosevelt.

Two of Audrey's eight children had come down from New England with her, and Mimi's and my three children were also there. These were the children of America in the good times, born in the middle of the twentieth century, destined most likely to know what the twenty-first holds.

And two of our granddaughters were there, Mimi's and mine, born in the 1980s, who would, all going well, reach far into the next century. I was aware of my life stretching across a great expanse of time, of reaching across some two hundred years inside this old house and connecting Ida Rebecca's Civil War America with whatever America might be in the middle of the twenty-first century.

My father's funeral procession had set out from another house just up the road from this one. Thirty-three he was at death. And now my daughter Kathy was thirty-two, my son Allen thirty-one, my son Michael twenty-nine.

Looking at them grouped with Audrey's children around the fireplace, I realized that if my father were mysteriously compelled to join us this day, he would gravitate naturally to my children for the companionship of his own kind. If he noticed me staring too curiously at him, he might turn to Kathy or Allen or Michael and whisper, asking, "Who's the old man in the high-priced suit?"

I was now old enough to be his father.

So it is with a family. We carry the dead generations

within us and pass them on to the future aboard our children. This keeps the people of the past alive long after we have taken them to the churchyard.

"If there's one thing I can't stand, Russell, it's a quitter."

Lord, I can hear her still.

There's an epidemic with 27 million victims. And no visible symptoms.

It's an epidemic of people who can't read.

Believe it or not, 27 million Americans are functionally illiterate, about one adult in five.

The solution to this problem is you... when you join the fight against illiteracy. So call the Coalition for Literacy at toll-free **1-800-228-8813** and volunteer.

Volunteer Against Illiteracy. The only degree you need is a degree of caring.